MW00880105

What Happened to Me???

Why People Become Addicted ---
our brain, genetics, and psychology
in addiction and recovery

Also by this author:

The Alcoholic / Addict Within:
Our Brain, Genetics, Psychology, and the Twelve Steps as Psychotherapy

A Trip Through the 12 Steps
With a Doctor and Therapist

Uplift Your Self-Esteem
A how-to guide to healthy, stable, unconditional self-esteem

Understanding and Helping an Addict
(and keeping your sanity)

These books are available in paperback and eBook versions from amazon.com

What Happened to Me???

Why People Become Addicted ---
our brain, genetics, and psychology
in addiction and recovery

Andrew Proulx MD

Contents

Introduction

What happened to us? Why are we alcoholics or addicts? Most people can drink or even use drugs once in a while, and they're fine. They'll go months without another drink or drug and not even think about it. But some of us have no "off" switch; one drink or hit, and we're done in. There are those who find themselves drinking or using drugs – or gambling or some other addictive behavior – too much and can shake it off, walk away from it, and never look back. Kudos to them; I wish I were one of them. But I'm not. I tried to be like them countless times, but I failed every time. Presumably, you're like me that way. What's the difference between those people and us? What happened to us? After you read this book, you'll be able to answer those questions with authority.

Part of the reason that we addicts deal with so much stigma is that people don't understand us and what happened to us. If you're like me, you were thoroughly sick of hearing: *Why don't you just stop?* Obviously, if we could "just stop," we would've done so long ago, when drinking or using was no longer fun and our life was disintegrating. But you can't really blame them, because to the non-addict it's an obvious question; they genuinely don't understand why we don't "just stop." That's why they say only an addict understands an addict.

You know what, though? When I was drinking and using, I couldn't understand why I couldn't "just stop" either. Or why I couldn't at least control my drinking and using. God knows I tried to stop. I kept telling myself and everyone around me that *this* time I got this, *this* time I've finally had enough and I'm done with it. And I truly believed it, every time. But, without fail, I'd last a few days, or maybe even a few weeks, but I'd be right back at it.

During my addiction, I couldn't understand what the hell was happening to me. I was saying and doing things that I ordinarily would never say or do. Never. And I didn't like who I'd become. I was lying, selfish, unreliable, deceitful, sneaky, and even criminal. I'd been practicing medicine and psychotherapy for nearly fifteen years, but I still couldn't understand what was wrong with me, what was making me into this self-destructive, irresponsible dickhead that I hated. It was like I was watching somebody else... but it was me.

When I finally got sober and found healing, I still didn't understand what had happened to me. But I needed to know. So, I started out on a process of researching addiction so I could find out about myself and the addiction that had taken over my life. I researched medical journals and textbooks, I interviewed other addicts, and I talked to experts on the subject. The learning journey was so personal and meaningful for me that I decided to make it my life: I became an addiction researcher and writer. I wrote my first book about addiction, and two more followed within two years. To boot, I even went back to school to do my Ph.D. in Addiction Psychology. So here I am, about to share with you what I've learned.

Why would anyone need to know about addiction and how it affected them? Good question. Well, for me, it was natural curiosity. Something had taken over my life and dominated my brain, my body, my behavior, and my life. It wiped out my career, my finances, my relationships with family and friends, and it very nearly killed me. I needed to know what that was. But there's more. As thinking beings, we have the power to use information to our advantage, and understanding addiction can serve us by helping us get sober and healthy, and maybe even help others. Knowledge alone won't get anyone sober – believe me. I know that if I took another drink or drug I'd be right back at it again. I've seen it happen to hundreds of better people than me with more time in sobriety than me. But, knowledge about addiction is one more tool we can use to help ourselves and others when we've accepted the help we need to get sober.

A word about terminology. I view addiction and alcoholism as one and the same. After all, alcoholics are addicted to the drug alcohol, which is in fact a mind-altering drug. The science of alcohol and other drugs is the same, so the information presented in this book applies to any mind-altering substance, and also largely to addictive behaviors, such as sex addiction, compulsive gambling, compulsive over-eating, and others. So, I'll use the word "addiction" to refer to addiction to any substance or behavior. Too, I refer to people who suffer from addiction to drugs or alcohol as "addicts," which some may find offensive. I call myself an addict; I long ago got over being offended by it. I use the term addict because it's short and easy, and everyone understands it. I hope I'm not upsetting anyone's sensitivities with this terminology. We're all brothers and sisters in recovery, and we should have no room in our hearts for outdated stigma.

Another note has to do with the term "addiction." The word "addiction" isn't a proper medical term. Until 2013, the accepted medical terminology for addiction was substance dependence and substance abuse. Since 2013 it has been substance use disorder (SUD). However, I prefer to use the term "addiction." It's unequivocal, to the point, and understood by everybody. The medical community keeps changing its terminology, but we always understand the word addiction.

With that said, let's get to it!

1

Why Some People Become Addicted... and Some Don't

I never planned on being addicted to drugs and alcohol, and I'm sure you didn't either. Nobody ever wakes up one day and decides: *today my goal is to become an addict.* Most folks can stop using drugs or alcohol when they realize it's becoming a problem. But some don't, even when they keep losing important things and can see that things are going downhill. So, what's the difference between someone who stops using drugs when it becomes a problem and someone who doesn't... or can't?

There are people who look at we addicts as weak-willed and self-indulgent. Even as a doc, I used to feel the same way. But once I myself was part of that world, that attitude didn't fit anymore. I've always been a driven person with tons of willpower, willing to endure hardship now for a pay-off down the road. Yet here I was, sick of using drugs and alcohol and desperate to stop, but my usual considerable willpower was useless. Drinking and using wasn't fun anymore, so I definitely wasn't drawn to it by an indulgent, weak-willed desire to feel good. Besides, even at the beginning of my addiction – when I still enjoyed the high – I couldn't explain why, suddenly, I had no "off" switch. I'd used alcohol and sometimes drugs lots before without any problems, so why was I now helpless over my substance use?

Addiction is about more than just drugs and alcohol making us feel good. After all, most people who try or use drugs and alcohol "recreationally" never become addicted even though it makes them feel good. The huge annual U.S. National Survey on Drug Use and Health (NSDUH) has found that by age 26, over 87% of Americans have used alcohol, and just over 50% have used illicit drugs. However, studies by the U.S. National Institutes of Health (NIH) show that about 10% of Americans develop drug addiction in their lifetime. Similarly, the U.S. National Epidemiologic Survey on Alcohol and Related Conditions III (NESARC-III) found that the lifetime incidence of alcoholism among Americans is 29.1% (although this statistic may be a bit high, according to other data). So, a minority of people who try drugs or alcohol become addicted, even though they find drug or alcohol use enjoyable. So, we may ask: *why do some people become addicted when they take drugs or alcohol, while most do not? Is there any way we can know who will become addicted? Could I have foreseen my addiction?* We're going to answer those questions in this chapter. Perhaps as you go, you can put a checkmark by any of the parts you identify with, to help characterize your addiction. If you've experienced any factors that you don't see in this chapter, I'd love to hear from you. As an addiction researcher, I'm always seeking input from the people who know addiction best – those who've been through it. My contact information is in the front matter of this book.

*   *   *

Our susceptibility to addiction depends on two factors: 1) our genetics, and 2) environmental factors. Environmental factors are all those things we're exposed to before and after birth that shape who and what we are. These include, for example, our nutrition, the quality of the parenting we experience as children, our education, and the friends we keep. It also encompasses our life situation, such as our income, living conditions, the quality of our relationships, and how much stress we face. Our genetics and environment act together to determine our susceptibility to addiction. For example, stress is a big factor in developing addiction – our genetics factor into how we react to stress, and our environment determines how much stress we have and what kinds of stress-coping skills we've learned.

Scientists sometimes refer to genetics as our "nature" – because our genes are part of us – and our environment as "nurture" – because of how our experiences shape us. So, the question is: how much of addiction is nature, and how much is nurture? Well, we know the answer quite well, thanks to research based on data collected from tens of thousands of people with addiction (such as from the annual U.S. NSDUH that I previously mentioned). It turns out that addiction is about half due to nature and half due to nurture. The influence of the two factors differs from person to person, but whether or not we'll become addicted when exposed to drugs or alcohol is 40-60% genetic, and 40-60% due to environmental influences.

Our genetics and environment interact in other ways, too. As we go through life, some of our genes can be switched on and off by specific environmental exposures – this is known as *epigenetics*. Epigenetics is very important in developing addiction, because many "addiction genes" are activated by outside influences, such as poorly managed stress, or repeated exposure to addictive substances.

The genetic and environmental determinants of addiction are collectively known as the risk factors for addiction. These risk factors influence our susceptibility to addiction when exposed to drugs or alcohol. However, risk factors are never a grand slam sure thing. I've met lots of people with all the risk factors who go through life without substance use problems, and others with very few risk factors who fell hard to addiction. Someone may go through life without any problems with substance use, then suddenly get into trouble when events make them cross their threshold. The lesson there: addiction can happen to anyone; no one is immune.

Of course, as we go through life our environment changes, so our predisposition to addiction can change too. My own story is illustrative. Throughout life, I was able to drink and even sometimes use drugs without any problems. I'd drink occasionally and even get drunk, then go months without even a thought about alcohol. I even kept a well-stocked bar in my house. The turning point was the stress of my divorce. I was embittered by the outcome in court, and I'd lay awake at night seething with anger, feeling like a victim. I felt I could only calm down and get to sleep by getting drunk. Soon, I was using drink and drugs daily to cope with stress and negative emotions, and my addiction soon followed. In other words, I never had any problems with substance use until life events pushed me to my threshold, and that was it for me.

Now that we've put them in context, let's talk about each of the major genetic and environmental risk factors, and how they play a role in determining our vulnerability to addiction.

*   *   *

Family history of addiction. Family affects us in two ways: 1) genes inherited from our parents ("nature"), and 2) the influence of our family, particularly during our formative years ("nurture").

Our DNA is organized into functional units known as genes. Each gene is responsible for a specific aspect of our makeup, and together all our genes represent the blueprint for much of who we are. In some cases, a single "bad" gene can cause a disease, such as cystic fibrosis or sickle cell anemia. However, most diseases and disorders are more complex and involve many different genes that together determine our risk of developing the disease. This is the case with addiction, where no single "addiction gene" determines if someone will become addicted when exposed to drugs or alcohol. Rather, many genes – probably in the hundreds – influence our vulnerability to addiction.

So, what exactly are these "addiction genes," and what do they do? Well, many affect the brain's *neurotransmitters*. These are the chemicals our brain cells use to communicate with each other to create thoughts, feelings, and behaviors. For example, the neurotransmitter dopamine is heavily implicated in addiction because it provides much of the "high" of drugs of addiction. Some addiction genes increase dopamine levels in the brain, or make the "high" from dopamine more intense. We'll talk more about neurotransmitters in chapter 3, when we look into the addicted brain.

Some addiction-related genes affect our response to specific drugs. For example, there are genes that affect how easily we can stop ourselves when we're drinking alcohol, how quickly we metabolize alcohol and get it out of our system, and whether or not we get sick when we drink a lot. Unsurprisingly, these genes have been associated with a higher risk of alcohol addiction.

Other addiction genes affect our emotional response to substance use, our ability to handle stress, how sensitive our brain circuits are to drugs, how badly we crave drugs or alcohol after we use them, and how impulsive we are.

There's a lot of overlap between genes that make us vulnerable to addiction and genes that make us susceptible to other mental health struggles. In many cases, it's the same gene. This is partly why there's so much co-occurrence of addiction with other mental health problems, such as depression, or anxiety. For example, genes that make people more likely to have an anxiety-prone personality type have been associated with an increased risk of developing anxiety disorders and an increased susceptibility to substance use.

However, even if we have a parent with many "addiction genes," that doesn't necessarily mean we also carry the same genes. Human reproduction has built-in processes to ensure we're not exactly like our parents. When parents' DNA combines during reproduction, the child's DNA will be a random mixture of both parents' DNA (through a process known as *homologous recombination*, for you science nerds). There are about 70,368,744,177,664 possible combinations that can result, which is trillions more combinations than there are people who've ever lived. That's why no two people are exactly genetically alike (except, of course, identical twins, who have the same DNA), why brothers and sisters are not totally alike, and why we're not exactly like our parents.

As if this wasn't enough possible combinations of DNA in parents' offspring, there's more biodiversity introduced through a process known as *genetic crossing-over*. When one parent's DNA is combined with the other's, some sections stick together and cross over from one to the other, further introducing billions of other genetic possibilities. Then, to top it off, genetic mutations also occur during reproduction, which further changes the baby's genetic profile. The end result is that none of us is a genetic copy of either of our parents, so just because one or both of our parents may have a particular "addiction gene" doesn't necessarily mean we will as well.

Lots of people in recovery from addiction carry guilt because they believe they have an "addiction gene" that they've passed on to their kids. However, as we've just discussed, there are many different addiction-related genes, and these are not necessarily passed on. Besides, there's no gene that's a guarantee of problem substance use. As such, I always reassure these people. The truth is that there's no way to know for sure what – if any – addiction-related genes anybody carries. Although we have lab tests that map out our genetic profile, these are expensive and not in routine use, and we're still lacking in knowledge about the genetics of addiction.

Guilt over possibly passing "addiction genes" on to our kids is misplaced. Even if someone does pass on a few genes, they can more than make up for it with their knowledge of addiction. They can ensure they provide a safe and caring environment for their kids, and do their best to reduce or eliminate environmental risk factors for addiction – the ones we're discussing in this chapter. As well, their own experience with addiction better equips them to talk to their kids about substance use, and to recognize early on when problems may be arising. As such, they can make good on any possible "nature" risks by optimizing the "nurture." The information in this book will further enhance your ability to talk authoritatively to your children and other loved ones about addiction.

Besides genetics, the other way a family history of addiction affects risk is the nurture aspect. A history of addiction in the parents can be protective, or a negative risk factor. If the parents are in recovery and knowledgeable about addiction, have good parenting skills, and are attentive to their children's needs, they may exert a highly positive influence over their children with regard to substance use. However, when children grow up in a neglectful, abusive, chaotic home, their risk for developing addiction (and other mental health problems) jumps significantly. Having parents who're in active addiction can be an absolute disaster for the children.

Data from the NSDUH show that about one in eight children in the U.S. live in a household with at least one parent with a substance use disorder. Certainly, not all children who live with a substance-using parent will be subjected to neglect or abuse. However, they're at higher risk of maltreatment and involvement of child protective services. People in active addiction often get to a point where they lose interest and even stop caring about their responsibilities and obligations, including childcare. As well, the addicted mind is typically ridden with anger, resentment, blamefulness of others, and frustration – a perfect recipe for abuse. Sometimes even previously excellent parents can become neglectful and even abusive when in active addiction.

Addiction is expensive, and drains resources. People in active addiction commonly lose their job, income, and health benefits before too long (if they had these to begin with), and quickly rip through their financial resources. Obtaining their drink or drug takes priority over everything else, and money intended for rent, groceries, and utilities gets diverted to substance use. The result can be raising a child in poverty, poor nutrition, and squalor.

As well, lots of people with addiction have a co-occurring untreated mental health disorder, which may further impair their parenting skills. Substance use worsens mental illness symptoms and prevents otherwise effective medications from working properly. This, too, may affect the home environment.

The overall result is that children with at least one actively substance-using parent are at higher risk of developing mental and behavioral disorders and addiction at some point in their life.

Childhood factors. Besides family history, other childhood factors increase the risk of problem substance use. These are:

- Early exposure to addictive substances – being around parents, family members, or peers who use drugs or alcohol or who break the law can increase a child's risk of future substance use,
- Early use – the earlier in life that individuals first try drugs or alcohol, the more likely they are to develop addiction,
- Social exclusion, poor social skills, social anxiety – attempts to gain social acceptance, show independence, and succumb to peer pressure is a common pathway to substance use among young people. Many find that drugs or alcohol help them overcome shyness, social awkwardness, or social phobia, which can lead to repeated use. As well, adolescents are more likely to use alcohol or drugs if they hang out with deviant friends, or friends who facilitate substance use,
- Poor school performance,
- Availability of drugs at school, and
- Lack of parental supervision – a recent study out of Iowa State University showed that parents can reduce the risk of addiction in their adolescent children simply by becoming involved in their kids' lives. Knowing what's going on with their kids and friends helps counteract negative social influences. You don't even have to be a "super-parent" to make a big difference; the researchers found that as long as parents are in the 71st percentile of parenting, they can counteract negative peer effects. The important thing is to invest time – especially in pre-adolescence and adolescence – to build a relationship and rapport. Open, respectful, and non-judgmental communication is key; if kids don't think talking things over with their parents is safe, they'll keep secrets.

Aggressive behavior. Although it may seem strange that being aggressive is a risk factor for addiction, many researchers consider it one of the most important. The Twelve Step program regards anger and resentment – the underlying elements of aggressive behavior – as the root of addiction. I tend to agree with them; addicts are typically angry, resentful, and defensive (if you don't believe me, ask your family!).

Aggressive behavior is an especially toxic risk factor for youth, because it's significantly related to early substance use (before age 14), and more than quadruples the risk of developing a substance use disorder by early adulthood.

To this end, one of the central focuses of addiction treatment is helping addicts to identify, confront, and find peace with their anger and resentments. Addressing the emotional dysregulation that leads to aggression significantly reduces the risk of relapse.

Chronic stress. Being overwhelmed by stressors is a common pathway to addiction. At its core, addiction is a dysfunctional coping mechanism, what psychologists refer to as *escape/avoidance coping*. By numbing their mind with psychoactive (mind-altering) substances and withdrawing into social isolation, people attempt to shut out the world and all its problems and stressors. Substance use provides temporary relief from stress, if only for a short while. Unfortunately, it inevitably worsens the stress because the effects of addictive substances on the brain lower stress tolerance, and avoiding problems never leads to a solution.

For many people, life stressors, conflict, and problems are their greatest trigger for substance use and relapse. However, it's unrealistic to try to avoid stress and difficulties in life; life will always have its ups and downs. Because of this, addiction treatment programs emphasize learning new, healthy ways to handle life on life's terms and cope with stress in a healthy and functional way.

History of trauma and adverse experiences. Some people use drugs or alcohol to cope with the ongoing mental effects of traumatic events, whether they happened recently or long ago. Many survivors of trauma – especially deliberate trauma at the hands of others – live with a deep sense of insecurity and mistrust. They don't view the world as a safe place, and they put up walls that prevent closeness with others. Their pain and haunting memories are a source of simmering anger and resentment, which is understandable, given that life has been so unfair. Some suffer intrusive thoughts and memories of their trauma, including nightmares and flashbacks, which keeps the pain fresh. These haunting memories and the assortment of negative feelings (such as anger, guilt, injustice, fear, anxiety, and shame) become a reliable source of pain and unhappiness, and they may seek temporary relief through substance use as a welcome break from their tortured thoughts and feelings.

Post-traumatic stress disorder (PTSD) has become a household name, largely due to veterans returning from conflict zones with terrible psychological injuries. Given the severity of the symptoms of PTSD, it's not surprising there's a high association between PTSD and addiction. About 20% of people who experience severe trauma will develop PTSD. However, people don't have to have full-out PTSD or even experience severe trauma to suffer disruptive and painful psychological symptoms that elevate their risk of addiction.

Significant trauma can come from one horrible event, but may also result from a pattern of events over time. For example, being bullied in school over a prolonged time, being subjected to repeated workplace harassment, living in poverty, or being neglected over an entire childhood can cause the same psychological trauma as a single horrifying event. What matters is how it affects the individual's thoughts and feelings, not the specifics of the trauma.

Too, we must recognize that living through addiction is, in itself, a profoundly traumatic experience. It ravages the psyche, and disrupts normal brain function. It's associated with devastating loss: material wealth, employment, family and friends, health, and happiness. It's a miserable and prolonged experience, a struggle of a lifetime.

Identifying and confronting past trauma is a necessary part of addiction therapy and relapse prevention – this is known as *trauma-informed care.*

Mental illness. Mental health disorders and addiction are closely linked. In fact, addiction itself is classified as a mental health disorder by the medical diagnostic manual (the DSM 5 – the *Diagnostic and Statistical Manual of Mental Disorders*). Addiction and other mental illnesses share genetic causes, risk factors, and many of the same symptoms. More than half of people with addiction also have a mental health disorder, most commonly depression or anxiety.

Addiction and mental illness are so closely tied together that one can cause the other, and it can be difficult to tell which came first. Many people begin their substance use to "self-medicate" their mental symptoms. Some aren't even aware they have a diagnosable and treatable mental disorder; they've been living with the symptoms for so long that it's just normal for them. Their doctor might not see it either, because addiction symptoms can overlap and conceal a concurrent mental health disorder.

The link between mental illness and addiction underscores the importance of early recognition, diagnosis, and treatment in anyone who struggles with mental health problems. This is especially so in children and adolescents, who tend to internalize their symptoms and may not recognize that something's wrong. They also fear the social stigma of mental issues, so they tend to be secretive and evasive about their symptoms. Most mental health disorders are easily treated, so it's truly a tragedy when anyone lives unnecessarily with such distressing symptoms, and doubly so if it results in addiction.

*   *   *

When we go from being healthy and thriving to caught up in life-consuming addiction, we may wonder: how did this happen? How did I get to this point? Could I have foreseen this? Well, most people who develop addiction get there through one or more of only a few pathways. Knowing these pathways to addiction helps us recognize our triggers to avoid when we're in recovery, and allows us to recognize when someone else may be heading down the same road as we once did.

It's tempting to believe that people get addicted because drugs and alcohol make you feel good, and everybody likes feeling good. While the euphoric effects of substance use are definitely part of it, we've already discussed how this doesn't fully explain addiction. It's also tempting to conclude that people develop addiction because of a lack of morals. However, if deciding to take a drink or drug makes a person immoral, then there are a lot of immoral people in America. In my work in addictions, I've encountered many very good and upstanding people who've fallen to addiction, including – if you take that to be an indication of morality – members of the clergy. For anyone who believes that addiction results from a lack of willpower or character, or from just not caring about life and health, then science would disagree. Let's put that point on hold for now, and in the upcoming chapters we'll see why addiction is a matter of biology, not a matter of morality, willpower, or character strength.

Addiction develops because of the effects of repeated substance use on the brain of susceptible individuals. The pathways to addiction are the reasons that individuals use psychoactive substances repeatedly, allowing addiction to develop. The risk factors are what make people vulnerable to addiction, and the pathways to addiction are how people get there. Let's now look at each of the pathways to addiction.

Becoming addicted to prescription medications. Lots of prescription drugs have a high addiction potential, and just because they're taken by prescription for a legitimate medical reason doesn't protect people from becoming addicted. The transition from taking prescription medications for their intended medical purpose to misusing them can be very subtle, and people may be unaware or in denial as this transition occurs. For example, people who take prescription pain medications (opioids such as codeine or oxycodone) may continue using them for their euphoric effects as their pain decreases and their need for pain medication ends. Even though their primary motivation is now the euphoric effects, they can easily rationalize it by telling themselves they still need the drugs for pain.

As people who misuse their prescription medications develop tolerance, they require more and more of the drug to get the same effect, and they may begin taking more of the drug and more often than prescribed. The prescriber will on flag this when the individual asks for higher doses, early refills, or reports "lost or stolen" prescriptions, and will probably stop prescribing the drug. Difficulty in obtaining enough drug causes desperation: people may resort to drug-seeking behavior with healthcare providers ("doctor shopping" by going to multiple prescribers in one day, or faking illness to get prescriptions), dealing drugs, obtaining drugs on the street, or resorting to harder drugs that are cheaper and easier to get (such as heroin).

This may sound extreme, but it happens. A lot. And it happens to good, regular people who may have never even thought of using drugs before. Most are caught off-guard and unaware, and may not realize they have a problem until it's too late. The U.S. is the highest consumer of prescription opioids in the world, with Canada being the second highest. In 2012, 255 million opioid prescriptions were dispensed in the U.S., making opioids the most frequently prescribed medications in America. That comes out to 81.3 opioid prescriptions per 100 people. The opioid prescribing rate has been falling since then, with 168 million prescriptions in 2018 (51.4 prescriptions per 100 people). Although the total number of opioid prescriptions has been declining, the dosages have been increasing, and the average daily dose is now about triple what it was in 1999. (These numbers have all been provided by the U.S. National Institutes on Drug Abuse (NIDA) and the Centers for Disease Control and Prevention (CDC) – see the reference list at the back of the book.)

The 2018 U.S. NSDUH found that eight out of ten heroin users began their addiction by using prescription opioids, and that people who become addicted to prescription opioids are 40 times more likely than the general population to end up as heroin addicts. About 21-29% of people who're prescribed opioids for legitimate medical reasons misuse them, and 8-12% develop an opioid addiction. About 4-6% of people who misuse prescription opioids transition to heroin.

In 2018, about 9.9 million people in the U.S. misused prescription opioids. "Misuse" means taking them without a prescription, in doses above what was prescribed, for longer than prescribed, or for reasons other than what they were prescribed for. More than half (51.3%) of the people who misused prescription opioids obtained them from a friend or relative. More than a third (37.6%) got the opioids by prescription or by stealing from a clinic. A further 6.5% obtained their opioids by purchasing them from a dealer or other stranger.

There's a lot of pressure on prescribers to stop putting so many prescription pain medications on the street, so many people who truly need them (such as people with severe cancer pain) have difficulty getting enough medications (or even any at all). This rebound effect of the opioid crisis has been called "the other opioid crisis." Reduced access to prescribed opioids for those who genuinely need them has driven many to seek opioids from illicit sources, or to resort to using cheaper, more easily accessible illicit opioids, such as heroin.

So far, we've been talking about opioid medications, but there are other types of prescription drugs that are addictive: sedative/hypnotics (such as benzodiazepines), stimulants (such as medications used to treat ADHD), and hallucinogen/dissociatives (such as the anesthetic ketamine). All are associated with addiction potential and a similar escalation as opioids.

Self-medicating symptoms of mental illness. Mental illness symptoms are uncomfortable, difficult to live with, and even excruciating. These symptoms significantly disrupt people's ability to function, costing them opportunities for jobs, education, relationships, and so on. Some don't even realize they have a treatable mental health problem, so they don't know to seek help. Some are too embarrassed to seek help. Some can't afford help, or don't have access to it. When people with mental illness symptoms try drugs or alcohol and experience relief from their symptoms, it makes them want to do it again. Thus can begin repeated substance use and addiction.

The ironic thing about self-medicating mental symptoms with addictive substances is that although there may be brief relief, the substance use worsens the symptoms afterward. Mental health disorders are primarily caused by abnormal levels of neurotransmitters in the brain, and substance use causes a rebound effect that worsens the abnormal levels. Thus, a vicious cycle ensues: mental health symptoms –> substance use to relieve the symptoms –> worsened symptoms –> more substance use –> and so on.

Self-medicating mental illness is a common pathway to addiction: just over half of people with addiction have a co-occurring mental health disorder.

Social Reasons. This is an especially prevalent pathway to addiction among adolescents and young adults. When people feel socially awkward or phobic, they may find that drugs or alcohol put them at ease in social settings. The calming and disinhibiting effects make them come out of their shell, and they like their newfound substance-induced social skills. Soon, they're resorting to substance use in more and more social settings, including work or school, and repeated substance use begins.

Peer pressure to use drugs or alcohol is also a significant factor, especially among adolescents, who wish to impress their friends, be part of the group, and demonstrate independence.

They like how it makes them feel. Addictive substances produce pleasurable effects, such as euphoria (an intense feeling of happiness and well-being), sedation (feeling calm and relaxed), a sense of detachment from the world, or even hallucinations. Some people enjoy these effects so much that they repeatedly seek them out.

When people repeatedly use drugs or alcohol, tolerance develops, and they may escalate how much and how often they drink or use as they "chase the high." After a while, they may feel little or no effect from their substance use, so they keep escalating. This can result in dangerously high levels of use, experimenting with more potent drugs, or trying other types of drugs.

Coping mechanism. Some people feel they can handle stress better when they're under the influence. Stress is a normal part of life – it helps us maintain alertness and ensures we direct our efforts toward problems that require attention. However, some people find stress overwhelming, particularly if they have a negative outlook or are prone to other negative feelings such as depression. Sometimes people face more stress than usual because of problems that suddenly pile up.

People who've previously been able to use alcohol or drugs without becoming addicted may suddenly find that things change when they're hit with overwhelming stress. As they repeatedly turn to drugs or alcohol to cope, their brain undergoes the changes that create addiction.

Similarly, some people resort to substance use to cope with negative feelings. Some folks live with overwhelming guilt, sadness, remorse, anger, and other painful emotions. Some experience grief they can't seem to come to terms with. As with mental illness symptoms, the brief relief from drink or drug may drive them to use repeatedly.

Substance use is often combined with another escape/avoidance coping mechanism: social avoidance. People shut themselves out from others and the world by disappearing on a binge or isolating themselves to avoid life and its problems. Noticing a person beginning to socially isolate is often one of the first red flags that they may be developing addiction or relapsing.

Adolescents are especially prone to internalizing their stress or negative feelings and trying to handle their troubles on their own. Their lack of life experience makes them vulnerable to the adverse effects of real-world stress.

Even people whose addiction didn't begin as a coping mechanism end up relying on their substance use to cope with the stress of their train-wrecking life, or to numb the negative feelings that typically accompany obsessive substance use.

Performance enhancement. This is a common reason for using stimulants, either prescription (such as medications used to treat narcolepsy or ADHD) or non-prescription (such as cocaine or crystal methamphetamine). These drugs make people feel more alert, energetic, and confident, so they feel they can perform better in life. Addiction may develop, which almost invariably ends up ruining their life rather than enhancing their performance.

Besides stimulants, some people also feel they can perform better with other drugs or alcohol, due to the relaxing, disinhibiting, and confidence-boosting effects. They may find stressful tasks such as job interviews easier to face, and their substance use can become a psychological crutch. Eventually, they may begin to rely on their substance use for everyday life, and addiction can develop.

Avoidance of withdrawal. Withdrawal from repeated substance use can cause agonizing or even dangerous physical and psychological symptoms and intense cravings that may last days or weeks. As addiction progresses and tolerance develops, avoidance of withdrawal usually becomes the primary driver of continued substance use. Addicts commonly describe a point where their substance use was no longer "fun," and became about avoiding withdrawal and trying to feel "normal."

Withdrawal symptoms may propel some people to continue using their prescription medications even though they no longer have a medical need. A tapering and detoxification plan should be part of the treatment plan when addictive drugs are prescribed. Unfortunately, this often doesn't happen.

*   *   *

So, addiction results from fundamental changes to the brain from repeated exposure to addictive substances. This is more likely to occur in individuals with genetic or environmental vulnerabilities, and who end up on one or more of the typical pathways to repeated substance use.

Treatment programs focus on addressing the factors that brought on the individual's addiction in the first place. For example, they'll identify specific risk factors that apply to each person, and address these. Some risk factors, such as our genetics, cannot be changed, but some can be corrected. For example, people with mental health problems can receive treatment, and those who struggle with the psychological effects of past traumas can be helped to stop the unkind past from "owning them." Treatment programs also address the brain changes and psychological pathology of addiction, which we'll discuss in upcoming chapters.

In the next chapter, we'll look at an important aspect of addiction, one that some people may initially turn up their nose to: the concept that addiction is a disease. If you recoil at the notion of addiction as a disease, then I ask that you keep an open mind and hear me out. I was once one of those people, too.

2

Why Do They Call Addiction a Disease?

Some people get really needled when they hear addiction referred to as a disease. After all: it's a choice, not a disease, *right?* When I was practicing as a physician, I didn't buy into the disease idea either, because I, too, believed that people with addiction were just bad people who woke up every day and made bad decisions. However, since becoming an addictions researcher, I've become convinced that the disease model of addiction is entirely correct. And it's not just my opinion; it's based on science. Who cares, though? Why does it matter if we call it a disease or not? Well, it does matter for a couple of important reasons.

Classifying addiction as a disease helps break down the terrible stigma that burdens people with addiction and presents a barrier to recovery. It helps people understand that by the time someone has crossed the line into addiction, they've long ago lost freedom of choice over their substance use, and are now displaying the symptoms of a brain disease. Although in the very beginning drinking alcohol or using drugs was a choice, the ability to choose has been lost. Otherwise, addicts would do what everyone else does – stop the substance use when it begins tearing apart their life.

In this chapter, we'll discuss why addiction qualifies as a disease. If you're skeptical, I ask only that you keep an open mind. I, too, was skeptical once, but developments in neuroscience over the past decade have provided irrefutable objective support for the "disease model of addiction."

*   *   *

The science community lacks consensus on a definition of what, exactly, constitutes a disease. Over the years, the debate about what defines a disease has taken some unfortunate and unscientific twists and turns. The disease definition has been manipulated for profit by private industry, and warped by societal stigma and prejudice rather than being established by science. Addiction has been caught up in this screwy process, often with disastrous effects.

Addiction is not the only condition that's suffered from unsound manipulations of the disease definition. For example, osteoporosis (pathological thinning of the bones) was long considered nothing more than a normal part of aging, until it was officially recognized as a disease by the World Health Organization (WHO) in 1994. Using the same logic, you could consider atherosclerotic heart disease (the process that causes heart attacks, the leading cause of death in the Western world) as a normal, unavoidable part of aging, but nobody would argue against classifying heart attacks as a disease.

Another unfortunate victim of the lack of a disease definition is homosexuality, which was long categorized as a pathological mental disease. Because of this, disastrous and humiliating attempts were made to "cure" homosexuality, using hormone treatments, hypnosis followed by a trip to a brothel, electroshock therapy, testicle transplants, shocks to the genitals while looking at gay porn ("aversion therapy"), and even brain surgery. It wasn't until 1974 that homosexuality was officially declassified as a disease by the American Psychiatric Association. As you can see, determining what qualifies as a disease often has nothing to do with science.

Unfortunately, government and private industry have often seized control of what constitutes a disease for reasons that have nothing to do with science or the public's best interests. It has (and still does) often boiled down to what will maximize profits for health insurance corporations or pharmaceutical consortia. This has been the case with addiction, where political and profitability concerns drive much of the opposition to the disease model. Insurance companies try to dodge the billions of dollars in payments required to cover addiction treatment and time off work to recover, and therefore oppose defining addiction as a disease. Likewise, government policy-makers have also often opposed the medicalization of addiction. Their opposition is based on various motivations, including the powerful lobbies of the health insurance industry and the privatized prison system. Politicians who become involved in advocacy for addiction may risk alienating much of their electorate, who may not be familiar with the nature of addiction. People in active addiction generally do not vote or make campaign contributions, and there's no well-heeled "behind the scenes" lobby that represents people with addiction.

Besides political and financial motivations, the social stigma of addiction also obstructs acceptance of the disease model. Even among healthcare professionals, addiction remains widely stigmatized as a failing of morality or just bad decision-making, rather than a pathological brain affliction. Even if that were so, it would not preclude the classification of addiction as a disease; lung cancer, for example, is uncommon outside of people who smoke, and few people would deprive lung cancer of disease status because it's based on a decision to use tobacco. However, addiction suffers from deep-seated stigma and bias that goes well beyond that of smoking.

The stigma of addiction arises largely from the behaviors that make up its symptoms. The most visible people with addiction are typically unkempt, pathetic-looking individuals who may behave aggressively, engage in criminal behavior, and act strangely and antisocially. Addicts at their rock bottom may be visible as dirty, homeless, scary people. However, as we'll see when we talk about the effects of addictive substances on the brain, these are simply manifestations of the symptoms of the disease of addiction; these very same scary and undesirable people were once ordinary, functioning people, and will be again if they succeed in finding their way into healthy recovery.

The stigma of addiction has been worsened by the so-called "War on Drugs." While the superhuman efforts of the men and women of the various agencies involved in eliminating sources of production, importation, and distribution of drugs are laudable, policy-makers also declared war on individual substance users by making possession of drugs for personal use a criminal offense.

The term "War on Drugs" has disappeared from official use, having been dropped by the U.S. Office of National Drug Control Policy (ONDCP) during the Obama administration. However, simple possession of drugs for personal use remains a crime in America and many other countries. This policy diverts people with addiction away from the medical system, instead channeling them into the criminal justice system. With addiction criminalized, people who're already socially isolated, stigmatized, and marginalized have been driven even further underground.

Many addicts refuse to admit their problem or even discuss it with their doctor for fear of being reported or arrested. Fear of arrest keeps many from calling for help in overdose situations; the criminalization of addiction has thereby almost certainly contributed to the massive overdose death rate. I recently conducted a survey among addicts at a safe injection site, and only one in five said they would call for help if they or a friend were overdosing. In every case, they said it was because of fear of arrest. Many of the people I've interviewed who just survived an overdose said their drug-using friends ran away from the scene without calling for help when the overdose occurred.

Humans Rights Watch reported (in their 2016 report *Every 25 Seconds: The Human Toll of Criminalizing Drug Use in the United States*) that every 25 seconds someone in the U.S. is funneled into the criminal justice system accused of nothing more than possession of drugs for personal use. Many are charged for "drug residue," where swabs of their belongings find "trace" amounts of drugs so small that they can only be detected by specialized laboratory equipment. A hollow victory that does nothing to help solve the addiction crisis.

The criminalization of drug possession results in many people – especially young people – being burdened with a criminal record that deprives them of opportunities to thrive once they've overcome their addiction. They're often alienated from opportunities for education and employment, and sometimes even stripped of voting rights. Single mothers may be barred from social supports they need to provide their children with a healthy environment.

Worldwide, healthcare systems desperately lack funding for addiction treatment programs, yet many of these countries spend tremendous amounts of public funds on policing and incarcerating addicts for simple drug possession. In some countries, the privatization of prisons has resulted in incarceration becoming a lucrative private-sector business that can afford lobby activity to keep the prisons full. As such, there's often considerable pressure on governments and financial incentive for politicians to maintain the *status quo* of the criminalization of addiction.

The point here is that there are powerful forces at work to maintain the pernicious negative stigma against those who suffer from addiction, and this plays a significant role in closing people's minds to the concept of addiction as a disease. People are led to view addiction as a crime rather than an illness. The disease model of addiction represents a significant, evidence-based step toward reducing this crippling stigma, and moving addiction from the criminal justice system to the medical system, where it belongs. However, speaking strictly from a medical perspective, addiction does indeed qualify as a disease. Let's discuss that now.

*   *   *

Although there's no widely accepted definition of a disease, a reasonable, all-encompassing definition may be: *a disorder of structure or function that produces specific signs or symptoms that affect a specific system, organ, or group of organs of the body*. A disease may be caused by various agents, such as infection (viruses or bacteria, for example), inflammation, genetic defects, toxins, or environmental factors, but usually does not include injury. Diseases disrupt the body's usual functions, and often usurp its natural processes to propagate themselves. For example, a virus causes disease by entering the body, then using the body's own physiological processes to invade cells and use the cells' DNA and protein synthesis apparatus to reproduce itself, resulting in the production of "baby viruses" that then leave the cell and carry on the disease process. The virus thereby "hijacks" the body's natural processes to propagate itself, disrupting normal bodily functions. The result is specific signs and symptoms that are caused by the virus's effects on a body organ or system, and these signs and symptoms are what we call a disease. Some viruses act mainly on the liver (causing hepatitis), some target the lungs (causing pneumonia), and some act specifically on the brain (causing encephalitis).

Like viruses, addictive substances are foreign toxins that enter the body and alter its natural functions to propagate their continued use. Like viruses, addictive substances use our DNA (through epigenetics) to promote their continued use. The result is the specific syndrome of signs and symptoms that we call addiction.

As with other diseases, addiction causes physiological and structural changes to the body. An overwhelming body of research evidence has shown that addiction involves physical changes in DNA and other molecular structures and functions in brain cells, and changes in the connections and activities of brain circuits (if you're not sure what exactly that means, don't worry – you'll be an expert by the time you finish this book). These are real changes that can be seen on MRI scans and under the microscope. As well, addictive substances trigger the brain's immune system, resulting in harmful inflammation, which also happens with viral infections. As such, addiction is demonstrably a physical disease that causes disruptive physical changes in the body, not at all unlike how viruses cause disease.

As with other brain diseases, addiction alters brain function in pathological ways. The corrupted brain functions result in aberrant thought processes and behaviors that promote continued substance use, create barriers to seeking and accepting help, and favor relapse in those who attempt to stop. At that point, the individual is under the power of a disease, and they're no more able to make it go away than cancer victims can make their malignancy go away.

Another factor that supports the disease model of addiction is that the symptoms and pathophysiology are remarkably uniform between different people, regardless of race, culture, age, gender, socioeconomic status, or country of residence. The same can be said of other diseases, like cancer or diabetes.

*   *   *

Why does it matter if we call addiction a disease or not? Well, there are several reasons. First, it helps medical practitioners and researchers to frame addiction in the proper context and give it the attention it deserves. It also opens the door for medical insurance organizations to provide coverage for treatment, and for employers to provide sick leave for treatment and recovery. As well, it's a big step toward quashing the stigma of addiction.

Systemic biases can also be better addressed when we use the disease model to understand addiction. For example, employers who understand addiction as a disease are probably more likely to hire people who're in recovery from addiction when they realize that the person was afflicted with a disease and not possessed of a flawed personality. Companies are more likely to view employees who develop addiction as treatable, rather than a lost cause suitable only for automatic firing. Policy-makers are more likely to make changes to keep people arrested for simple drug possession out of jails, and to loosen the purse strings for treatment programs.

The disease model also helps people in active addiction understand that they're not a lost cause, that treatment is available, and that recovery is possible. When society sees addicts as criminals rather than people with a treatable medical condition, addicts may see themselves the same way.

The disease model of addiction offers benefits that will help our efforts to overcome the substance use epidemic. However, viewing addiction as a disease boils down to a simple matter of science. When addiction is viewed through the lens of science and without the fog of societal stigma, it is fundamentally a disease process. As we progress through our review of addiction together, you'll see that understanding this disease process allows us to get to the bottom of what happened to us.

3

The Addicted Brain

There really is such a thing as the "addicted brain." Although substance use sickens other parts of the body, addiction is primarily a disease of the brain. Because of new techniques for studying the living brain (such as *functional magnetic resonance imaging* (fMRI), and *positron emission tomography* (PET) scanning, for example), our understanding of the addicted brain has advanced considerably over the past two decades. Until recently, we could only study the brain directly through dissection during an autopsy; now we can watch the brain working in real-time, right down to different molecules as they go about their business in brain cells. So, we now know *a lot* about the addicted brain, and everything we've learned has confirmed the disease model of addiction. Our newfound understanding of how addiction transforms the structure and function of the brain provides explanations for the symptomatology of addiction, and offers new insights into how we can treat this horrible disease. Addiction really is a matter of biology.

Besides brain changes, the symptoms of addiction also result from the effects of substance use on the mind. We'll discuss the addicted mind (as well as what, exactly, the difference is between the brain and the mind) in the next chapter.

Addiction occurs simply because addictive substances overwhelmingly activate and adulterate key brain structures and processes in a way that propagates substance use. Two particular brain systems are primarily involved:

- **The executive control system** – this is the part of the brain that allows us to engage in higher-level thinking, such as reasoning, planning, and decision-making. It protects us from harm by giving us judgment and self-control, and helps us achieve our goals by coordinating our behaviors so that they're goal-directed. The executive control system decides what we do, how we do it, and when; therefore, it may be thought of as the "CEO of the brain," and

- **The learning system** – this is the brain system that enables us to adapt to our environment and achieve our goals by learning new information and behaviors. It helps us learn from our mistakes and successes, so that our future actions are improved by lessons learned from our past actions. Much of the brain's learning is driven by a "reward system" that releases feel-good chemicals that give us a bit of a "high" when we accomplish something good. We learn to repeat behaviors that earn us a reward and to avoid behaviors that don't. As such, much of our learning is reward-based (reward-based learning is known as *conditioning*). The learning system is thus involved in memory and motivation.

Once the brain has undergone the physical changes that create addiction, the effects occur independent of intoxication, so they disrupt brain function even when the person is sober. Unfortunately, many of these brain changes are long-lasting and time-stable. Nevertheless, these effects can be effectively countered, and people in recovery can return to normal function and behavior. *But...* the addicted brain can be re-activated by re-exposure to addictive substances years – even decades – after the last drink or drug, resulting in a rapid resumption of the same behaviors and dysfunction. In my work in addiction, I've seen countless cases of people with many years of sobriety relapsing right back to where they were with even one drink or drug. In my work in a detox center, I hear the same thing time and again from people coming back from relapse: *I picked up right where I left off!*

*   *   *

The human brain is a fascinating contraption. It has justifiably been described as the most complex object in the universe. It's a collection of 86 billion nerve cells – known as *neurons* – that work together in ways we're only beginning to understand. This most formidable of machines – capable of the most wondrous of achievements – can be manipulated by addictive substances into shattering lives.

The brain is not simply a big lump of brain cells. Rather, it consists of many parts with different structures and functions that operate together in different combinations, depending on the task at hand. Because of this, there are wondrously complex and intricate interconnections between the various parts.

The human brain weighs 3.3 pounds – half of what our skin weighs – making up about 2% of our body weight. It contains 86 billion neurons – the gray matter – and billions more nerve fibers – the white matter. Each of these billions of neurons has up to 10,000 connections to other neurons. A piece of brain the size of a grain of sand contains 100,000 neurons and one billion interconnections. Despite the trillions of inter-connections that crisscross and run in all directions, the brain's functions are harmonious and sophisticated beyond measure; its abilities are boundlessly greater than the sum of its parts. The entire body is there to support the brain, and it alone is responsible for all humankind's actions and interactions, society, history, and accomplishments.

Even though the brain makes up only 2% of our body weight, it uses up to 60% of our total energy and oxygen intake. It's composed of 73% water, yet it takes only 2% dehydration to disable it. The brain is the fattiest organ in the body, being 60% fat. A quarter of all the cholesterol in our body is contained in the brain, which needs it; without enough cholesterol, brain cells die. Maybe cheeseburgers are brain food, after all.

The brain works by transmitting information between neurons, which explains why there are so many interconnections. None of the neurons actually touch. There's a microscopic gap between them, so neurons communicate by releasing various chemicals across the gap. These message chemicals are known as *neurotransmitters*. Each of the many different neurotransmitters means different things to different neurons at different times and in different amounts. The sending brain cell produces and releases the neurotransmitters, and the receiving cell picks up these signals on *receptors*, which recognize the signal and understand the message. The receiving neuron then passes the signal to the next neuron in the pathway. Thus, the message is passed along the neuron sequence that forms a pathway. There are pathways for every kind of brain function: producing emotions, moving our arms, thinking about what to have for lunch, everything.

There are many different neurotransmitters, each with various functions. Of course, if the neurotransmitters become disrupted, the messages will get mixed up and brain function will be altered. Neurotransmitter disruptions are responsible for many problems and disorders, such as Alzheimer's disease, Parkinson's disease, depression, schizophrenia, and so on. Addiction is also on the list. Alzheimer's disease causes specific neurotransmitter disruptions that cause the specific symptoms of Alzheimer's disease. The same is true for Parkinson's disease, and depression. Likewise, addiction results from specific neurotransmitter disruptions that cause the specific symptoms of addiction. Besides using neurotransmitters, neurons can also pass messages along by direct electrical impulses, and these, too, are affected in addiction. However, the main problem in the addicted brain derives from the disordered neurotransmitters.

Although the various drugs of addiction each have different ways of disrupting neurotransmitters, the neurotransmitter dopamine is the common end-point. Dopamine is also the culprit in addictive behaviors, such as compulsive gambling, compulsive shopping, and so on. Dopamine is responsible for the feel-good euphoria of the high, which provides positive reinforcement for continued drug use. Conversely, removing the drug causes reduced production and release of dopamine, which causes the opposite of a high: depressed mood and low energy, which makes the individual seek the drug to stop the negative feelings. Thus, there is positive and negative reinforcement involved in drug-seeking behavior. Reinforcement, positive and negative, is a form of learning known as conditioning.

In normal life, rewards usually come only with time and effort. For example, going out and earning a paycheck gives us a good feeling (from dopamine release in our brain), but earning this reward takes a lot of time and effort. Substance use gives the brain a much bigger and faster burst of dopamine reward without all the work, providing a shortcut, flooding the brain with dopamine and other feel-good neurotransmitters.

The brain is not naturally exposed to such massive bursts of dopamine, so it compensates, trying to get things back to normal – a process known as *homeostasis*. The brain sharply cuts back the production of dopamine and reduces the number of dopamine receptors, and the individual becomes sensitized to dopamine so that it produces much less of a pleasurable feeling. As a result, people who repeatedly use substances need more and more of their drug to get the same effect. This is what's known as tolerance.

The reduced dopamine and receptor levels result in rock-bottom dopamine levels when the substance isn't present. Therefore, when addicts are not high or drunk, their baseline dopamine levels drop way below normal, and they feel the opposite of high – depressed, lifeless, lacking energy, and unable to feel pleasure. Eventually, even such ordinarily rewarding things as eating, accomplishing a goal, or finding a fulfilling relationship no longer bring them pleasure. They need their drug just to feel normal, let alone high. As we discussed in chapter 1, withdrawal is a major cause of addiction because it induces people who may not yet be addicted to escalate their substance use. It's also a major driver of continued substance use among those who are addicted.

Anything we put in our body that messes with our neurotransmitters is referred to as *psychoactive*. All substances of addiction are psychoactive, including anabolic steroids. Some drugs, such as marijuana and heroin, have a chemical structure that mimics neurotransmitters, especially dopamine. This "fools" receptors and allows the drugs to activate the feel-good reward system directly. Although these drugs mimic the brain's natural neurotransmitters, they don't activate neurons in the same way, resulting in abnormal message transmission through the neural networks. Other drugs, such as stimulants, cause neurons to produce and release abnormally large amounts of natural neurotransmitters or prevent their normal breakdown. This produces a greatly amplified message, disrupting communication channels.

In addition to its role in the reward system, dopamine is also involved in other brain processes, including those that regulate movement, emotion, motivation, and, oddly enough, screening our thoughts. Because of this, imbalances in dopamine, such as the highs and lows brought on by addictive substances, can have other serious consequences. For example, high levels of dopamine cause the symptom of psychosis, which may include a loss of touch with reality, visual or auditory hallucinations, receiving weird but compelling instructions from inner voices, paranoia, ideas of reference (believing that people on TV and the radio are talking about you), and generally weird behavior. Some addictive substances are particularly tied to psychosis – such as marijuana, MDMA, and methamphetamine.

There are other effects of the extreme highs and lows of dopamine from psychoactive substance use. For example, low dopamine levels cause Parkinson's disease, so the lower-than-normal dopamine levels when withdrawing from substance use may cause shaking and unsteadiness similar to Parkinson's disease. Dopamine is also involved in regulating emotions, so the ups and downs of dopamine have much to do with the sudden alterations and extremes of emotions we see in addicts as they cycle through their substance use and withdrawal.

Although dopamine is the neurotransmitter most relevant to addiction, addictive substances also affect various other neurotransmitters, most of which are involved in crucial brain functions. Notably, the neurotransmitters that cause depression, anxiety, obsession-compulsion, and other mental health problems (neurotransmitters such as serotonin, norepinephrine, and GABA, for example) are also affected, partly explaining the considerable overlap between mental health disorders and addiction.

Now, let's take a closer look at the first of the two brain systems that are hijacked by substance use: the executive control system, the "CEO of the brain."

*   *   *

The executive control system is the section of our brain that gives us the ability to think, reason, plan, self-monitor, exercise self-control, make decisions, and adapt to what's going on around us (these are referred to as our *cognitive functions*). Importantly, it's also responsible for inhibition, so we don't get derailed from our long-term goals by choosing immediate gratification when it interferes with our goals. As such, it's how we control and regulate our behaviors in a way that allows us to survive and thrive.

The executive control system is seated in the *pre-frontal cortex* (PFC). The PFC is the forward-most part of the brain – sitting in the front part of the frontal lobe – located directly behind your eyes and forehead.

Disruption of circuits in the PFC from the toxic effects of addictive substances results in profoundly erratic executive control functions. This is why addicts are virtually incapable of goal-directed behavior (for any goal other than substance use), and their judgment, self-control, flexibility, inhibition, and decision-making abilities are unhinged. The PFC also regulates our personality expression, how we go about social interactions, and how we interpret our interactions with others. It's not hard to imagine why disruption of the PFC would result in someone seeming to have a different personality, choosing immediate gratification despite the consequences, and being prone to bad decision-making – all hallmarks of addiction.

The discombobulation of the PFC from repeated substance use is extensive – so much so that it produces symptoms that closely resemble "dysexecutive syndrome," which occurs in people who have a stroke or other serious brain injury to the PFC. See if any of these symptoms of dysexecutive syndrome remind you of yourself or others during active addiction:

- Impulsivity,
- Euphoria,
- Impaired inhibition,
- Untruthfulness, confabulation,
- Poor ability to plan,
- Difficulty with time and sequencing,
- Lack of insight into one's own dysfunctional behaviors,
- Aggression,
- Restlessness,
- Apathy and lack of drive,
- Perseveration (obsessive or repeated thoughts or actions),
- Knowing-doing dissociation (i.e. undertaking unwise actions despite knowing better),
- Distractibility, poor concentration,
- Poor decision-making,
- Lack of social awareness, and
- Lack of concern for social rules.

Sounds a lot like the behaviors we see in addicts, *right?* Some of the PFC's functions are also disrupted in some mental health disorders, which further explains the overlap between addiction and other mental health disorders.

*   *   *

The other major brain system that's disrupted by addictive substances – the learning system – uses motivation and reward to direct our attention toward things that matter and that will help us achieve our goals. It enables us to learn from experience and adjust our behaviors to improve our performance and adapt to change. It's a critical mechanism for enabling us to survive and improve our situation in the world, providing us with a process for remembering information and behaviors that help us function better and avoid calamity.

Addiction utterly corrupts the otherwise beneficial learning process, so that it directs behavior exclusively toward a single goal – obtaining and consuming addictive substances, at the cost of all other goals and motivations. As such, addiction takes the brain's learning system – which is designed to help us adapt and thrive – and usurps it so that it does the opposite. The learning system in the addicted brain is maladaptive and motivates us to learn self-destructive behaviors, leading to sickness, dysfunction, and perhaps even death. Let's look at how the brain learns, and how addiction takes over this process.

Earlier, we talked about the many connections that exist between brain cells (neurons). When neurons connect in a series, we call that series of connections a pathway. When we learn something, new neuron connections form, creating a pathway that becomes part of our memory. When we access that memory, the neurons in that pathway fire (activate), and we recall the memory. These neuronal connections allow us to learn, store memories, remember things, understand the present based on what we've learned in the past, and interpret those memories to apply them to our present actions.

Learning is driven by motivation. There must be an attractive goal to motivate the mind to learn to behave in a way to attain that goal. When there's a barrier to that goal, the mind is motivated to learn how to overcome the barrier. When we achieve something that helps us survive – such as finding food when we're hungry – or that improves our situation in the world – such as getting a job promotion – our brain rewards us by releasing feel-good neurotransmitters (including dopamine) that provide us with a reward. This little "high" motivates us to do things that'll get us another reward. That's how our mind teaches us to repeat good behaviors and work toward our goals. Our executive brain functions allow us to use judgment and self-control to put off immediate gratification (such as goofing off at work) to achieve a more significant gratification later on (such as a job promotion).

Psychologists refer to this reward-based learning as reinforcement – positive reinforcement when we get a positive reward for doing something good, and negative reinforcement when we learn to do something to avoid punishments. For example, if we touch a hot stove, we get a painful burn (a negative reinforcement), so we learn to avoid touching hot stoves. To illustrate, let's look at some basic learning that's important to our survival: food acquisition.

We need food to survive. So, to ensure we learn to give our body food, our brain gives us a nice shot of our feel-good reward chemicals when we eat when we need to. That's why we feel pleasure when we have a good meal when we're hungry. Because of the reward, we learn to seek food when hungry. Conversely, if we don't seek food, we get hunger pains and feel weak and unwell – a punishment. So, we learn to obtain food when we're hungry because it helps us to feel pleasure (positive reinforcement) and avoid the punishment of hunger pangs (negative reinforcement).

The link between addiction and learning is that addictive drugs stimulate our brain's reward system to release feel-good chemicals at levels far higher than natural, creating euphoria. Because the reward from addictive substance use is so ultra-heightened, obtaining and consuming them becomes the dominant motivation in vulnerable individuals. This is why addicts will sacrifice all other motivations – including eating, sleeping, and accomplishing goals – to pursue their substance use.

Conversely, once substance use becomes regular, agonizing withdrawal symptoms occur – a punishment – after the drug wears off, driving addicts to seek their drug to avoid punishment. In early addiction, drug use is primarily driven by reward (positive reinforcement) because the "high" is still huge and there's little withdrawal. However, as addiction progresses the "high" diminishes as tolerance develops, while withdrawal symptoms become more pronounced. As such, later in addiction motivation is primarily driven by avoiding punishment (negative reinforcement). By this point, the brain's normal thought processes, logic, needs, motivations, and control functions have become derailed. The brain has been conditioned to focus on one goal: obtaining and using substances. The brain is now addicted.

Of course, most people who use alcohol and drugs become high and have the same rush of feel-good neurotransmitters, but they don't become addicted. Why is that? Well, as we discussed in chapter 1, addiction occurs in people who're vulnerable to the brain changes and have something driving them to seek repeated highs.

The usurpation of the brain's learning system is so complete that even the threat of loss of employment, savings, family, home, and friends doesn't stop the substance use. It's why addicts will use their rent and grocery money to buy their drug. It's why they'll even forsake the care of their children, even if they were previously dedicated parents. This is why nagging and cajoling addicts with threats won't make them stop their substance use or commit to treatment. It's also why addicts learn to be sneaky and deceptive and even criminal to overcome barriers to their drug use, such as lack of money, or family trying to interfere with the substance use. These are not liars or criminals; they're addicts displaying the symptoms of the addicted brain. Regardless, people must answer for their criminal behavior because being addicted is generally not accepted as a defense in court. When we're in recovery, we must own up to our past doings if we are to heal ourselves, our relationships, and our life. More on this in chapter 6.

The type of learning we've been discussing is called *operant conditioning* – learning through positive and negative reinforcements. There's another type of learning that's important to addiction, known as classical conditioning. Let's take a look at that now.

*   *   *

You may recall the story of Pavlov's dogs from high school biology or psychology. Ivan Pavlov was a Russian psychologist who first described associative learning, where our brain learns to connect things in our environment to rewards. Pavlov noticed that when he rang a bell every time he fed his dogs, after a while the dogs began salivating as soon as they heard the bell, even though they hadn't yet been given any food. This is because the dogs learned to associate the sound of the bell (the cue) with being fed (the reward). We now refer to this kind of learning as *classical conditioning*. Classical conditioning plays a big role in addiction and relapse.

As addiction develops and people become increasingly motivated to obtain their substance-based "reward," they devote more of their attentional resources to their substance. Anything associated with their drug gets their attention, and they become conditioned to associate these cues and the reward. As such, they come to subconsciously relate certain people, places, and things with their substance use, just like Pavlov's dogs associated the sound of the bell with the reward of being fed.

As addiction develops, substance use may become a daily occurrence, often many times a day. As it continues over the weeks, months, and even years, these learned cues become deeply embedded in the brain's memories. The extreme levels of reward and emotion associated with substance use further cement the learned cues. Soon, exposure to these cues triggers powerful cravings and extraordinary efforts to satisfy the cravings. For example, an alcoholic may learn to associate her favorite bar's street with drinking, so that simply seeing the street triggers cravings.

One of the unfortunate consequences of addiction learning is that these substance-related cues become permanent memories embedded in the subconscious mind. Even decades into recovery, people can be triggered by exposure to their cues, especially if they're vulnerable at the time. Avoiding people, places, and things associated with our substance use is an essential part of recovery.

Conditioned cues and triggers become so deeply embedded in the brain that they create automatic behaviors, by-passing our brain's

"CEO" (executive control system) so that addicts react without thinking first. Overriding these automatic behaviors and re-asserting thinking control over behavior is one of the main goals of addiction treatment. This is only possible when addicts are substance-free, so that their brain's "CEO" can begin functioning properly again. More on that in chapter 5.

*   *   *

Social learning is another way the brain learns addiction. However, it's of particular interest to us because it can be turned around and used decisively in recovery. Social learning is our brain's innate mechanism for learning new attitudes and behaviors by observing and emulating other people. We're born without any experience of the world, so our brain is designed to notice, register, and model the behavior of important others, almost right from birth. This instinct continues as we grow and learn to survive and thrive in a complex world. Social learning is especially important in childhood and adolescence, but continues throughout our lifetime.

Social learning can be intense among addicts. As they become alienated from their "nagging" family and friends and increasingly rejected and marginalized by society, addicts crave acceptance with some group of people – *any* group. Of course, the group most likely to accept them as they are is other addicts. Being around other people engaging in the same behaviors helps addicts feel better about themselves because it reduces their bad feelings about what they're doing (this is cognitive dissonance, which we'll talk about in the next chapter). After all, when you're doing something "bad," it can't be all *that* bad if everyone else is doing it too, *right?*

Social learning tends to escalate substance use as addicts push each other to new lows. It's also a common pathway to trying new drugs, when using-buddies expose each other to new drugs and ways of doing drugs. Social pressure from the group is a powerful deterrent to recovery, due to a phenomenon I call the "misery loves company effect." Addicts don't like it when their using-buddies get sober and healthy because it highlights their own continuing substance use and magnifies their bad feelings about themselves (their cognitive dissonance). They'll try hard to talk their friend out of recovery and push them to relapse. I see this happening a lot in my work with people in early recovery. Misery loves company, and the addict's selfish mind can't stand seeing someone else escape the misery of addiction. It's yet another reason that addicts in recovery need to stop associating with their old substance-using friends.

Social learning is a fundamental part of all credible addiction treatment and relapse prevention programs. The application of social learning to recovery includes:

- Ceasing contact with the people and places that previously served as models, triggers, and peer-driven influences for substance use,
- Developing a new network of friends and family who support recovery,
- Inclusion in a recovery support group, during treatment and after, that involves immersion in a culture of recovery, where recovery-based attitudes, behaviors, and values are modeled and rewarded,
- The use of vicarious experiences for providing modeling and motivation for recovery, to increase self-efficacy beliefs (we'll discuss this in chapter 6), and to show the way to recovery,
- Establishing and using a supportive network for a healthy approach to dealing with stress and adversity, and
- Learning skills and the self-confidence to respond appropriately to negative peer pressure.

Let's quickly recap how the brain's learning system is involved in addiction. There are three ways that the learning systems are adulterated in the addicted brain – operant conditioning (seeking substance-related rewards and avoiding punishments), classical conditioning (making associations between substance use and cues), and social learning (observing and mimicking others). The obvious question is: *if addiction is a learned behavior, can it be unlearned?* In short, yes! We'll discuss how that happens in chapter 6.

*   *   *

You may have heard the term neuroplasticity, as it's one of those medical terms that's rightfully gotten a lot of attention in the popular media. All it refers to is the brain's ability to adapt. The term "plasticity" in general refers to the ability of our body tissues to modify themselves according to our needs. For example, muscles have plasticity: if we lay around and don't use them, they shrink and lose tone. They become weak and diminished. After all, our body sees no point in maintaining big muscles if we never use them. However, if we exercise and stay active, our muscles respond by growing in size and strength to meet the demands we place upon them. Likewise, laying around and watching TV requires little brain effort, so our brain will respond accordingly by diminishing in capacity. After all, why spend all the energy on a robust brain if it's not needed? However, if we use our brain and challenge it, it will grow in capacity and ability. It really does work like that. This is neuroplasticity – brain plasticity.

The brain is one of the body's most "plastic" organs; it's built to adapt. The brain is geared to re-wire itself, and modify or form new connections so that we can learn and adjust rapidly to what's going on around us. We can see examples of neuroplasticity throughout life: every time we learn new information or a new skill, our brain has changed. As we develop from infancy to adulthood our brain learns how to control our muscles, communicate in the language of those around us, and behave appropriately in society. Without neuroplasticity, none of this would happen, and we'd go through life as infants.

Neuroplasticity is both friend and foe when it comes to addiction. As we discussed in this chapter, the addicted brain has become adapted to optimize the addict's ability to obtain and use drugs or alcohol. As such, addictive substances use neuroplasticity to entrap the person into addiction. However, neuroplasticity can also be used to overcome addiction and prevent relapse, and all credible addiction treatment programs leverage neuroplasticity to great effect.

The neuroplastic changes that result in addiction are deeply imprinted in the fabric of the brain, right down to the molecular level inside neurons. They include changes to how neurons respond to addictive substances (through alterations in intracellular signaling), how DNA is expressed (epigenetic changes), how DNA is used (DNA transcription), how neurons communicate with each other (by adulterating neurotransmitters and their receptors), and by forming new networks of neurons – pathways – all of which promote obsessive, repeated substance use. Addiction even causes neurons in addiction-related pathways to become larger and more dominant. The brain essentially becomes physically geared toward substance use as its priority occupation.

We're not exactly sure how addictive substances take control of the brain and alter it in such fundamental ways. However, it appears to have to do with these toxins triggering epigenetic changes, and activating the brain's immune system (the *neuroimmune system*). Neuroimmune activation can seriously impact brain function, and appears to play a role in many neurodegenerative diseases, psychiatric disorders, as well as addiction. Repeated exposure to drugs of addiction triggers a low-grade brain inflammation as the brain tries to fight off these foreign toxins. The inflammation irritates neurons, making them vulnerable to the neuroplastic changes we see in addiction. The resulting alterations fundamentally change how the brain responds to addictive substances: they enhance the rewarding effects, increase craving, magnify withdrawal symptoms, and promote the development of substance dependence.

People in recovery can live normal lives and be just like other people, but with one fundamental difference – in most cases their brain's response to addictive substances will always be different than in non-addicts. So, while other people can have a beer after work, the addict in recovery cannot, lest the enduring addictive changes in the brain be triggered once again. I've seen this play out hundreds of times in my work; the same old story over and over – *I thought I could handle it this time.* Fortunately, just as neuroplasticity is involved in the development of addiction, so, too, can it be used to beat addiction – we'll talk about that in chapter 5.

*   *   *

People with the most plastic brains (more prone to changes) are especially vulnerable to addiction-related brain changes when exposed to addictive substances. Sadly, that happens to be children, adolescents, and young adults, whose brains are still "under construction." The brain doesn't finish maturing until about age 25. Until then, it's super plastic and sensitive to the adverse effects of drugs and alcohol.

Pathways laid down in the developing brain tend to become permanent, like tracing a line in wet cement with your finger. This is because children and adolescents learn information and behaviors they'll need to use for the rest of their lives. This is why early onset of substance use is particularly ominous. Even the fetal brain may develop pathways related to addiction due to maternal substance use, increasing the risk for addiction later in life, often not so far in the future.

So, adolescents who drink or use are more likely to develop brain changes that cause addiction. To make matters worse, adolescents are also more prone to risky behaviors, including substance use. There are social and psychological reasons for this, such as peer pressure, boredom, a need to fit in with the crowd, and a need to show independence from parents and authority. However, the as-yet un-matured brain also plays a role in their propensity for risky behaviors. While this can have benefits – such as making teens more likely to try out sports, more courageous in social situations, and better able to make risky decisions such as choosing career paths – it can also result in some unwise decisions, such as trying out drugs and alcohol, engaging in unsafe sexual practices, and dangerous driving. Unfortunately, the pre-frontal cortex (PFC – the brain's "CEO") is among the last parts of the brain to finish maturing.

Largely because of these brain factors, the earlier the age of onset of substance use, the higher the likelihood of developing problem substance use and addiction. For example, data from the NSDUH have shown that when an individual begins using alcohol at age 12, the risk of developing alcohol addiction is nearly double that of someone who starts drinking at age 21 (7.2% versus 3.7%). Similar findings have been made for other addictive substances, including marijuana. Moreover, earlier age of onset of substance use is a strong predictor of a more rapid onset and progression of addiction.

Exposure to one addictive substance in individuals with a developing brain increases their risk of addiction for all substances. Even "vaping" (e-cigarettes) has been shown to create addictive brain changes in adolescents, and increase the likelihood of developing an addiction to other substances. The resulting elevated risk of addiction lasts into adulthood.

The adolescent brain also responds differently to addictive substances. Studies have suggested that adolescents feel more of a high and less sedation than adults, particularly with alcohol. Because of this, they're less subdued, more energetic and aggressive, and more likely to engage in risky behaviors.

Research has established that alcohol and drug use in adolescence is associated with reduced brain volume, and disruptions to the connectivity and communication between brain regions, especially between the higher-level brain functions (i.e., the executive functions in the PFC) and the rest of the brain. These effects likely persist for life, and there's reason to believe that they impact the ability to succeed in education, career, and other important life functions.

Most of the research into the effects of drugs on the developing brain has been focused on alcohol and marijuana because those are by far the most commonly used drugs in this age group (besides nicotine). The fact that marijuana and alcohol are legalized may make people view them as "soft" drugs, but their effects on the brain can be significant and long-lasting. Both have been linked to problems with learning, memory, attention, and executive function. The risk increases with younger age of use, frequency and amount of use, and duration of use, but binging patterns of use – commonly seen among young people – has been identified as a particularly nasty contributor to persistent brain problems. People don't even have to develop an addiction to experience these adverse brain effects.

Substance use during adolescence has also been associated with functional problems, such as externalizing disorders (such as attention-deficit hyperactivity disorder (ADHD), conduct disorder (CD), and oppositional defiant disorder (ODD)), other "heavier" substance use, difficulties in school, accidents and injuries, family conflict, and problems with social functioning. Of course, there's the "chicken and the egg" question: which causes which – substance use or social problems? Well, both go hand-in-hand. Social conflict and poor parental/family relations are risk factors for substance use, and the behavioral problems brought on by substance use tend to cause social conflict, especially within the family. One thing is sure: regardless of which causes which, substance use among adolescents worsens things and may bring on other more enduring problems.

*   *   *

We've discussed the two brain systems primarily involved in addiction: the executive control and learning systems. However, neither operates in isolation. All parts of the brain are interconnected to provide a complex control mechanism for how we think and act.

Other parts of the brain also contribute to the obsessive, all-consuming substance use of addiction. For example, the area responsible for assigning our attention also becomes corrupted. Although our brain can remember a lot of stuff and think about a wide variety of things, we have limited attentional resources; we can only really focus on one thing at a time. The addicted brain assigns undue attentional resources to obtaining and consuming the drug. Individuals become increasingly unable to focus or concentrate on anything else, and little or nothing can override that for long. Addicts have told me that once they were deep into addiction, even when talking to someone, their mind was focused entirely on their drug.

The area of our brain that creates and regulates emotions (the *limbic system*) is also involved. Our brain assigns emotional states to our motivations; we experience joy with achieving our goals, and disappointment, anger, and sadness with failures. When substance use becomes the brain's almighty motivation, the emotions that accompany the highs and lows can be extreme. The neurotransmitter fluctuations in the limbic system caused by substance use and withdrawal are far more dramatic than those that naturally occur. Extremes of emotional behavior, such as aggression and violence are not uncommon. The emotions felt with any success in obtaining drugs are so profound that even physical effects occur – such as rapid heartbeat, sweating, and goosebumps. The positive emotions experienced by obtaining drugs add to the reward effect.

*   *   *

Have you ever noticed how some complex behaviors take a lot of concentration and focus, while others take none at all? For example, if you're baking cookies for the first time, a number of steps are involved. You must read through the recipe, plan your actions, and think about what you're doing. Only then will you get a proper batch of delicious cookies. However, making coffee – which also takes a number of steps – is automatic for most of us. We do it day after day, time after time, and the process becomes so ingrained into our brain that we can be totally distracted and thinking about something else and still make a perfect pot. The sequence of steps is so automatic that ten minutes later we might not even remember doing it. The difference between the two behaviors is that coffee-making is a much-repeated behavior, so the brain has entered the sequence of steps and movements into its memory banks. The brain does this so that we can be efficient and perform our routine behaviors without having to think our way through them every time. Imagine having to figure out and think through unlocking your car, adjusting your seat, and starting your car every morning.

Brain scientists refer to "bottom-up" and "top-down" brain processes. Brain processing that controls behaviors and actions that have become automatic for us is called "bottom-up" processing, because the behaviors are remembered and controlled by the lower, more primitive, unthinking parts of our brain (the brainstem), which happen to be located at the bottom of our brain. Behaviors and actions that we have to put conscious thought into and think our way through are referred to as "top-down" behaviors, because they involve the higher, thinking parts of our brain (the cerebral cortex), located at the top of the brain.

As addiction develops and the behaviors around obtaining and using substances become repeated over and over, they become automatic "bottom-up" behaviors; just like making coffee becomes an unthinking "bottom-up" behavior once we've repeated it enough. When this happens, responses to cravings and cues become automatic, unthinking, and further removed from the control of the thinking part of our brain. For example, I've spoken to one individual in recovery who used to go to the liquor store every day after work. While he was in active alcoholism, he went to the liquor store after work so often that the complex set of behaviors involved in driving to the liquor store became automatic. One day about four years into recovery, he was at work and became very stressed during a particularly tough day. He got in his car after work and his mind was entirely focused on his problems and stressors. He said he felt like he was kind of in a daze. The next thing he knew, he was at the liquor store. He swears he didn't plan on going there; it was an automatic stress response when his mind was distracted, left over from his long-passed addiction days. Fortunately, he used his recovery tools and drove away without going inside (we'll discuss these recovery tools in chapters 6 and 7).

Addiction becomes very much an automatic behavior or set of behaviors that are difficult to break. Although I hate using the term "habit" when referring to addiction, addiction really does become a habit.

Disrupting these automatic behaviors and re-establishing "top-down" control is a major goal of addiction therapy. Despite the deep-seated nature of addiction-related learned habits and behaviors, this is surprisingly easy to do once a few principles have been adopted. We'll discuss this more later.

*   *   *

While we're on the subject of the brain, we should briefly talk about the phenomenon of "blackouts." Many non-addicts aren't sure what to believe when a substance user denies remembering things they

50

did – after all, lying and deceit are a hallmark of addiction. However, it's not always lies. Although blackouts famously occur with alcohol, they can also happen with other drugs that act on the neurotransmitter *GABA*. This includes primarily drugs that are central nervous system (CNS) depressants (such as opioids and barbiturates). Most notably, the sedative-hypnotic drugs known as benzodiazepines (such as diazepam or lorazepam) are highly associated with blackouts, which is why they're used as "date-rape" drugs.

People don't have to be addicted to alcohol or drugs to experience blackouts. They can occur in anyone who binge drinks (i.e., has more than two or three drinks at a time), or takes even one dose of a CNS depressant drug, even if they only do so occasionally. Studies have shown that about 40% of college students have experienced blackouts during a binge-drinking episode.

When people experience a blackout, their brain is incapable of forming memories, but is otherwise capable of performing purposeful tasks reasonably well. They can have complete conversations and perform complex actions such as driving a vehicle, but later have no memory whatsoever of the time they were drunk or high. They don't forget what they've done; they just don't record any of it in memory. This is why, no matter how hard they try, they can't remember what they did during a blackout, even when given an account of events.

Blackouts appear to be caused by the speed at which blood alcohol/drug levels rise, rather than the amount used. Some people appear to be more predisposed to blackouts than others; anyone who's had one blackout is more likely to have another, those who were exposed to alcohol *in utero* are predisposed, and there's likely a genetic component as well.

There are two types of substance-induced blackouts: 1) total blackouts (*en-bloc blackouts*), and 2) partial blackouts (*fragmentary blackouts*). En–bloc blackouts involve total amnesia of the entire period of intoxication. Fragmentary blackouts (sometimes called brownouts or grayouts) involve missing pieces of memory from the period of intoxication, although the missing gaps may be recalled when prompted. Fortunately, brownouts are much more common than blackouts.

En bloc blackouts can be distressing and scary. I've heard more than a few blackout drinkers say that the first thing they'd do in the morning would be to go to a window to see if their car was in the driveway. Some found their vehicle damaged, or parked across the neighbor's lawn, or not even there, and they had no idea whatsoever about what happened. Because alcohol (and other drugs) are associated with disinhibition and risky behavior, many people with no memory of the event have faced serious consequences due to their actions while intoxicated, including killing someone while driving, assaulting someone, or damaging property. I've spoken with lots of addicts who've woken up in jail with no idea of how they got there or why they were there. Not a good feeling. Having no memory of the event, or being intoxicated at the time of a crime carries no weight in a court of law, nor does it excuse anyone of liability for damage.

Although people don't have to be addicts to experience blackouts, anyone who has blackouts is likely engaging in risky, problem substance use and should consider re-evaluating their drinking or drug practices.

Even when blackouts or brownouts don't occur, being intoxicated affects perspective, attention, and memory formation, so many individuals have an incomplete or inaccurate memory of their doings. An essential part of the healing process in recovery includes taking responsibility for our past actions rather than trying to use our substance use as an excuse. As such, I suggest that people in recovery be open to hearing from their loved ones about their behaviors during their addiction, and be ready to take responsibility. We must confront our past to heal; hiding behind being high or having a blackout just keeps us sick. I frame it like this: substance use puts our ugly behaviors in context, but doesn't excuse them.

*   *   *

In chapter 2, we talked about why addiction is widely considered to be a disease. As you can see from our present discussion, the addicted brain is beset by pathological and enduring physical and physiological changes that can be seen on brain imaging studies, as well as under the microscope, and these correlate with the behaviors that we know as the symptoms of addiction. This provides powerful support for the disease model of addiction. The overall message is – I'll say it again – that addiction is a matter of biology, not a matter of morality or weakness of character. Despite the offensive and irresponsible behaviors and outbursts, we must strive to separate the disease and its symptoms from the person if we wish to recover and take back our lives.

Although addiction is primarily a disease of the brain, we can't simply isolate brain function alone as being responsible for the symptoms. It's brain function, together with genetic make-up, environment and experiences, and the mind (our psychology) that all come together in addiction. We must look at all those aspects together to get the whole picture. That's why this book covers all these inseparable topics under one cover. In the next chapter, we'll discuss the addicted mind – the psychology of addiction – and how the workings of the mind contribute to the thoughts and behaviors that make up addiction. *Wait, what?* What's the difference between the brain and the mind? Well, the brain is an organ, while the mind is not. The brain is a physical object that can be studied under a microscope, while the mind is all the intangible things that come from the brain. The mind is our consciousness, awareness, sense of self, imagination, creativity, and instinct. Now let's look at how it plays a role in addiction.

4

The Addicted Mind

In the last chapter, we talked about the effects of repeated substance use on the brain, and how these result in physical changes that create addiction and produce its typical symptoms. While the biological effects of drugs and alcohol on the brain explain much of addiction, they don't explain everything. To fully understand addiction, we must also consider the impact of substance use on the mind.

As mentioned at the end of the previous chapter, the brain and mind are different things. While the mind comes from the brain, the brain is a physical thing – a body organ – and the mind is not. While it's the workings of the brain that somehow produce the mind, unlike the brain we cannot touch the mind, look at it under a microscope, or see it on imaging scans. Unlike the brain, the mind has no shape or form. The mind is all those things that surround our consciousness and awareness, our creativity, and imagination.

The brain and mind are certainly intertwined; when the brain is sick or damaged the mind is usually affected. In the last chapter we discussed how the substance-sickened brain causes addicts to think and act differently. In this chapter we'll examine the psychology of addiction – psychology is the science that studies the mind and its functions, and how the mind affects our behaviors.

Although every person is unique and you can never generalize rules to all people, the psychological mindset and symptoms we'll be discussing in this chapter apply to the vast majority of people in addiction, particularly as their substance use progresses to the point where it's causing them significant life dysfunction. Please don't be offended if you find that some of the symptoms I describe don't apply to you; I would never presume to paint everyone with the same brush. I will say this, though: I've interviewed hundreds of addicts and alcoholics in various stages of their addiction and recovery, and my experience has been that if anyone stays on the substance use road long enough, they'll display the symptoms we'll talk about in this chapter. I know I certainly did during my time in addiction. So I ask that you keep an open mind, and see if our discussion applies to you!

*   *   *

Addicts are excellent actors. As their using-focused life becomes increasingly divorced from normality, they lead a double life, going to great lengths to present a false front, as if all's well. However, they're hurting inside, and their mind is so consumed by constant intrusive thoughts about substance use that they find it hard to think of anything else. They're wracked with worry, fear, guilt, and shame. They don't want anyone to interfere with their drinking or using, so they'll go to any lengths to guard their secrets and protect their access to their drug. Indeed, secretiveness and denial are among the cardinal symptoms of addiction.

As a result of this false front, it's impossible for non-addicts to truly appreciate the depths of dysfunction that people endure in addiction. Although most addicts can maintain a reasonable level of function for a while – some call them "functional" addicts or alcoholics – as the substance use becomes increasingly dominant, it pushes out all other aspects of ordinary life, and life becomes a moonscape of a single focus – substance use. By that point in their addiction, addicts may be able to carry out a relatively normal conversation with others – and even smile and laugh – but obtaining and using their drug and avoiding withdrawal has become the sole focus of their thoughts and actions. Addiction is a full-time job, and it's a miserable way to live.

Before I experienced addiction myself, I had patients who I knew or suspected were "problem" substance users, but they always portrayed themselves as living a fairly normal life. When I began working in addictions, I encountered some of the same people I had once seen as medical patients, and I could see first-hand what their lives were *really* like. Many lived absolutely miserable, destitute lives while they were in active addiction. They sure had me fooled when I saw them as medical patients, because I had no idea what their life and mindset were like. The lesson here is that when we interact with someone engaged in "problem" substance use, all may not be as it seems.

*   *   *

A few core dysfunctional psychological processes occur in the addicted mind. These are heavily involved in developing and propagating obsessive substance use, and drive many of the odd thoughts and behaviors we see in addicts. We'll look at each of these in this chapter. They are:

- **The "dissonant self"** – this is the gnawing guilt that people feel when their behavior deviates from how they believe a good person should behave,
- **Negative psychology** – this is a mindset that's dominated by negative feelings and thoughts, such as pessimism, self-loathing, and depression,
- **Low self-esteem, but elevated pride** – when self-esteem is low, the addicted mind tries to compensate by projecting an exaggerated false, defensive pride,
- **Usurpation of motivation** – substance use becomes the sole, over-riding motivation,
- **Dysfunctional coping** – rather than coping with stress through healthy de-stressing approaches (such as exercise or recreation) or

solving the problem causing the stress, the addicted mind copes by avoiding problems and escaping from reality. This is known as escape/avoidance coping,

- **Cognitive bias** – this is the tendency of the addicted mind to make up and believe reasons to justify or rationalize behaviors that are harmful and unwise, even if those justifications are obviously untrue,
- **An "external locus of control"** – this is where people feel like helpless victims of the world, and they come to believe that their fate is determined by outside forces or people, so that there's no point in trying to solve their problems or make their life better, and
- **Pathological need for control** – the addicted mind is characterized by a strong need for control; so much so that addicts are unwilling to put themselves into the hands of people or a program that can help them. This is based on their psychological need to keep a pathway to substance use always open, "just in case." The addict's need for control is a significant barrier to the commitment needed for recovery.

Let's now look at each of these dysfunctional mental processes.

The Dissonant Self. Nobody dreams of one day becoming a drug addict or alcoholic. When it does happen, it can produce profound and painful disappointment in the self. Addiction is burdened with a sanctimonious social stigma, and addicts apply that stigma to themselves.

Humans have a fundamental need to feel good about themselves. We need to see ourselves as useful, competent, and needed. We also need to see ourselves as fundamentally good. By the time we reach our late teens, we all have a deeply established set of beliefs, standards, and values about what's right and wrong, and what makes a person good or bad. We subconsciously apply these standards to ourselves in everything we do, and in order to feel good about ourselves, we need to see our personality and behavior as consistent with these beliefs.

Living up to our beliefs and values is so important to our psyche that it becomes a defining part of our self-identity. For example, a cherished part of most people's identity includes such things as being good at their job, being a loving parent, conducting themselves with honesty and integrity, and so on. People are comfortable with their self-identity when their behaviors are consistent with their values. If they don't see themselves as good parents, good at their job, or honest, they suffer considerable psychological pain because their real self is dissonant (inconsistent) with their ideal self.

As addiction progresses, the obsessive substance use becomes increasingly incompatible with living up to our standards for ourselves. We usually abandon our self-defining roles, such as work, parenting, and connections with others. Some really unlovely dissonant behaviors become our norm – such as shirking responsibilities, lying and deceiving, driving impaired and other risky behaviors, neglecting our children, and even crime. Such behaviors create a huge chasm between the ideal self and the actual self; in other words, it creates an enormously dissonant self. Disapproval from family and friends, failure to meet important responsibilities and obligations, censure and firing at work, loss of income and savings, and a feeling of lack of self-control add to the negative self-evaluation.

Addicts usually report reaching a point where their substance use is no longer "fun," and they're thoroughly miserable and genuinely want to stop, but can't. I commonly hear from them that they've tried multiple times to quit on their own, each time believing that this time they could do it, but repeatedly failing. I can identify with that because I went through the same thing. Just as other people don't understand why addicts can't "just stop," addicts don't understand either. They may see themselves as weak, immoral, and lacking in self-control. Addicts don't like what they've become, and it causes them tremendous psychological discomfort. Guilt, remorse, shame, and self-loathing become the norm in the addicted mind, all resulting from the dissonant self.

Cognitive dissonance theory is one of the fundamental models of human motivation. The theory tells us that the mind experiences great distress (this psychological distress is called cognitive dissonance) when our behavior doesn't match our beliefs and values, so we're driven to seek to reduce or stop the offending behaviors that create the dissonant self. In other words, we feel bad when we behave badly, so our mind pushes us to stop the bad behavior. The drive to reduce cognitive dissonance is one of the main reasons people generally try to behave in a good and moral way.

There are two ways we can stop the psychological pain when our behaviors don't match our beliefs about what's good and right: we can change the offending behaviors, or we can change our beliefs. For people in active addiction, neither of these options is viable; they can't stop their substance use, and it's too much of a stretch to try to believe that substance use and related behaviors are good and right. As such, the only option left for resolving the psychological pain from the dissonant self is avoidance and escape, which they try to accomplish by numbing their mind through substance use and isolating themselves from anything that reminds them of how bad their behavior is. That's why addicts hate being lectured by family and friends about their behavior – they're already well aware of it, and they're trying to escape from anything that reminds them of it.

Sadly, cognitive dissonance and substance use form a vicious circle that propels addiction to deeper, darker levels. The pain created by cognitive dissonance worsens the substance use, which worsens the cognitive dissonance, which further escalates the substance use, and so on. As such, addiction – regardless of how the substance use began – soon becomes a snowballing cycle of negative feelings and using drugs to cope with the negative feelings. I consider cognitive dissonance to be one of the primary psychological drivers of addiction. Breaking this cycle is a major focus of addiction therapy.

Negative Psychology. "Positive psychology" is a relatively new area of psychology research – it's the study of what makes life most worth living. The concept is pretty cool: rather than the traditional focus on what makes people unwell, positive psychology focuses on what makes people happy and fulfilled. People whose minds are in a state of positive psychology are happy, grateful, and have a positive outlook on life – in good times and in bad. It's hardly surprising that positive psychology has been correlated with multiple measures of physical and mental health.

On the contrary, "negative psychology" describes a gloomy and pessimistic mindset. The addicted mind typically exists in a state that's an extreme example of negative psychology. Addicts feel like victims of the world; they blame their situation on other people and things (*you'd drink too if you had my spouse*), and it makes them angry and resentful. They're pessimistic, and ruminate on their misfortunes. They're consumed with guilt, shame, and remorse, and obsess over past events. Their self-identity is utterly conflicted and unfulfilled, and their self-esteem is gutted. They feel helpless and hopeless about their life situation, and have an external locus of control (which we'll discuss shortly). They have no capacity for coping with stress – other than by substance use and running away. They experience significant fear and anxiety, seeing the world as a cruel and unfair place, and believing their world can come crashing down at any minute. These negative thoughts and feelings constantly weigh on their mind, making them deeply unhappy and providing ample impetus for further substance use and isolation.

Of course, it's not difficult to understand how someone trapped in addiction could develop a negative mindset when their life is crashing down around them and they're troubled by self-destructive substance use that feels out of their control. However, the physical effects of addictive substances on the brain further make addicts feel inherently downcast and melancholy. Here's why.

As you may recall from the previous chapter, the cycle of highs and withdrawal that come with drug or alcohol use results in massive fluctuations in multiple neurotransmitters, including the ones that generate mood disorders. The result is that addicts will undergo bouts of overwhelming depression and feelings of anxiety and impending doom that contribute to an overall negative outlook.

Negative psychology is a common pathway to addiction *and* a consequence of addiction. As such, negative psychology can be both cause and effect of addiction, and – as with cognitive dissonance – a vicious cycle of painful feelings and substance use can develop. As with cognitive dissonance, breaking this cycle is a central focus of addiction therapy.

Low Self-Esteem and Elevated Pride. The failure to live up to one's own standards, beliefs, and values – the dissonant self – causes addicts to get down on themselves. The additive effects of the disapproval of others, the stigma of addiction applied to the self, and a negative mindset push their self-esteem to new lows. The mind tries to compensate for this low self-esteem by projecting exaggerated false pride.

Psychologists identify two types of pride: *authentic* (good) pride, versus *hubristic* (bad) pride. Hubristic pride is the kind that's arrogant, boastful, self-absorbed, conceited, and narcissistic. Authentic pride is when we're proud of a legitimate accomplishment, but we aren't shoving it in everybody's face. The dysfunctional pride at work in the addicted mind is hubristic. The mind needs to feel good about the self and to be well-regarded by others, so this false pride is an attempt to cover up for rock bottom self-esteem.

Good pride (authentic pride) isn't a bad thing; we're right to be proud of our accomplishments. In fact, authentic pride is a valid part of healthy self-esteem and positive psychology, and it can be a great motivator.

The pride that's commonly seen in people in active addiction is a defense mechanism driven by low self-esteem. Typically, they compensate by projecting a fabricated positive view of themselves by inflated demonstrations of pride, and conversely by criticizing and nit-picking others. They become consumed by being "right" and can't acknowledge their own shortcomings. Others find them obnoxious and difficult to be around.

For most people, pride is a by-product of accomplishments and feelings of self-efficacy and self-worth. In other words, they have something to at least partly back up their pride, over-inflated as it may be. In people in active addiction, displays of pride are bloated and defensive in nature, with nothing to back it up.

When people rely on hubristic pride, they become heavily dependent on validation from others to prop up their sense of self-worth. That's why many people with low self-esteem overspend on expensive cars, houses, and other showy items; they need to be noticed, admired, and praised in their drive to prop up their fragile ego. Criticism cuts through them like a knife. So it is with addicts; they tend to be unwilling to admit they have a problem, and even if they do they'll insist they don't need anybody's help. This presents a serious barrier to treatment because they may interpret efforts to help them as an ego-threat. Their very feelings of self-worth are at stake, so they may become defensive – sometimes even aggressive or violent – at attempts to help them.

This masquerade of pride requires tremendous effort; maintaining fake pride and trying to sell it to others (and to themselves) can be exhausting. And it brings out some ugly behaviors. To maintain appearances, they'll lie, cheat, and exaggerate. They're intensely jealous of others. They're judgmental and look for fault in others, always trying to cut others down to elevate themselves. They become defensive and aggressive when anything or anyone challenges their delicate ego or when they don't get the praise and validation they seek. It's an ugly, dysfunctional coping mechanism that makes addicts ugly to be around.

The hubristic pride of addiction contributes to negative psychology, and presents a barrier to recovery. As such, the low self-esteem underpinning this false pride is a major target of addiction therapy.

Disruption of Motivation. We talked in chapter 3 about how the brain's system for creating our priorities and motivations becomes badly corrupted in the addicted brain. This becomes one of the most life-disrupting effects of addiction, as addicts sacrifice more and more of their life in favor of their substance use.

In 1970 psychologist Abraham Maslow worked out a model of motivation that explains much about human behavior. Despite being almost 50 years old and simplistic, Maslow's "Hierarchy of Needs" remains highly regarded and applicable, as it has largely stood up to scrutiny. If Maslow's name sounds familiar, it's because his ideas are taught in every introductory high-school psychology and biology course. Maslow's Hierarchy of Needs theory says that our basic needs must be met before our attention is diverted to more elaborate, less biologically necessary needs. Specifically, our most basic need is our physiological essentials. This is the stuff we require for basic survival, such as food, water, shelter, and sleep. Our attention will be laser-focused on obtaining these things, and only when these physiological needs are met can our attention turn to satisfying our higher needs, which are, in order: safety needs (safe and secure environment), love and belongingness, self-esteem, and finally self-actualization (achieving self-fulfillment, becoming what we want to become).

However, everything changes when addiction takes over the mind; the drug becomes the number one physiological need. This is utterly odd and illogical since our hierarchy of needs is a basic survival instinct; but, such is the nature of addiction.

Dysfunctional Coping. Lots of people find drugs or alcohol a relaxing escape from stress, which is why some will go out for a drink (or whatever) after a stressful day. Others turn to exercise, or watching a movie, or meditation, or some other distracting activity as a preferred way to unwind. Some of us find it helpful to bend a trusted someone's ear when we're upset. Most of us have some way that we wind down from stress and negative feelings; these are our coping mechanisms.

Some people who feel overwhelmed by stress or negative thoughts or feelings may turn to drugs and alcohol repeatedly as their escape. They may find the euphoric feelings and the sedating, numbing, soothing effects of the high their only escape from tortured and intrusive thoughts, stresses and worries, negative feelings and emotions, and mental illness symptoms. They may also find the sense of detachment they get from drugs or alcohol to be a welcome escape from an unkind world. This is the "escape/avoidance" coping that's already come up a few times.

This escape from reality draws some people into the repeated substance use that brings about the brain changes that beget addiction. However, even people whose addiction started for other reasons usually end up relying on substance use as a form of escape. It's what famous Swiss psychiatrist Dr. Carl Jung meant when he referred to addicts as: *people [who] will do anything, no matter how absurd, to avoid facing reality.*

Besides substance use, the other dysfunctional coping mechanism we see in addiction is social isolation. Addicts tend to prefer the company of other addicts, because other addicts' pathetic situation makes them feel better about their own pathetic situation, and the group effect reduces their guilt and cognitive dissonance. As such, *downward social comparison* is preferred, while *upward social comparison* – being around people who're healthy and thriving – is avoided because it magnifies their own terrible actions and situation.

If people hope to succeed in recovery, they must learn to cope with life's highs and lows in a healthy way. Addicts are people whose go-to coping mechanism was running away through social isolation and substance use, and they can easily return to the same behaviors and relapse if life again becomes stressful. As such, addiction treatment focuses on learning to accept life's ups and downs as a normal part of life and to handle stress and disappointment in a healthy and functional way.

Cognitive Bias. A "cognitive bias" is a mental distortion the human mind uses to protect its beliefs and what it wants to believe. The human mind manipulates information through these biases to fit with its pre-existing beliefs and attitudes, even if that information is suspect. People see what they want to see.

Cognitive biases are a natural feature of the human mind, and occur mainly subconsciously, although they can also occur purposely. These biases affect our decision-making and behaviors, as we act on faulty, biased assessments of available information. This doesn't just happen with addicts; it happens with everybody.

For example, let's say a guy named Michael takes art lessons and paints a portrait of his wife. Michael's very proud of his painting and hard work, and he really believes (and wants to believe) that it's quite good. Because of cognitive bias, Michael's mind will tend to ignore obvious mistakes or bad points in the painting, and his mind will instead focus more on the positives. He'll also tend to de-emphasize comments from others that suggest that the painting isn't good, and place undue emphasis on information that suggests that it's terrific.

Although cognitive bias occurs to some degree in everyone (nobody's capable of being 100% objective), these mental distortions are pushed to extremes in the addicted mind.

The addicted mind uses cognitive bias to warp facts and reality to rationalize and substantiate what cannot be logically substantiated – self-destructive substance use and its related behaviors. The addicted mind also uses cognitive bias to reduce cognitive dissonance by making excuses for all the dissonant behaviors. However, because such behaviors cannot be truthfully rationalized, the truth must be deconstructed and the facts profoundly distorted. That's why family and friends of addicts get tired of the excuses; they're so obviously distorted as to be ridiculous.

Additionally, addiction-related cognitive biases generate thoughts that support ongoing substance use, to the exclusion of other, more rational and productive thoughts that may lead the addict to recovery. Essentially, the addicted mind uses cognitive bias to talk the addict into continuing to use.

One of the most dangerous aspects of addiction-related cognitive biases is that they can arise even years into recovery, so that individuals who don't pay attention to their recovery tools may actually talk themselves into relapse (this is the subject of my Ph.D. research). We'll talk more about that in chapters 6 and 7.

There are lots of different types of cognitive bias, but only four that are especially relevant to the addicted mind:

- **Attentional bias** – this is where the mind assigns excessive attentional resources to information and cues related to obtaining and using substances. If an addict enters a room where there's one tiny substance-related cue, they'll pick up on the cue and their mind will be laser-focused on it. For example, if an alcohol addict enters a room and there's a half-empty glass of wine sitting in a corner on a table, the alcoholic will quickly pick up on it and may be unable to concentrate on anything else due to attentional bias,

- **Optimism bias** – in this type of bias, the addicted mind clings to the belief that the individual will be able to control or stop their substance use on their own, despite multiple previous failed attempts. The optimism bias is paradoxical, given that the addicted mind is deeply pessimistic. The optimism bias is profound in addiction and a significant barrier to recovery because individuals stubbornly believe they don't need outside help. It's also a significant cause of relapse because people develop the belief that they can safely try drugs or alcohol again after a period of abstinence,
- **Approach bias** – this is the tendency to choose behaviors that lead to obtaining or using substances, even if those behaviors are harmful or unwise. The approach bias causes addicts to engage in unsafe or risky behaviors to get their drug. Impaired driving, prostitution, and other crimes or dangerous behaviors may be chosen and the risks ignored or rationalized. This is commonly seen in relapse situations, where individuals choose small steps that lead back to substance use, substantiating the reason for each small step even though they're fully aware that they're headed for trouble, and
- **Memory bias** – this is the tendency to recall information in a way that supports substance use. This bias is a significant cause of relapse, as people in recovery will tend to remember substance use as "fun," even though they were thoroughly miserable during their addiction. The memory bias persists and even worsens as people progress in recovery. The further they are from their last drink or drug, the more likely they are to remember their substance use in a positive light. Combatting memory bias is a focus of relapse prevention.

Addiction treatment and relapse prevention programs address cognitive bias by making addicts aware of these harmful mental distortions so that they can identify and challenge them as they occur.

External Locus of Control. As addiction deepens and problems and consequences accumulate, addicts may feel overwhelmed by life and the world. They begin to feel like victims of the world – like they're being picked on – a condition known to psychologists as *self-victimization*. Research has identified self-victimization as a significant cause of psychological pathology, such as emotional pain, depression, anxiety, substance use, and suicide.

Like any victim, addicts who perceive themselves as victims are angry and resentful, with their ire directed at other people, institutions, and even God. Unfortunately, the people who bear the brunt of this are usually those who're closest to the addict.

When people feel like victims of the world, they begin to believe that their problems and fate are outside their control and that their actions won't change anything. Psychologists refer to this mindset as an *external locus of control*.

People with an external locus of control may feel helpless and hopeless, and resign themselves to being passive observers of their own life. They begin to believe that any effort they put into improving their lives would be pointless. They may give up on trying to deal with their problems and become withdrawn. Some withdraw into avoidance and escape behaviors, such as substance use and social isolation. This state of mind is referred to by psychologists as *learned helplessness*.

When the mind descends into learned helplessness, the individual believes they can't change their situation, so they won't even try – even when opportunities to do so arise. That means they'll pass up on offered help for their addiction.

Addicts' external locus of control also impairs their self-efficacy beliefs – beliefs that they can accomplish a given task – so they believe they're incapable of recovery and won't even try. An external locus of control makes addicts believe they drank or used because their spouse is such a tyrant, or because their finances had gotten so bad, or because they didn't get that great job they interviewed for. As long as they maintain these beliefs, every new stressor in recovery will be seen as another reason to return to their drug.

For addicts to heal and achieve the mindset they need to succeed in recovery, they must take responsibility for their own lives and actions, and an external locus of control prevents that. If they continue to believe that whether or not they drink or use is determined by other people and things, they'll relapse as soon as the next life challenge comes along.

Pathological Need for Control. Despite their external locus of control, there's one area of their life where addicts cling to an obsessive need for control: their freedom of movement. While we all like to have freedom of movement, with addicts it reaches pathological proportions.

The addict's need for control is based on the fear that something may prevent them from having access to obtaining and using their drug. This need is so paramount that they attach great emotional salience to it – anyone who's tried to come between an addict and their drug has likely found this out. This is why when a family member finds the addict's stash and flushes it there's inevitably a volcanic reaction that follows. This is why addicts don't like going away on trips, or they don't like holidays where everything is closed down (alcoholics really hate that). It's also largely why addicts fear checking into a detox or drug treatment facility.

Even when they do want and accept help, addicts who still cling to their need for control will pick and choose which parts of the help they want – they want to make sure they retain the freedom of movement to get and use their drug "just in case."

*   *   *

Although the tangible brain and intangible mind are separate entities, they're intertwined, and each contributes in its own way to determine our behaviors, including self-destructive substance use. As such, the effects of repeated substance use on the brain and on the mind explain the symptoms of addiction, and give us an understanding of why addicts behave the way they do. Otherwise, the mindset, personality changes, and behaviors of addiction are so illogical as to defy understanding.

As you can see, the addicted mind is a dark place. Although addicts are great actors and can put on airs that everything's okay, they're hurting inside. Their mindset, negative thoughts and emotions, non-stop obsession with substance use, and crippling outlook on life amount to a troubled person. No one can be happy and at peace and have any reasonable chance at recovery unless these psychological burdens are nursed back to health.

However... as dark as that may sound, people do recover. I've met hundreds of people who're years and even decades into recovery after being completely caught up in addiction and its lifestyle. In most cases, their life had train-wrecked and their situation felt helpless. However, I've been singularly impressed by how quickly and thoroughly people regain a vibrant and full life when they take care of one thing – their recovery. I've lived that story myself. In the next two chapters, we're going to talk about what happens to the genetics, brain, and mind of an addict in recovery, and how addiction's effects can be successfully overcome for a lifetime of recovery.

5

The Brain and Genetics in Recovery

Luckily for us, the brain is a very forgiving organ. Although there may be lingering or even permanent injury from all the abuse we've piled on it, when we finally give our brain a chance to heal, it works hard to recover. Thanks to neuroplasticity, our brain has a tremendous capacity for remarkable feats of recovery, particularly if we take care to optimize the conditions for its healing. We'll talk about that in this chapter, but first let's talk about what happens to all those "addiction genes" once we're in recovery.

Our Genetics in Recovery

We can improve our addiction-related genetics in recovery. While it's true that we can't change our genes (at least not yet), there's much we can do to improve how our genetics affect us. In chapter 1 we talked about addiction-related genes, and how many of them function through epigenetics. To refresh your memory, epigenetics is where certain genes are "switched on" by some environmental factor. We believe that many addiction genes operate through epigenetics, and that the primary environmental factors for switching them on are: 1) exposure to addictive substances, and 2) the effects of poorly tolerated stress. By abstaining from substance use and learning to handle life's inevitable stressors in a healthy way, we can eliminate both factors, thereby switching off many of our addiction-related genes.

The Addicted Brain in Recovery

In chapter 3, we talked about the profound adulterations to structure and function that change the brain to the addicted state. Changes occur within brain cells (neurons), to the structure of the neurons, how they communicate (through the various neurotransmitters), and how they connect in pathways. As we discussed, these changes occur because of neuroplasticity – the brain adjusting to the injurious stress of repeated exposure to toxic substances (drugs or alcohol). The good news is that just as we suffered harmful changes due to neuroplasticity, we can also have very positive changes in recovery due to neuroplasticity. Neuroplasticity is about the brain adapting to what we're doing, so if we stop exposing it to toxins and instead expose it to healthy, challenging behaviors and habits, it'll respond in kind.

I refer to these healthy, challenging behaviors and habits as "brain hygiene." Brain hygiene is where we use the brain's plasticity to enhance its performance for improved physical, mental, emotional, social, and spiritual well-being. For addicts in recovery, it's also about forming and nurturing new neural pathways that allow us to re-orient our brain toward recovery and good life function, rather than toward obsessive substance use.

After months or years of inadequate diet, poor and irregular sleep, lack of exercise, and repeated exposure to toxic substances, the brain is a sick organ. The rest of the body is unhealthy, too, and it takes a healthy body to house a healthy mind. The brain hasn't been challenged for a long time either, so it's like a flabby muscle desperately in need of some exercise. When we begin treating our brain and body to activities that boost their health – such as regular physical activity, yoga, deep breathing, quality sleep, relaxation, socialization, positive thinking, hobbies, a healthy diet, sports, listening to music, meditation, reading, and mindfulness – we're participating in brain hygiene. This is why most addiction treatment programs include a wide range of activities in their curriculum – they're using brain hygiene to promote brain health and set the conditions for positive neuroplasticity.

Although the brain changes that caused addiction will likely remain for life and can be re-activated at any time by drugs or alcohol, neuroplasticity allows us to learn new ways of thinking, new behaviors, and new habits that lay down new neural pathways that by-pass the unwanted pathways.

To demonstrate the impressive therapeutic power of neuroplasticity, I'll illustrate with the scenario of a stroke victim. A stroke occurs when the blood supply to part of the brain gets cut off by a blockage of the artery. The affected brain tissue dies, rots away, and never grows back, leaving a vacant cavity in the brain. If the affected part of the brain is the part that controls the individual's left arm, they'll be unable to move their left arm. However, over the next eight months or so, with the proper therapy, the stroke victim can regain the function of their left arm, often just as well as before the stroke. But how is that? The part of their brain that controls the left arm is dead and rotted away. The answer is neuroplasticity. The stroke victim's brain – with the proper therapy – can adapt and form alternative pathways around the dead brain tissue to regain control of the left arm. However, if the stroke victim had just sat around and not participated in therapy to develop new brain pathways, their arm would've ended up permanently paralyzed.

Like stroke rehab programs, addiction treatment programs rely heavily on neuroplasticity to help addicts recover their proper brain functionality. Addicts are taught new ways of thinking, reacting to people and situations, handling stress, and new behaviors that promote recovery and counter the addicted brain.

As we begin repeating these healthy, recovery-focused thoughts and behaviors, new brain pathways get laid down, and old unwanted brain pathways whither as they go unused. The new pathways become stronger and more prominent with time and practice, and soon become our go-to brain pathways. Neuroplasticity is about our brain adapting to what it needs to do; if we need to do healthy, functional things, it will adapt positively. Elderly stroke victims can form new pathways with practice, and so can we. We're "unlearning" addiction. We'll talk more about unlearning addiction later in this chapter.

*   *   *

During early recovery, the brain is in a state of chaos. The poor thing's been desperately trying to correct for the repeated exposure to toxins that keeps disrupting its best efforts to do its job, and it's been losing the battle. Tightly regulated neurotransmitters are the brain's bread and butter, and these have alternated between ultra-high spikes and rock-bottom plunges, leaving the brain constantly scrambling to figure out what's going on and trying to get things back to normal. Ultimately, the brain has pushed its natural production of neurotransmitters way down, and reduced the number of receptors for these neurotransmitters. Fortunately for us addicts, the brain can handle a lot of abuse and still recover normalcy when we finally give it a chance – but it takes a little while.

When people stop using psychoactive substances, it takes time for the brain to understand that this is more than just a temporary reprieve from the drugs, and to start restoring things to normal. Despite the absence of drugs, the neurotransmitters and their receptors remain low for a period that varies depending on the duration, type, and amount of substance use, and the physical characteristics of the individual. As such, there'll be a period in early recovery where these feel-good neurotransmitters and their receptors are bottomed out.

The result is that the individual may – depending on how their brain responds after detox – feel the opposite of "high" – depressed, listless, unmotivated, and fatigued. They may experience *anhedonia*, which is the inability to feel pleasure, even when doing something that would otherwise be enjoyable. They may also experience anxiety and emotional volatility as the abused brain struggles to regain normal neurotransmitter levels. These effects are most pronounced during the immediate withdrawal while the body and brain detoxify, but they can last weeks or months. Although it can happen with any drug, neurotransmitter volatility may be especially prevalent in methamphetamine withdrawal, due to that drug's especially harsh and long-lasting effects on brain chemistry.

Anhedonia is also a common symptom of a number of mental illnesses, such as mood disorders (depression, bipolar disorder, anxiety disorders, dysthymia, etc.), schizophrenia, and PTSD. Anhedonia is almost always accompanied by other symptoms caused by the same low neurotransmitter levels. These are referred to as *vegetative symptoms*, and may include low energy, lack of desire to do anything (even things that are usually enjoyable), and excessive or disrupted sleep. Because of the overlap in symptoms, there's a fine line between anhedonia and clinical depression. Often, it's difficult for a doctor to tell the difference.

These symptoms are sometimes severe enough to make it difficult to function normally and may be a risk factor for relapse; anhedonia is strongly associated with increased craving and intensity of withdrawal. Therefore, treating anhedonia may be important for success in recovery, especially during that tough initial period of sobriety.

Most people experience mild anhedonia or other depressive symptoms, but for those who find it a struggle, different therapies are available. There are two main approaches: psychotherapy, and low-dose antidepressant medications that correct the abnormal brain chemistry. Psychotherapy, particularly cognitive behavioral therapy (CBT), has a role in treating depression, although it's very time-consuming and expensive to properly pursue. Often a short course of a once-a-day, non-addictive antidepressant medication called an *SSRI* (selective serotonin reuptake inhibitor) is appropriate, as it returns the brain chemistry to healthy levels. Usually, only about four months of this medication may be required, maybe longer in some individuals (particularly former meth users). A medication closely related to SSRIs – called *bupropion* – has proven particularly effective for anhedonia and depression associated with withdrawal. It's known as an "energizing" antidepressant because it's particularly helpful with low energy levels. Some cases are tougher to treat than others, and medication doses may have to be titrated, or other medications used. Interestingly, research has shown that recovery support groups that involve face-to-face meetings also have a significant effect on reducing anhedonia.

I encourage recovering addicts at any stage of their recovery to visit their doctor and be honest about their symptoms and their history of substance use if they're experiencing any mood disorder symptoms, such as depression, anhedonia, and anxiety. Trying to tough it out results in needless suffering and an increased risk of relapse.

*   *   *

Of course, not every person experiences anhedonia or depressive symptoms. Some will have only mild symptoms, and some will bounce back quickly. Some experience the opposite, where they feel high on life – a phenomenon known as the "pink cloud effect." The pink cloud effect, first described by Alcoholics Anonymous in the 1930s, is a psychological anomaly commonly seen in early recovery. It's a state of unusually elevated happiness and grandiosity despite difficult life circumstances. Most of the psychology literature views it as an undesirable and negative influence on recovery, despite the positive feelings it entails. It's great to feel happy in early recovery, but the pink cloud effect is a state of delusional elation, to the point where it impairs the ability to accept and meet life circumstances. It's dangerous to recovery because individuals can lose sight of and ignore problems and become over-confident and complacent in their recovery. This may lead them to stray from their plan of action for recovery, and bring on the feeling that it's OK to drink or use again. As well, the pink cloud effect doesn't last forever – seldom longer than three to six months – and when individuals "fall off the cloud," they can fall hard.

It's important to distinguish between the pink cloud effect and the normal elation that's perfectly natural from newfound freedom from addiction. People in early recovery are finally free of the horrible, life-consuming compulsion that had stolen their happiness. For the first time, their mind is clear. Their time, energy, and thoughts are their own again. Every one of their senses is alert and alive – they feel re-born. Long-forgotten emotions awaken. They can live again, connect with people, and do things. Yes, they may have many problems to clean up, but they're learning to tackle their problems one day at a time, so they're no longer overwhelmed. They're learning to forgive themselves and even feel good about themselves, for once. They're feeling good physically and mentally, people and things they've lost are returning, and they're slowly regaining the trust of themselves and others. So it's only natural that they're going to feel a little high on life in early recovery.

So how do we know if someone's riding a dangerous pink cloud? The pink cloud effect likely occurs because addicts' emotions have been anesthetized by drugs and alcohol for so long that the sudden awakening of normal feelings can be intense. But there's a fine line between the perfectly normal elation of early sobriety, and the pink cloud effect. There's no blood test or set way to determine if someone's too high on life, but it's usually clear when things aren't right. The line is crossed when people have lost touch with reality, their emotions aren't adjusting to reflect their real-life situation, and they're in denial about their problems and challenges. Overconfidence in their recovery is another red flag.

If someone in recovery is experiencing the pink cloud effect, it's not a disaster. They just need to be watched to ensure they remain in touch with reality and don't get so cocky about recovery that they stop doing their recovery activities. Also, individuals "riding the pink cloud" should be watched for a crash when the euphoric effect wears off. This usually occurs no later than 3-6 months into recovery, and if the brain's neurotransmitters haven't yet normalized, the result can be a crash from an elevated mood to a low mood, sometimes in a matter of hours. This sudden drop can knock them off their feet and bring on a depression that'll keep them off their feet. This terrible outcome elevates the risk of relapse.

Even people whose neurotransmitter system has normalized by the time the pink cloud wears off can run into problems. They may feel boredom after the high emotions give way to more modest feelings, and stop doing the things they need to do to stay sober. They may feel despondent, fearing that something's wrong, and they may question if recovery is worthwhile – or even necessary.

It's proper for recovering addicts to be happy in sobriety and to be proud of their amazing accomplishment, but when it gets to the point of distraction from real life and the necessary efforts for recovery, then it becomes dysfunctional and should be addressed. There's no magic way to directly address the pink cloud effect, other than an awareness of the problem so we can watch for it. Often people don't recognize they're "clouding," and might resist the suggestion. Once people accept that they're on a pink cloud, they can't be talked off it, but they can be talked through it. Discussing their immediate life issues and a plan for addressing them helps them face reality. Addiction recovery support groups know about the pink cloud effect, so participants watch for and recognize when a fellow recovering addict is in trouble. They're very good at helping each other through such problems. As well, it's not a bad idea to let family and friends know about the pink cloud effect, so they can also keep an eye out. I explain the pink cloud effect and other aspects of recovery in my book "Understanding and Helping an Addict (and keeping your sanity)." The book explains to family and friends what their addict loved one is going through, and how they can best help out, without being invasive.

*　　　*　　　*

I'm often asked about relapse dreams, because they're a common phenomenon among people in recovery and can be terribly distressing. These are vivid and intense dreams of drinking or using, and the individual often wakes up feeling like they really did relapse. They usually report feeling the same emotions as if they actually had relapsed: guilt, shame, and disappointment. It often affects them physically, too: waking up sweaty with a racing heart, and even feeling drunk/high or hung over. A minority are left with a craving to drink or use, but almost all are gripped by a fear that they really will relapse. People usually report a deep sense of relief at realizing the dream wasn't real, and thankfulness to be still in sobriety. Even then, however, the dreamer is quite shaken by the experience. These are powerful dreams.

Relapse dreams occur most frequently during detoxification and early sobriety, but tend to sharply decrease as we progress in sobriety, especially after the first six weeks. However, they can persist for a lifetime, albeit usually only occurring occasionally. One unfortunate peculiarity, however, is that although they decrease in frequency, they don't decrease in intensity and believability. I've spoken with people who've experienced them just as vividly decades after their last drink or drug.

People come forward and talk to me about their relapse dreams because they fear that the dreams mean something – that they subconsciously want to relapse, or they're not doing their recovery activities well enough. However, my professional opinion is that they're not indicative of anything we've been doing wrong in our recovery and are not a sign of impending relapse. I still get them occasionally, and I've been in recovery a long time. I'm used to them now, and they don't mean anything to me. They're just dreams. I encourage people not to read too much into them, lest they become a self-fulfilling prophecy.

Nonetheless, research has shown that the more relapse dreams a person has, the more likely they are to relapse. However, relapse dreams occur by far most often in early recovery, when relapse rates are highest with or without dreams. Having said that, it certainly makes sense that they could trigger a relapse because people sometimes wake up from them with an urge to relapse.

Sleep experts widely discredit the idea that our dreams are packed with disguised meanings. Rather, dream researchers are – I believe –

spot-on with the *activation-synthesis theory* of dreaming. This suggests that our brains produce random electrical discharges during sleep, and these impulses stimulate memory and thought pathways. Our brains then weave these thoughts and memories into a coherent story (our dream). Any brain pathway can be stimulated, which is why our dreams can be bizarre combinations of random memories, abstract thoughts, and imagination.

Our drinking and using memories are of events on which we were intensely focused, held profound emotional impact for us, and were repeated multiple times, so the memory pathways involved are deeply ingrained. When one of the random electrical discharges hits one of these deep memory pathways it plays the whole memory rather than skipping around, as in an ordinary dream. Think of the memory pathways related to our drinking and using as deep grooves in our memory banks, like a bad scratch on an old vinyl record. When the needle hits that groove it gets stuck and follows it to the end. Thus, the relapse dream is realistic, vivid, and complete – tastes, smells, emotions, hang-over... everything's there. Of course, as these memories fade, we're less likely to hit them with these random brain electrical discharges as we sleep, which is why our relapse dreams decrease as we progress in sobriety.

So, relapse dreams are the result of random electrical discharges that happen to hit a deeply ingrained memory. Reducing them is best accomplished by neuroplasticity: making the addiction-related pathways less prominent, and new, healthy brain pathways more well-traveled. However, because relapse dreams are so visceral, realistic, and emotional, I suggest people get past the associated guilt and discuss their dreams. Talking to a family member or friend who understands, or – for those who belong to a recovery group – calling their sponsor or sharing their experience at a meeting is helpful. It helps put things back in perspective and lets us get the experience off our chest. Addicts are people whose natural tendency is to seek drugs or alcohol when they have negative emotions or thoughts, so keeping the guilt, fear, and shame of relapse dreams locked up inside is a bad idea.

*   *   *

Let's talk about abstinence and recovery for a moment. There are two models of recovery: one is abstinence-based, and the other is "harm reduction," which involves the controlled use of addictive substances. I firmly believe that the only way for people who're truly addicts to recover and get back to good health and function is through abstinence from *all* addictive substances. After all, one of the defining characteristics of addiction is the inability to control or stop substance use despite obvious negative consequences. People who can control their substance use are not truly addicts, or they would've done so long before drug or alcohol use ruined their life.

Overwhelming research evidence and decades of documented experience have shown that the brain changes discussed in chapter 3 are time-stable, probably lasting a lifetime. That means that once the addicted brain develops, that person will likely never again respond normally when exposed to addictive substances. Even after years of working with people in addiction and recovery, I'm still always amazed at how quickly individuals in recovery revert to the addicted brain's thought processes and behaviors after even a single exposure to drink or drug. In my work at a detox center, I've heard the same thing time and again from recently relapsed addicts and alcoholics, often with years of recovery behind them: *I picked up right where I left off!*

The psychology of the addicted mind includes a penchant for finding the easiest, least effortful way to beat their addiction. That means that if there's a way to beat addiction without having to go through detox, participate in treatment, put in the effort of recovery activities, and – best of all – not have to give up their substance use, then addicts are all for it. Naturally, *right?* When the addicted mind hears of "harm reduction," it immediately likes the sound of it: *you mean I can keep drinking and using? Sign me up!* However, research studies and abundant clinical experience have shown that this seldom works. By definition, addicts cannot control their substance use, harm reduction or otherwise.

"Harm reduction" – a return to substance use in a "controlled" fashion – is flawed for true addicts in several fundamental ways. It's dependent upon self-control in a group of people who have a severe impairment of their self-awareness and self-control brain circuitry as soon as they're exposed to addictive substances, and it relies on accountability and self-reporting in people who've in the past been entirely deceitful and dishonest about their substance use. Besides, what's the definition of "controlled" or "acceptable" substance use? How many lines of cocaine are "acceptable," and how many times a week of smoking meth is considered "controlled?" How much potentially fentanyl-laced heroin can people put in their arm that "reduces harm?" What's the line between acceptable intoxication and unacceptable drunkenness? How do you keep alcohol intake from creeping up, as it has in the past?

Recently I ran into Hamid, a guy I know who's in recovery from heroin and alcohol addiction. I met him when he was in our local detox center, and I've run into him a number of times at recovery meetings and around town. He was doing well in recovery – he married his longtime girlfriend (who's also in recovery), he had his son back in his life, and he had a decent job and a nice place to live. Then, about a year and a half into recovery he told me he was thinking of smoking pot. I told him I thought it was a bad idea, and why. He did it anyway; his addict's mind rationalized it: *it's a harmless drug, it's legal, I've never had a problem with pot, everybody does pot*, and so on. Before long, every time I saw him, he was stoned. He even made a fool of himself at a couple of meetings because he was so stoned, and once even had to be escorted out. His wife left him because they were fighting over his pot use, and they were broke. He'd lost his job (I'm sure it had something to do with him being stoned all the time), and he was spending their rent and grocery money on pot. It's sad to see someone doing so well in recovery give it all up because he made himself think he could safely use drugs again. He convinced himself that *this* time doing drugs would be different.

Let's look at another story to further illustrate. Another guy – Liam – was a low-bottom cocaine and alcohol addict, nearly ten years into abstinent recovery when he relapsed. During his initial addiction he was using $1,200 a day in cocaine, and went broke despite his considerable financial resources. While in recovery, he had once again done well for himself financially. When he was only a few weeks from what would've been ten years in recovery, Liam was traveling through Italy with his girlfriend. They'd stopped for the night in a little Italian town and were having dinner at the Locanda (inn) where they were staying. In that town there was a specific traditional liqueur that had been made locally since the 19th century, and the innkeeper came to Liam's table and offered Liam and his girlfriend a shot of this special liqueur, on the house. Liam declined, of course, but the innkeeper appeared nettled by the refusal, so Liam's girlfriend pressed him to take it. *It's just one shot, Liam!* She knew he was an addict, but she didn't know him back in his drinking and using days and didn't understand the nature of addiction. So, Liam acquiesced and took the innocuous-looking little one-ounce shot. After all, what harm could it do? He'd been in recovery ten years, *right?* Liam had stopped participating in his recovery activities over a year before, and that kind of thinking was seeping back into his addict's mind.

For the next three days, as Liam and his girlfriend toured Italy, Liam was utterly rocked by an obsession with that one innocent little shot of alcohol; he could think of nothing else. No matter what they did or saw, Liam could only think of that shot of liqueur. On day three after the drink, he got so drunk on the plane ride home that he had to be helped off the plane in a wheelchair when they landed. So started an eight-month bender of alcohol and cocaine that again took him to his bottom. Fortunately, Liam is back with us in recovery, with his life back on track.

Maybe there are addicts out there who can return to "responsible" substance use, but personally and professionally, I doubt it. As for me, you couldn't pay me to even try; there's no way I'm going to risk sacrificing everything that's important to me and going back to that horrible, miserable life in addiction. I've seen too many friends and patients in recovery fall again after talking themselves into having a few drinks, or doing a hit at a party, or taking up a "soft" drug, and I've seen too many of them die from it.

*   *   *

Because of addiction's enduring brain changes, the term "addiction treatment" is a bit misleading. After all, it's not like what we traditionally think of as "treatment," such as when you take an antibiotic for an ear infection and it's all over. Nobody walks out of a treatment program cured of addiction; recovery is a lifelong commitment that requires ongoing care and attention. Successful recovery depends upon remaining mindful of the potential for relapse, and doing the things we need to do to stay in recovery (we'll talk about what these are shortly). Even people with years of recovery must use their tools to prevent relapse, particularly in moments of stress or other times of vulnerability. As such, I liken addiction to other illnesses that can be controlled but not cured. Diabetes is the perfect example. Undiagnosed or untreated, diabetes can cause serious health problems and even premature death. However, when properly treated and controlled, people with diabetes are at no higher risk than anybody else, and can live a normal and long life. Like addiction, diabetes can't be cured, but it can be managed with daily care. So, to stay healthy, diabetics must take daily care to manage their disease. If they don't, their disease can flare up and cause health problems and even death. So it is with addiction; addiction should be viewed as a condition that's *managed* rather than *cured*.

Attending an addiction treatment program isn't enough to "unlearn" addiction. These programs are designed to get addicts away from their using/drinking environment and help them address their issues and learn some tools for recovery. These tools are the things we can use to stay on top of the things that once drove us to substance use – for example, how to deal with stress in a healthy way, and an action plan in case of a flare-up of mental health symptoms. These tools also include regular activities that keep healthy brain pathways fresh and robust while keeping addiction pathways from re-asserting themselves.

To learn recovery we must live it. That means going home from treatment and adopting the things we need to do to stay in recovery into our daily life. I've been in recovery a long time now, and my recovery activities have become a part of my everyday life. I don't see them as a pain or a burden, any more than I see brushing my teeth or eating lunch as a burden. They're all just activities I need to do to stay healthy. In my work I've seen way too many people gradually slide into relapse because they got cocky and figured enough time had passed that they no longer needed recovery activities. That was the case with Liam, and I've heard the same time and again from others who've relapsed. The way I put it is this: *when we're in recovery, we're privileged to be able to go back into the world and live like normal people – have a job, be a parent, enjoy a fine summer day, all that stuff. However, we must remember that we're different from other people in one important way – we have an addict's brain, and we have to take care to ensure we remain healthy and in recovery.*

*   *   *

So, what are these recovery activities that retrain our brain, these "things we need to do to stay in recovery?" Well, everybody's different, but I suggest there are some basic recovery activities needed to retrain the brain and keep the addicted brain in its place on an ongoing basis. The first is finding new people, places, and things that support recovery. Being around old drinking or using cues and influences serve as triggers for our addiction pathways, and inevitably place us in relapse situations.

Another is by becoming part of a "culture of recovery." This leverages the potent human learning and brain remodeling driven by social interaction. It provides us with a close group of friends we can lean on in times of trouble and can help when we're at a low point. Reciprocally helping others has also been shown to have a strong positive effect on our recovery. As well, attending meetings and interacting with others in recovery allows us to "keep our head in the game." Addicts who relapse commonly report that they gradually forgot "who they are" as addicts and how they have a fundamental difference from others. Participation in a recovery support group keeps us oriented toward recovery and alert for red flags.

Learning about recovery also helps retrain our brain by providing a basis for more insightful metacognition (this is a powerful psychological therapeutic tool, which we'll be discussing in the next chapter). I'm in the habit of reading about addiction and recovery daily. Not for long; just a few minutes a day is all it takes. Reading this book is a great recovery activity, but there's much more to learn. Every recovery support group has excellent recovery-related literature available.

Another important recovery activity is putting together an action plan that includes early disruption when we begin addiction approach behaviors. "Approach behaviors" are steps that bring us closer to a situation where we may be exposed to drugs or alcohol. Many people relate that their relapse began with tiny steps that slowly led to their relapse situation even though they knew they were headed for trouble. For example, they might begin talking with an old using buddy, then meet them for coffee, then start hanging around with them and their friends, then go to a party with them, and so on. We know when we're doing something wrong, little alarm bells go off in our head. The sooner we interrupt the chain of tiny approach behaviors, the easier it is. It's much easier to ignore an out-of-the-blue text from an old buddy we know is still using than it is to say "no" to a hit when we end up at a party together. It may take courage and determination to break the chain of events, but it gets easier every time. We'll talk more about relapse prevention plans in chapter 7.

Good brain hygiene is also important because a healthy and well-looked-after brain heals much better and faster and learns new behaviors more effectively. Besides, being good to ourselves feels good and elevates our self-esteem; it's the least we can do after abusing our brain for so long.

The brain goes where the body goes. That means that when we act a certain way, our brain and mind will fall in line and believe in what we're doing. When we take on a new identity as a person in recovery, it helps direct our motivations, thoughts, and actions. It's easier to act our way into thinking than to think our way into acting.

One of the most potent techniques for re-writing our brain pathways and preventing old addiction pathways from re-asserting themselves is a technique (borrowed from the Twelve Step program) called "remember when meditation." It's nothing fancy: it just involves spending a minute or two focusing the mind on specific incidents that occurred during our substance use days that were especially miserable. People in early recovery should do this daily and repeat it anytime their addict's brain tries talking them into drinking or using again. My experience has been that this works exceptionally well for helping addicts overcome cravings and urges. So why does something so simple work so well? Well, let's use our knowledge of the addicted brain to find out why.

We previously talked about how our brain becomes conditioned to cues and behaviors that support substance use, and how the conditioned responses become automatic (bottom-up) behaviors. The brain has been conditioned to seek drugs or alcohol during times of stress, and to view substance use as a relief, as something positive. The addicted brain quickly forgets all the misery that we lived through and how desperate we were to escape the obsessive substance use. This learned association in the addicted brain is remarkably persistent and dominant, and even years into recovery can push us toward relapse. I've seen this with virtually every addict I've ever known or worked with, and I've experienced it myself.

These weird, persisting, unwanted, false memories of drinking and drugging as a good thing occur because of memory interference, where older learned memories, thoughts, and behaviors interfere with our efforts at new healthy thinking. There are two types of memory interference: *proactive* and *retroactive*. In proactive interference, strong older memories will interfere with our recall of newer information. That's how these unwanted conditioned memories persist and assert themselves even though we know we're much better off and happier without substance use.

The other type of memory interference – retroactive interference – occurs when stronger new information that we place in our memory will interfere with the recall of the old. When we "remember when," our focus on these memories strengthens them, which engages retroactive interference to smush out unwanted false positive memories of our addiction. We're "unlearning" addiction by replacing old, dysfunctional learned associations between drugs or alcohol and fun, with associations between substance use and the pain and misery it brought us.

I'll tell you about my own experience. I was a low-bottom drunk and addict by the time I was carried into a detox center. I had long ago accepted that I was way too addicted to be able to ever stop, so I had resigned myself to my miserable existence and was even planning my own death. However, when I was in the detox center, I finally gave up my need for control and secrecy, and accepted the help I needed. I began "remember when" meditation right away... once or twice a day, just a few minutes at a time. For me, this is the skill that most contributed to taking away my obsession and cravings for alcohol and drugs. Now, years on, once in a while I still get ambushed by thoughts of drinking or using, and my addict's brain tries to convince me that it would be OK, that it would be fun. When that happens, I do a quick "remember when" in my mind, picturing how miserable and sick I was when I was drinking and using, how I couldn't control it, and how desperate I was to stop. It really works for me.

Another benefit of "remember when" meditation is that it leverages what neuroscientists call *creative re-imagination*. This is when our memory recall is greatly influenced by new suggestions we insert into old memories. By repeatedly "remembering when" in early recovery, we overwrite our false memories with the truth. These addiction-related memories are deep, so it takes time, but it works.

*   *   *

As we've discussed, our learned cues, triggers, and behaviors became bottom-up brain processes – automatic, unthinking. In recovery, as our brain heals and begins functioning properly again, we can re-assert our brain's executive control system (the brain's "CEO") so that we can stop thinking like addicts and instead think and behave in a healthy and functional way again. In other words, we can assert top-down higher thinking over instinctual bottom-up thinking. The best way to do this is to pause before we act. Automatic thoughts and behaviors come to mind instantaneously, but our top-down thinking takes a few seconds. So, if we pause before acting on impulse, we give our higher brain functions a chance to do their job. Psychologists refer to this as "critical thinking," and they teach anyone with bottom-up thinking problems (such as anger issues) to use this thinking pause. Many of the recovery tools we'll discuss in chapter 7 are based simply on critical thinking.

*   *   *

I'm often asked if substance use causes any permanent damage to the brain. Well, maybe. It depends a lot on the type, amount, and duration of substance use, and personal characteristics, such as overall health, genetics, age, and so on.

Studies into the enduring brain effects of substance use have only recently begun, and even these are generally small studies. At this time, we don't know how long physical brain changes persist and how many may be irreversible. Nonetheless, some of the studies have found that there may be a prolonged reduction in the size of the cerebral cortex (the higher functions part of our brain, the "grey matter"), although the white matter (the deeper, older portions of the brain) may not suffer any significant reductions. Methamphetamine is especially hard on the brain, but even with this drug, studies have shown that many (but not all) adverse brain effects recover after about 14 months of abstinence, although some appear to be very long-lasting.

Methamphetamine and cocaine can cause an ischemic stroke (death of part of the brain following a loss of blood supply). When this happens, the brain damage is permanent, although much function can be regained if intensive therapy is started right away. Meth use has also been linked to a later elevated risk of stroke and the development of Parkinson's disease.

When people overdose on opioids, they may stop breathing and therefore develop anoxic brain damage (tissue damage from lack of oxygen). These effects are permanent if they survive the overdose.

A few types of brain damage are specific to alcohol use. You may have heard of "wet brain," which refers to an alcohol-induced affliction called *Wernicke-Korsakoff syndrome* (WKS). Wet brain, WKS, is almost exclusively seen in alcoholics, but isn't directly caused by alcohol. It's actually a disease of malnutrition, specifically the deficiency of vitamin B_1 – thiamine – that commonly occurs in the "advanced" alcoholic. Thiamine is a vitamin, which means that our body can't produce it, so it must come from food. The body's available supply runs out with advanced malnutrition, as we see in advanced alcoholics. Lack of thiamine interferes with the delivery of proper nutrition to the brain. The brain is a hungry organ, and when it's not adequately fed it'll start to digest itself. The brain progressively withers, and WKS results.

Someone with WKS is usually a sad spectacle. They suffer from severe confusion, lack of interest in anything, inability to concentrate, and lack of awareness of their immediate situation. Their eyes and vision are affected, and they're unsteady on their feet. Eventually, they develop hallucinations, memory loss, confabulation (making up stories to compensate for memory loss), inability to form new memories, and nonsensical speech. Left untreated, WKS leads to coma or death.

You may have seen someone with WKS. These unfortunates are usually dismissed as "crazy drunks." They're disheveled and unkempt, and appear thin and poorly nourished. Their eyes vibrate and often don't line up properly. They seem to be in another world, and it's difficult to get and hold their attention, although they will follow simple commands. They talk to themselves, often repeating the same random phrase. They stagger when walking and fall easily. They're the extreme endorsement of the truth that no one ever drank themselves smart, successful, or happy.

Although WKS is treatable, requiring a couple simple injections of vitamin B_1, most do not get any treatment or get it late, and about 75% end up with permanent brain damage.

Another disease that may affect the brain in advanced alcoholism is known as *alcoholic cirrhosis*. Although this is a liver disease, it can also affect the brain. The diseased liver produces toxins that travel in the blood and poison the brain, resulting in a condition known as *hepatic encephalopathy*. This brain impairment occurs in 70% of people with cirrhosis. Fortunately, it resolves with treatment, which is easily done with inexpensive medications. Unfortunately, it'll return unless the individual stops drinking and has their liver disease cared for.

All told, we can't predict precisely how past substance use will affect the brain once an individual is in recovery. It depends from person to person so much that we may never be able to say as a general rule what the long-term effects are. As well, permanent changes to the brain may or may not cause symptoms, because neuroplasticity enables us to bypass some brain injuries.

The most important issue isn't what damage occurs to the brain, but how it affects our ability to function. Some of the persisting effects on brain function that are commonly reported include delayed reaction time, slowed thinking, difficulty thinking clearly, memory problems, hallucinations (primarily in meth and hallucinogen users), and lack of coordination. Unfortunately, there's not much we can do to treat most of these symptoms if they occur.

So, what do we do with this information? I suggest taking the following attitude: *there's no way to know for sure how much our brain has been affected, how long any effects will last, and whether they'll impact our ability to function. The important thing is that we're in recovery now, and that's how we can function to the best of our ability.*

6

The Mind in Recovery

In this chapter we look at the changes to the addicted mind that are consistent with healing, successful recovery, and a return to happiness and good function.

Recovery isn't simply the absence of using drugs and alcohol. Rather, the underlying causes of the addiction must be identified and addressed, and the effects of substance use on the brain and mind must be taken care of, or relapse is almost certain. If not, the addicted brain and mind will continue their work, and any abstinence from substance use will be from sheer willpower. And we know how willpower works in the addicted mind... it doesn't – or at least not for long. However, when care is taken to heal and restore the addicted brain (as we discussed in the previous chapter) and the addicted mind to proper function, the need and desire to drink or use falls away. It really does work like that.

Addiction therapy is based on the *biopsychosocial* model of healthcare, which recognizes that disease affects people in many domains of their life: biologically, psychologically, socially, and spiritually. This model of care is used for all healthcare today, not just addiction treatment. It acknowledges that good health isn't simply the absence of disease; rather, health is determined by all aspects of our life. The biopsychosocial model of care – properly done – remarkably improves outcomes in treating all types of sickness and disease. Few diseases demand this all-encompassing approach to care more than addiction.

The spiritual dimension is the least understood of the four factors of the biopsychosocial model. Most people equate spirituality to religion, but this is incorrect. Spirituality is about connections outside ourselves, such as connections with other people, the world in general, and – for some – some kind of a higher power. A huge volume of research has shown that these connections are a powerfully therapeutic aspect of all healing, including addiction recovery. Ph.D. psychologist and noted addictions researcher Wayne Skinner provides a good explanation of the spirituality dimension of recovery: *when people find connection to a larger frame of meaning that allows self-transcendence and meaningful engagement in recovery practices and social re-engagement, they are more likely to change from addictive preoccupation to increased behavioral self-control, mindfulness and reconnection with others in ways that are meaningful for the person* (Skinner, pages 2-3).

*　　　*　　　*

Counseling in addiction treatment is heavily focused on *metacognition*, which is a big word for a simple concept: learning to understand how we think, so that we can challenge and change dysfunctional thinking. By reading this book, you're getting a jump on metacognition because you're learning about how the addicted mind works. Metacognition is a powerful modality for achieving positive neuroplasticity.

Earlier, we discussed how the dysfunctional thoughts and behaviors that constitute addiction are largely due to "bottom-up" brain processes, meaning they've become automatic, without involving any prior thought or consideration. In other words, once addiction gets going, the brain's executive control system (our ability to think, plan, consider consequences, and make sound decisions) is removed from the loop. Metacognition is a powerful technique for re-asserting the executive control part of the brain after it's been disabled by chronic substance use. As the brain detoxifies and recovers its ability to function properly, metacognition allows addicts to use their thinking abilities to challenge what had been automatic reactions. Quite literally, addicts go from the infant brain to the adult brain.

Fortunately, recovery from the adverse psychological effects of addiction is the norm among those who've taken care to heal. Indeed, my experience has been that people who take their healing from addiction seriously end up in much better psychological health than before their addiction. This is because they may have dealt with pre-existing issues, such as mental health problems, the effects of previous trauma, and toxic negative psychology. As well, they learn new life skills that they may not have previously used.

In this chapter, we'll talk about characteristics of the mind in recovery that lead us to success in recovery, positive psychology, and a return to good function. Let's begin by talking about what must happen to the addicted mind to become ready to heal and recover from addiction.

The Addicted Mind Going Into Recovery

Recovery from addiction begins with becoming mentally ready to seek and accept help, and to make the commitment necessary to beat addiction. I included in the appendix my description of the stages of addiction, including when someone is mentally ready for recovery.

Readiness for recovery requires overcoming some significant psychological barriers. Chief among these is the addict's need for control. As we've discussed, this is rooted in the need to retain the freedom of movement to be able to return to substance use "just in case:" just in case recovery is too hard, just in case we're having a bad day. Addicts who haven't let go of their need for control will approach recovery with one foot in, one foot out. They'll seek the easiest possible way to stop their substance use, which is pretty much always inadequate. They'll try to do recovery their own way, picking and choosing what help they accept. However, "their way" has always failed in the past. "Their way" has gotten them into this mess.

Fear presents another psychological barrier to recovery, and a few fears stand. First, addicts have a pathological fear of withdrawal. Most have repeatedly gone to great lengths to avoid withdrawal during their addiction. I've heard addicts say they were long ago ready to stop their substance use, but fear of withdrawal kept them from pulling the trigger. In virtually all these cases, the individuals had tried self-detoxing by tapering themselves off their drug, but this never works; self-tapering requires an ability to control our drug use. However, detox and withdrawal can be made much safer and more comfortable by taking advantage of medically assisted withdrawal by checking into a detox center for a week or seeing an addictions doctor, for those who plan on detoxing at home.

Addicts commonly speak of their fear of living without drugs or alcohol, which may have been their "safety" crutch for a long time (*how will I deal with life without drugs or alcohol?*). And there's the fear of failure at recovery. Many are kept from recovery because of the fear of taking responsibility for their past actions. And there's fear that their life is such a train wreck that life in recovery will suck. Then, there's the fear of the unknown (*what's going to happen to me in treatment?*), the fear of giving up control and giving themself over to the care of others (*what if treatment is too hard and I need a drink or drug?*), and the fear of being exposed as an addict and branded by stigma.

My experience in my work in addictions – and my personal experience as an addict in recovery – has been that these fears are largely unfounded, uninformed, or exaggerated, so let's talk about that. To begin with, telling someone our fears has a remarkable calming effect, especially if that person is someone who cares and we can trust. As we've discussed, the neurotransmitter abnormalities in the addicted brain generate a state of anxiety and fear that exaggerates reality. As well, the addicted mind is secretive and prone to denial, so letting go of the secret-keeping is difficult. A leap of faith is necessary to let go of our fears and secrets to begin recovery, and people invariably feel better once they've done that. People in the Twelve Step program say that our secrets keep us sick, and that's very true. Getting our fears off our chest is a potent way to ease our anxieties and find the courage to face up to our angst.

We don't have to clean up the mess we've made of our life in one day once we're in recovery. Treatment is designed to help addicts with a train-wrecked life ease their way back into the world and handle their problems one day at a time. And it works very well. I've heard many addicts in recovery say that their worst day in recovery was way better than their best day in addiction – even though in recovery they've had to face their problems and fears. We don't need to fix our whole world in a day. Easy does it!

When addicts are facing criminal charges, debts, and the shame of having mistreated others, remaining in social and mental isolation by hiding out with their substance use is their security blanket. However, when they've had a chance to clear their substance-soaked minds, finally facing these issues lifts a tremendous load off their shoulders. Finally stopping the running, hiding, and lying is a tremendous relief.

My experience and the experience of hundreds of addicts in recovery whom I've interviewed has been that judges, police, debtors, landlords, and other authorities greatly respect recovery, and they're tremendously pleased when someone in recovery has the courage to come forward and own up to their responsibilities. They're always predisposed to give them a break. It might not save someone from jail time or other consequences, but it always makes a difference. Owning up to past wrongdoings – even if it means going to jail for a while – is a powerful and necessary aspect of healing from addiction. Debtors are almost always predisposed to cut addicts in recovery some slack and arrange a reasonable repayment schedule. Judges and debtors are so accustomed to addicts running away from their responsibilities that they greatly respect one who comes forward – sober – wanting to put things right. People respect recovery.

A powerful way of allaying addicts' fears is through *vicarious experience.* This term refers to the uplifting effects of hearing the success stories of other people that we identify with. In the case of addiction, vicarious experience comes from hearing the stories of fellow addicts who were as bad – or worse – than we were and have beaten their disease and found a happy and healthy life again. Because it's someone who's shared their experience, addicts can identify with the person sharing the story and visualize themselves succeeding. Recovery support groups provide an excellent opportunity for positive vicarious experience.

The turning point for addicts is when they're so thoroughly sick and tired of being sick and tired that they're ready to do *anything* to get better, including "surrendering" their need for control and secrecy, and facing their fears. People in the Twelve Step program refer to this as "reaching our bottom."

Healing the Addicted Mind

Finally healing the tortured addicted mind is one of the great rewards of recovery.

As we've discussed in previous chapters, addiction arises from significant disruptions in thought processes (cognition) that result in dysfunctional and harmful behaviors. As such, *cognitive behavioral therapy* (CBT) – or a variant of CBT – forms the basis of most addiction therapy programs. CBT refers to various counseling approaches that focus on changing how individuals think and respond to their environment. Some of the various counseling techniques have different names (such as *dialectical behavioral therapy* (DBT), *rational emotive behavioral therapy* (REBT), *motivational interviewing*, and *psychodynamic therapy* (PT), for example), but they all boil down to targeting cognition (how people think), and behaviors (how people act and react).

The primary technique used by CBT is metacognition, but you don't need to undergo CBT to practice metacognition. Just learning to recognize "stinking thinking" when it arises and challenging and changing it is all you need to do. With practice, metacognition soon becomes automatic, and addiction-related stinking thinking just dies out. And it works very well; not only for overcoming the addicted mind, but a whole variety of other psychological problems, such as low self-esteem, anger problems, and relationship issues.

When it comes to addiction treatment, rehab, or therapy – whatever term we use, they all mean the same thing – we're talking about a therapeutic program that identifies and addresses the causes and effects of the addiction and provides the "tools" needed to return to sober, healthy, functional living.

Just as I find the term "addiction treatment" to be misleading, I'm also disappointed by the word "rehab." The term is a bit loaded, with implications that an individual is being rehabilitated or corrected after misbehaving, as if they were in prison. However, both terms are in general use and widely understood, so we should take them in the correct context.

The best data about addiction treatment centers are from the U.S. These data show that the majority of addiction treatment centers are Twelve Step based, which research has shown to be by far the most effective approach to psychological healing and recovery. Some treatment centers are not Twelve Step based, which doesn't necessarily mean they lack validity. However, not all addiction treatment programs are created equally, and some are absolute nonsense and lack any validity. Sadly, many make outlandish claims of success on their websites, citing success rates that have no basis in reality. Frankly, I've been appalled by some of the nonsensical addiction treatment programs that prey on unknowing victims.

As a doctor and research scientist, I'm impressed by the Twelve Step program for two main reasons: 1) even though the program was developed in the 1930s, it's entirely consistent with the current science of addiction, and 2) it amounts to a singularly effective form of CBT, even though it predates the invention of CBT by nearly 50 years. Its time-tested methodical and straightforward approach is refreshingly simple and amenable to all. Studies have shown that people who've completed the Twelve Steps score higher on measures of positive psychology than do normal, high-functioning non-addict individuals.

The Twelve Step program also provides a robust system of social support and recovery activities for ongoing recovery support and relapse prevention for a lifetime. It's a complete package. Best of all, it's free; anyone can attend the meetings and participate, and it's widely available.

Resistance to the Twelve Step program lies primarily in the criticism of it being a "religious" program. This misunderstanding derives from the fact that the Twelve Step literature often uses the word "God." However, I've interviewed many agnostics and atheists who've found sobriety and health through the Twelve Steps, and they're entirely comfortable with how the program fits with and respects their beliefs. Personally, I am not a religious person, and I find that I don't have to sacrifice any of my beliefs to participate in the program. I don't want to spend too much time on the issue, but the Twelve Step program is intended for and respects people of all cultures, beliefs (or non-beliefs), languages, races, and backgrounds. Anyone interested in learning more about this fantastic program may wish to check out my book, *A Trip Through the 12 Steps with a Doctor and Therapist.*

"Unlearning" Addiction

We talked in chapter 3 about how the brain's learning system is involved in addiction; let's just quickly recap. There are three ways that learning contributes to creating the addicted brain and mind – classical conditioning (making associations between substance use and cues), operant conditioning (seeking rewards [the "high"] and avoiding punishments [withdrawal]), and social learning (other people influencing how we think and behave).

Through neuroplasticity, we can "unlearn" addiction. The addiction brain pathways are prominent and well-used, so making new pathways our go-to way of thinking and acting will take some conscious practice, just as any learning requires practice. However, the effort pays off: with time these new, healthy pathways become more and more prominent, while the unused addiction pathways wither away. Nonetheless, the old learned pathways may re-activate in times of vulnerability (such as times of high stress), or with future exposure to addictive substances, so we must use our recovery tools (we'll discuss these more in chapter 7) when we feel things may not be right with us. As addicts in recovery like to say: *I have to use my recovery tools, because my addiction is out in the parking lot doing push-ups.*

The first type of learning – classical conditioning – can be unlearned through a psychological technique known as *extinction*. A learned association – a cue we associate with drinking or using – will naturally diminish when we stop reinforcing the association. In other words, when we abstain from using or drinking, the learned associations will begin to fade. The extinction process is gradual, and spontaneous recurrence is common. For this reason, avoiding people, places, and things that were associated with our substance use is essential, lest they trigger cravings or urges. This important recovery principle taps into *cue-dependent forgetting*, which is the decay of memories when the cues that trigger them are no longer encountered.

The second type of learning – operant conditioning – is partly reversed after detox because we no longer need our drug to avoid punishment (withdrawal). However, cravings and urges can continue well beyond detox, so using recovery tools is very important until these extinguish. The "remember when" technique we discussed in chapter 5 is probably the most effective tool for eradicating cravings and urges. As you will recall, "remember when" taps into a psychological process known as interference. By forcing our mind to recall the misery of our addiction, we interfere with the old learned associations of substance use as "fun."

The third type of addiction learning can be turned around and used with great effect in recovery. As we've discussed, social learning involves learning new attitudes and behaviors by observing and emulating other people who matter to us. When we cease being among people related to substance use, the previously learned behaviors will begin to fade. Instead, we spend time among people who're associated with recovery, and their healthy ideas and behaviors become internalized for us. This is one of the potent benefits of recovery support groups – they allow us to become part of a "culture of recovery," and we benefit from the influence and experience of people who've succeeded in recovery. Recovery groups are also a rich source of vicarious experience that fills us with self-efficacy and motivation.

Social learning is a fundamental part of all credible addiction treatment and relapse prevention programs. The application of social learning to recovery includes:

- Ceasing contact with the people and places that previously served as models, triggers, and peer-driven influences for substance use,
- Developing a new network of friends and family who support recovery,
- Inclusion in a recovery support group, during treatment and after, that involves immersion in a culture of recovery, where recovery-based attitudes, behaviors, and values are modeled and learned,
- The use of vicarious experiences for providing modeling and motivation for recovery, to increase self-efficacy beliefs, and to show the way to recovery,
- Establishing and using a supportive network for a healthy approach to dealing with stress and adversity, and
- Learning skills and the self-confidence to respond appropriately to negative peer pressure.

*   *   *

Maintaining a positive mindset is an important part of recovery. Anything that returns the mind to negative feelings, or poorly tolerated stress, or re-emergence of mental health symptoms increases the risk of relapse, as the mind may return to its past ways of escape/avoidance coping in its desperation for relief. In such cases, addicts in recovery need to use their recovery tools. Just as there's a mindset associated with addiction, there's also a mindset that's associated with success in recovery, good health, and happiness. Let's now talk about the key aspects of this positive mindset.

Correcting the Dissonant Self

As you may recall from chapter 4, when people violate their personal beliefs, standards, and values, they experience the dissonant self and suffer considerable psychological distress. We need to see ourselves as useful, competent, and needed. And we need to see ourselves as fundamentally good and moral. When we don't behave as we believe a good person should, we view ourselves negatively – and even dislike ourselves – which significantly erodes our self-esteem. Besides diminished self-esteem, the dissonant self creates gnawing feelings of guilt, remorse, shame, and self-loathing.

We also experience the dissonant self when we don't fulfill the roles in life that make up our self-identity. For example, if one of an individual's identity roles is being a parent, but they're selfish and neglectful toward their children, they'll experience the dissonant self. The more important the role, the more it produces dissonance if we don't fulfill it as we believe we should.

Addicts create a dissonant self that stands out for its severity. They deviate so far from how they believe a good person should behave, and they shirk and abandon their self-defining life roles so completely, that they suffer considerable psychological pain that is a significant driver of continued substance use. To heal, an addict must correct the dissonant self, and make amends for their past wrongdoings.

We can resolve the dissonant self by changing our behavior to match what we believe is right and wrong. However, we don't need to try to be monks. We're human, not flawless robots, and if we set impossible standards for ourselves we're setting ourselves up for failure. Instead, we should seek progress rather than perfection; our mind judges us based on our intentions rather than the outcomes. By committing to doing our best to better align our words and actions with our values, standards, and beliefs, we earn our own respect.

We all know when we're about to do something inconsistent with our values; we have a little alarm that goes off in our mind, and the mind doesn't like it. With a sober mind, we have the power to make choices; doing the right thing isn't always easiest, but it's consistent with healing and our new identity as addicts in recovery.

An old parable of uncertain origin – although it probably originated with the Cherokee Indians – illustrates what we can do about the dissonant self. The story goes: a young Cherokee boy came home one day angry and determined to get revenge against another boy who had just wronged him. He expressed his anger to his grandfather:

> The old Cherokee chief said to his grandson: *I too, at times, have felt a great hatred for those who have taken so much with no sorrow for what they do.*
> *Hatred wears you down, and hatred does not hurt your enemy. Hatred is like taking poison and wishing your enemy would die. I have struggled with these emotions many times.*
> *It's as though a fight is continuously going on inside me. It is a terrible fight and it is between two wolves.*
> *One wolf is good and does no harm. He is filled with joy, humility, and kindness. He lives in harmony with everyone around and does not take offense when no offense was intended. He will only fight when it is right to do so and in the right way.*
> *The other wolf is full of anger, envy, regret, greed, and self-pity. The littlest thing will set him into a fit of temper. He fights everyone all the time and for no reason. When blinded by his anger and hatred, he does not have a sound mind. It is helpless anger, because his anger will change nothing.*
> *It is hard to live with these two wolves inside me. These two wolves are constantly fighting to control my spirit.*
> *Young man, the same fight is going on inside you and inside every other person on this earth.*
> The grandson thought about it for a moment and then asked his grandfather: *Which wolf will win inside you, grandpa?*
> The old Cherokee chief smiled and replied: *The one I feed.*
> *Dear reader, which wolf inside are you feeding?* (Belludi, 2014).

So, think of correcting the dissonant self as separating the two wolves within us and making a conscious decision to commit to feeding the good wolf. Our healing depends upon it.

Making meaningful amends to people we've harmed during our active addiction is essential to correcting the dissonant self. It takes courage to approach someone we've harmed and apologize, or pay them back, or fix what we've done, but the psychological rewards are enormous. We gain respect for ourselves, and show others that we're not defined by our addiction. People respect recovery, and they tremendously respect those who seek to right past wrongs. It's a rare quality these days.

Altruism – giving to others and expecting nothing in return – will come up later in our discussion. Altruism has powerful healing properties, including for survivors of trauma. For addicts in recovery, engaging in selfless acts not only reduces the dissonant self, but absolutely crushes it. Altruism *exceeds* everyone's expectations about how a person should behave, so it has an especially potent effect in purging toxic dissonance. We become positive citizens of the world, and it's much easier to like and respect ourselves.

Being human, we cannot simply eliminate our natural instincts, and they'll sometimes get the better of us. But, at the end of the day, we shouldn't ask ourselves: *was I perfect today?* Instead, we should ask: *was I better today than I was yesterday? Can I be proud of how I lived my life today? Did I learn something today that I can use to make myself better tomorrow? If I couldn't speak, would people know by my actions what I stand for?*

Self-Forgiveness

Correcting the dissonant self, especially making amends for past wrong-doings, provides the basis for forgiving ourselves. Our mind won't permit self-forgiveness if we keep on with the wayward behaviors that were part of our addiction.

Self-forgiveness also requires that we give ourselves a break by working on correcting our inner critic. The so-called inner critic is one of the most self-defeating mental workings of the human mind. Most people have an inner "voice" – although it's usually really thoughts, not an actual voice they hear – that provides a running dialogue as they go about their day. Most of us aren't even fully aware of it, unless we consciously pay attention to it. Self-talk includes our conscious thoughts and our unconscious beliefs and assumptions about ourselves and what we're doing. Our inner voice can be helpful and nurturing, or fault-finding, nit-picking, shaming, and self-defeating. When our inner voice is self-critical and pessimistic, that's our inner critic speaking to us. Unfortunately, for some people the dominant internal dialogue is their inner critic. The addicted mind is particularly susceptible to a harsh inner critic.

What we say to ourselves affects how we feel about ourselves and how effective we are in life; so much so that our inner dialogue is a major determinant of whether we succeed or fail at our endeavors, how happy and adjusted we are, and how we interact with other people. Sadly, many people are held back from their true potential because of their inner critic. When we talk to ourselves negatively, we damage our confidence and self-esteem, and we're less likely to take on new challenges. It makes it more difficult for us to project a positive image to others. Worst of all, the inner critic chews away at the positive mindset that's so important for success in recovery and our overall happiness and well-being.

People tend to view self-criticism as a positive thing, as something that helps them learn from their mistakes and improve themselves. They may even fear they won't be able to achieve the standards of behavior they want unless they're hard on themselves. Some even gain a sense of security or control from their inner critical voice. However, while we all should learn from our mistakes, the inner critic is a dysfunctional and damaging way to attempt to do so. The problem is that the inner critic doesn't provide a logical, objective breakdown of who we are and how we did in a particular event or task; instead, it's a deceitful beat-down that focuses unduly on and exaggerates what went wrong, seeking to find reasons that we're inferior or unworthy. The inner critic exaggerates our shortcomings, and sees failure where none exists. Indeed, research has shown that the practice of self-criticism is a result of skewed information processing in cortical brain circuits.

Similarly, some people are reluctant to let go of their inner critic because they confuse it with their conscience. However, the inner critical voice is not the same as our conscience, by no manner or means. Our conscience is what we believe is right and wrong and how our actions fit with our beliefs. The inner critic is neither trustworthy nor is it any kind of a moral guide.

We should definitely be aware of our shortcomings, learn from our mistakes (and our successes), and strive to better ourselves. However, listening to the inner critical voice is not the path to cultivating growth and success. In fact, the inner critic has been linked to all kinds of life difficulties, including performance anxiety, fear, low self-esteem, reduced self-confidence, dysfunctional relationships, and even mental and physical health problems. The inner critic generates stress by increasing people's mind-taxing reactions to ordinary life stressors, turning even benign events into upsetting hassles. It often leads people to making unhealthy decisions. As such, people are mistaken when they believe that the inner critical voice is somehow helpful in improving their performance in life; to the contrary, self-criticism is known to psychologists as a maladaptive personality trait, one well worth curbing.

Psychologists refer to the inner critical voice as *toxic self-criticism*. And toxic it is. Research has demonstrated that self-criticism adversely affects our mental and physical health. One researcher describes self-criticism as: *a formidable dimension of vulnerability to a wide array of psychopathologies* (Shahar, 2016). More than just an association with psychopathology, the inner critic is a defining characteristic of many mental health disorders, such as eating disorders, obsessive-compulsive disorder, depression, anxiety, and – you guessed it – addiction. Addressing their self-destructive inner critic is a major focus of therapy for people with such struggles.

So, have I convinced you that putting the inner critic in its place is worthwhile for fortifying your recovery? OK, but does this mean we stop evaluating our performance and behaviors? No, not at all. In fact, conquering the inner critic helps us to better evaluate and learn from our mistakes and shortcomings. Self-criticism impairs our ability to improve ourselves – like the teacher who demeans and screams at a child who got their math question wrong versus the teacher who explains the mistake. It leads to frustration because we see our very nature as a person as the cause of our failure.

If we want to be happy and positive, we must talk to ourselves in a positive and affirming way. It's about strengthening a nurturing and encouraging inner voice and refusing to accept the scolding and self-shaming voice; that is, it's about choosing to feed the right wolf. Our job is to recognize our inner critic as a toxic pest and to become willing to do our utmost to free ourselves of its power over us. As always, this begins by engaging our metacognition and challenging the skewed opinion and bad advice that this inner enemy tries to force upon us. This may take some practice, because the inner critic may have been part of your internal dialogue for a long time. When we mindfully notice our inner critic trying to bully us, we must change the channel immediately. Refuse to listen to that crap.

Most people recognize the value of being loving, kind, generous, supportive, and tolerant toward others; likewise, we must also be loving, kind, generous, supportive, and tolerant toward ourselves. Psychologists know the value of cutting ourselves some slack – *self-compassion* – for our emotional and psychological well-being. So much so, that replacing dysfunctional self-criticism with self-compassion is a major focus of CBT. Research has shown that self-compassion is associated with improved inner strength, resilience to stress, physical health, motivation, interpersonal relationships, and overall psychological function.

We must take a realistic view of what we expect from ourselves by adopting an attitude that we're not perfect creatures. We must accept that we may fall short sometimes, and that even what constitutes "falling short" is a matter of perspective. We use acceptance – in this case acceptance that we'll sometimes perform less than superbly and sometimes may even fall flat on our face. To hold expectations that we'll somehow go through life and perform perfectly in everything we do is to set ourselves up for disappointment and frustration. Our attitude should be that we're striving for progress – learning from our mistakes – rather than perfection. Maybe we've fallen short somehow... so what? Can we learn from it and progress somehow, so we'll be better and wiser next time? Yes. Are we gaining anything by ruminating on the event – going over and over it repeatedly in our mind? Nope.

If we find ourselves ruminating over past events, we should pull the plug on this waste of brain-power. Change the channel. When we ruminate, it's our inner critic at work. The inner critic loves to live in the past and go over things again and again. It prevents us from finding self-forgiveness. It loves to make us lay awake at night, replaying all our supposed mistakes and doing the "what-if" and "should-have" thing. It's just wasted brain-power, and manufactured stress. It does nothing to help us. The past has happened, and there's nothing whatsoever we can do to change it. So, we must accept it. We can either ruminate over it, blow it out of proportion, and beat ourselves up, or we can accept the past, learn from our mistakes and successes, and then move on. Even our supposed failures have advantages if we acknowledge them. Putting the toxic inner critic in its place requires a few attitude changes:

- Stop expecting perfection from ourselves in every situation,
- Accept that we tend to blow our own failures out of proportion,
- Accept that ruminating about past performances accomplishes nothing, and
- We should aim for progress rather than expect perfection.

Psychologists teach their patients a technique known as *dis-identifying*. This is where we separate that inner critical voice from being a part of us and look at it as a foreign, unwelcome entity. Sometimes it even helps to give it a name. Then, when we hear that inner critic starting with its unhelpful browbeating we can dis-identify – detach – ourselves from it. Essentially, we look at the inner critical voice as an individual separate from ourselves and tell it to bugger off. Clinical studies have shown that it works!

We can also challenge the inner critic by examining the evidence. If we look at the situation objectively, we can see that our inner critic focuses only on the bad, and makes it look worse than it was. So, we examine the evidence and challenge the inner critic. If we're upset over something that we just did and our inner critic calls us an idiot, it's best to wait until our initial emotional outburst has cooled and then take a realistic look at what just happened. *What were the positives? Was my action really that stupid, or that bad? What would it have looked like through another person's eyes? Would I call a friend an idiot in this situation?* And, even when there are negatives, we accept that no situation will ever be 100% pure positive. There will always be some negatives, so why get hung up on them when they occur? Our inner voice seems to think that any negatives are unacceptable, but we know better, so we can challenge that notion.

Effective self-evaluation is about admitting that we faltered, learning from it, and committing to improving. We reject self-criticism and turn to self-correction. However, it's also about acknowledging when we do well, and putting our perceived shortcomings in perspective. Did we really do as badly as our inner critic is telling us? The answer is almost always: no!

Using self-talk to challenge the inner critic is another strategy for overcoming the self-sabotage. Repeating to ourselves: *my mistakes do not define me!* is a good self-talk technique. Try picking out a mantra that works for you and repeating it to yourself when your metacognition skills alert you that you're getting down on yourself. Here are a few more:

Easy does it!
Does it really matter?
Nobody's perfect!
I did the best that I could!
Everybody makes mistakes!
Some days are good, some aren't. I don't let a bad day change who I am.
Did I learn from this? Good, then time to move on.

When we correct our addiction-related dissonant behaviors – such as selfishness, intolerance, impatience, and irresponsibility – and make amends to those we've harmed with our behaviors, we're in the correct frame of mind for self-forgiveness. This is further fortified by correcting the self-destructive inner critical voice and engaging in self-correction instead of self-criticism. The end result we're looking for is self-forgiveness and a release from the guilt, shame, self-loathing, and regret that have been plaguing our minds and driving our addiction for so long. Self-forgiveness is one of the great rewards of recovery.

Humility

Everybody knows that humility is bad, *right?* Well, hold on a minute. There's a widely held belief that humility is the opposite of confidence and self-esteem. People believe that to take on humility means to degrade oneself; after all, "humility" sounds a lot like "humiliation." However, that's not what it means.

Rather, humility is a realistic appreciation of our limitations as well as our strengths. Humility is a key virtue for mental well-being because it allows us to see and understand our true value as a person, so that our self-worth stands unshakeable through our successes and failures, and doesn't depend upon whether or not other people treat us well or give us praise. In other words, humility is the basis of a consistent positive self-regard that comes from within and doesn't depend on outside people or events.

By recognizing our strengths and weaknesses, we can use good judgment and take on goals that are consistent with our abilities without over-stretching ourselves by overestimating what we can do. With humility, we can be disappointed with failures and setbacks, but we don't allow it to affect how we feel about ourselves. When you hear people describing someone as "secure," or "grounded," or "selfless," chances are the individual they speak of practices humility.

Humility is one of the most important outcomes of CBT. Psychological studies have supported and confirmed humility as a therapeutic tool and key to happiness, health, and overall well-being.

Psychologists describe humility as a "foundational virtue," in that it's a requirement for other positive personality traits to develop.

Studies in the behavioral sciences have shown that humility is a highly desirable virtue, a character trait that can advance our fortunes in the world. Humility is associated with a number of improved outcomes in life, including pro-social behavior, academic excellence, better job performance, and receiving respect from others. None of those things involve "humiliation." However, most importantly, humility allows us to crush the addict's false pride as we transition to recovery.

Humility is a complex personality trait, so rather than trying to define it in a few sentences, let's look at the characteristics of humility:

- an accurate (not overinflated or underestimated) sense of our abilities and achievements,
- a willingness to share due credit for accomplishments,
- the ability to acknowledge and accept responsibility for our mistakes, imperfections, gaps in knowledge, and limitations,
- openness to new ideas, contradictory information, and advice,
- keeping our abilities and accomplishments in perspective,
- relatively low focus on the self, and little self-preoccupation,
- empathy, gentleness, respect, and appreciation for the equality, autonomy, and value of others,
- lack of a desire to distort information to make ourselves look and feel better,
- a non-judgmental and open-minded disposition to considering new and divergent ideas and seeking new information,
- a general desire and openness to learn,
- gratitude,
- appreciation of the value of all things, as well as the many ways that people and things can contribute to our world,
- an awareness of our place in, and connection to, the world, and
- a willingness to consider or connect with God or some higher power.

By looking at these characteristics, we can see that humility involves overcoming our natural tendency to see ourselves as a priority or privileged above all others. As well, humility is about seeing ourselves more objectively, as one among many other worthy people, which means that we don't criticize or treat ourselves more harshly than anyone else. Humility is based on a realistic understanding of our capabilities and limitations, not on a merciless critical inner voice.

But does living with humility mean we must become meek and mild and allow people to walk all over us? Does it mean that we can't be ambitious and competitive? What if we have a job that requires us to be aggressive and uncompromising? Do we have to quit our jobs to stay right with our humility? Does it mean we can't stand up for ourselves in a dispute? Does it mean we can't be tough and negotiate with someone for a better deal? No, not at all. Humility is no bar to doing what we need to do in life, including being tough and assertive when necessary. The difference is that when we behave in such a way, we do so with humility. We still treat others with the respect they deserve, and we don't allow our actions to be governed by anger, resentment, jealousy, greed, or a need to boost our ego. Being tough, assertive, and confident is consistent with humility.

And what about pride? Must we throw pride under the bus if we seek humility? Again, not at all. Remember: humility is just as much about acknowledging our awesomeness as it is about recognizing our limitations. It involves a shift in our pride from the dysfunctional hubristic pride (boastful, self-aggrandizing pride) of people of low self-esteem to a healthy authentic pride, where we're rightfully proud of our legitimate accomplishments, but we aren't shoving them in everybody's face. Pride in our achievements is healthy as long as it's coupled with humility and gratitude.

Gratitude

It's human nature to take what we have for granted, and to covet what we don't have. When we receive something we want, we're soon focused on obtaining the next thing. Even a certain dissatisfaction sets in when we get what we want. It's healthy to want things, set realistic goals, and work toward achieving what we want – that helps us succeed in life. However, when wanting something becomes a focus of envy, anger, jealousy, resentment, and self-pity, we're hurting ourselves. The antidote to constantly feeling like we don't have enough... is gratitude.

Gratitude is an issue of perspective. A little exercise in empathy helps to illustrate this. The next time you see someone who has less than you, imagine yourself in their shoes, looking at you and what you have. Maybe it's a homeless person, or someone dying of cancer, or someone who's blind or in a wheelchair. Try seeing yourself from their perspective, and how they could envy you because of what you have. Maybe also resent you for it. Now, does what you have suddenly seem a little more fulfilling? Do you think the person in the wheelchair will be able to walk again or be happier by burning in resentful envy over you and your ability to walk? These people with glaring deficits in their life have long ago learned to be grateful for what they do have so they don't spend their lives chained to the green-eyed monster and his good buddies anger, resentment, and self-pity. We can do the same if we have an attitude change.

Gratitude is a therapeutic emotion. Having gratitude means being aware of what's good in our life and having an appreciation for our life. It's the difference between having a day filled with regret and envy or a day filled with contentedness and appreciation. Anyone who hasn't tried it should do a "gratitude list." This simple exercise – sitting with pen and paper and listing what we're grateful for – always has a healing impact. Many people don't do well with their list until they've been exposed to people less fortunate than themselves. That's one way that giving of our time to help others helps us: it makes gratitude come a lot easier when we need it to chase away the self-pity monster.

Many people do a gratitude list whenever they feel down on themselves and experience the "poor me's." I do a gratitude list in my mind a couple of times a week, usually when driving or walking. It keeps me grounded and contributes to my happiness and peace of mind. No matter what's got me down, it always makes me feel better.

Some of the most content people I know are people in recovery who have glaringly little in terms of material treasures. Their peace of mind comes from acceptance, and gratitude fills them with appreciation. Their perspective is that they're a success today if they don't drink or use, so they feel like a success every day. They've chosen to rid themselves of the unhappy yoke of unsatisfiable envy. Let me tell you about one guy in particular, Lucas.

I was fortunate in that before my drinking and using misadventures I was able to put together a life: get educated, surround myself with wonderful family and friends, and put together a good work history. Lucas wasn't so lucky. His drug and alcohol use started as a teen, so he never finished high school, never got an education or a trade, never built up any kind of positive work history, and never developed any meaningful relationships. When he finally got sober, he was nearly 60, alone, and had the same employability as a teenager who hasn't finished high school. As a result, he does minimum wage manual labor jobs, barely survives paycheck to paycheck, and lives a simple life. He does without a lot of things that some of us take for granted. However, he's by far one of the most grateful people I've ever met, and that's the basis of his happiness. If he began comparing himself to others with more possessions, a better life situation, or a better job, his happiness and peace of mind would quickly evaporate. However, Lucas does volunteer work with people on the street who're struggling with addiction, and that helps him keep his perspective healthy. He's so wonderfully grateful for life, his sobriety, and the few material things he does have that I find him to be an inspiration, especially when human nature gets the better of me and self-pity creeps in.

Taking Responsibility for Ourselves

The addicted mind is characteristically angry, resentful, and defensive. Addicts see themselves as victims and blame everybody and everything (except themselves) for their life situation. The self-pity and blamefulness of the addicted mind are incompatible with recovery. Until we accept responsibility for ourselves and our situation, we'll easily slip back into that seething "poor-me" mindset that got us into trouble in the first place.

When we blame our misery on others, we're engaging in learned helplessness and an external locus of control, as we discussed in chapter 4. Just to remind you, these are a mindset where we believe we're helpless victims of outside forces and events, and nothing we could do would help our situation. So… we don't even try. Taking responsibility for ourselves allows us to develop self-efficacy and an internal locus of control, where we acknowledge that our actions can affect our life. It's how we go about becoming people who govern our affairs instead of allowing our affairs to govern us.

Correcting the dissonant self helps us cut out the poor-me, self-victimization attitude. Cognitive dissonance propels the addicted mind to dodge responsibility for our life situation, because the substance-soaked mind seeks to lessen our guilt about what we've become by blaming others for our situation.

Regardless of how we got where we are, and even if other people were somehow to blame, we must take responsibility for our life and our situation, and for cleaning up our own mess. Even if other people or events contributed to our downfall, obsessing over it and burning with anger and self-pity does nothing to help us get ourselves out of our predicament. The substance use that causes an individual to become addicted occurs because they put a drink to their mouth or a needle in their arm, not because of what anyone else did or said. There are risk factors for addiction – such as genetics, past traumas, and so forth – but these are not causes. Many people with unbearable stress and horrible life situations never turn to obsessive substance use to cope. Likewise, many people with terrible family relationships never become addicted.

The turning point for my addiction was the stress of my divorce; I felt I got a raw deal, and that was when I began using drink and drugs to cope with my anger and stress, and my addiction developed from that. But that's on me; it's not the fault of my divorce, or the judge, or my ex-wife. Lots of people get divorced and go through horribly tough times without doing what I did. However, when I was in active addiction and my addict's blamethrower was in full swing, I pointed my finger at everybody but myself. It's what addicts do. It kept me angry, and it kept me trying to put out that fire with drink and drug. I'm happy and at peace now (and sober) because I learned to unload my anger, resentment, and self-pity and take responsibility for my own life.

I know a woman – Cheryl – whose addiction began when she was smoking crack at home with her mother when she was nine. By age twelve she was living on the street and turning tricks to buy drugs. She would pick up a "John," then take the money to buy crack. When the drugs ran out, she'd find another "John" and repeat the process. That was her whole life. Of course, her mother holds the blame for Cheryl's miserable life in addiction, but it does Cheryl no good (she's now in her thirties) to walk around with anger and resentment burning in her brain. She's succeeded in recovery largely because she's learned to unburden herself of those self-defeating emotions and take responsibility for herself.

Unlike Cheryl, most of us blame people and things that really don't deserve the blame for our addiction. Anyone who feels like a hapless victim is angry and difficult to be around, and those closest to us usually bear the brunt of it. In recovery, we owe it to our loved ones to make amends for all the misery we brought them, including all the anger we heaped on them.

For some among us – me included – letting go of anger, resentfulness, self-pity, and blamefulness is easier said than done. This may especially be true for those who were truly victimized, such as victims of abuse. However, this angry mindset is a tremendous barrier to overcoming addiction and finding happiness and positive psychology. As long as we cling to these toxic emotions, we'll always be sick. We can't change other people or the past, but we can change how we react. It's about making a conscious decision to stop allowing other people and the past to live in our head rent-free, continuing to victimize us every day. The Twelve Step program is, in my opinion, the most potent form of CBT for unburdening people of happiness-killing negative emotions, particularly for those who really struggle with the past. Some individuals may benefit from the care of a trauma counselor.

In the end, we're responsible for our recovery, for cleaning up the mess we made, and we're accountable for our own behaviors. If we sit around waiting for those who've wronged us to come to us on their knees and apologize, we'll probably stay addicts for a very long time. Cheryl's mother has never apologized to her or even acknowledged her responsibility for what happened to Cheryl. Thankfully, Cheryl didn't wait for that, and she's been happy and successful in recovery for over a decade. Taking responsibility for ourselves is an important requisite for recovery; after all, nobody else will do recovery for us – least of all the people who've harmed us in the past.

Self-Esteem

Our self-esteem takes a beating during our addiction. We don't like what we've become, and neither does anyone else. The arrogant, false, know-it-all hubristic pride of the addicted mind doesn't fool anybody, and it doesn't fool us – our sense of self-worth is in our boots. I've heard many addicts new to recovery say that their self-esteem was so low that they didn't feel they deserved recovery and a good life.

The great thing is that everybody is capable of honest, stable, and unconditional self-esteem. Many people are under the mistaken belief that self-esteem depends upon our level of success, physical attractiveness, and social popularity. However, healthy self-esteem doesn't depend upon any of those things. It's a psychological construct that comes from within and survives the onslaught of the external world. Ego and narcissism, on the other hand, are frail and depend entirely upon outward displays of success and social tactics designed to garner the attention of others.

Self-esteem largely comes back to us when we begin living according to our principles again; in other words, when we correct the dissonant self. It also helps us regain our self-worth when we remember the disease model of addiction, which tells us that addiction is a matter of biology, not an issue of lack of morality, weakness of character, or willpower. Addicts are sick people who need to become well, not bad people who need to become good.

When we live according to our principles and make amends to those we've wronged, other people respect us, and we respect ourselves. True self-esteem naturally blossoms when we do the things we're discussing in this chapter, regardless of our income, or education, or the kind of car we drive.

Resilience to Stress

Resilience to stress is among the most critical life skills for success in recovery. I liken the mind's ability to handle stress to a glass of water, where the glass represents the mind's capacity for stress, and the water represents stress. If our glass is nearly empty, we can add lots of water before it overflows and makes a mess. However, if the glass is filled nearly to the top, even adding a little water will overflow. So it is with our mind and stress. If our mind is filled with lots of unresolved stress, adding even a little more will create a mess: we'll blow up with anger and rage at what might otherwise be a minor stressor. All that compressed, unresolved stress with no outlet seeps out of every pore until we explode when that little bit more puts us over the top – overfilling the glass.

However, we don't have to have a stress-free life to keep our glass low or empty. In fact, many people who face tons of stress have their stress glass nearly empty all the time, while others with low-stress lives have theirs constantly full and ready to overflow. The trick is to reduce the amount of water in our glass by draining the water periodically, before the glass gets too full. The way we keep our stress-glass low is through healthy stress-coping skills.

The negative disposition of the addicted mind keeps the stress glass full all the time. The anger and resentment, guilt, shame, self-loathing, and low self-esteem – for example – keep addicts on edge and thin-skinned to anything that doesn't go their way. The addicted mind's need for control will perceive anything that gets between the addict and their freedom to drink or use as an extreme stressor. The low self-esteem will perceive even a trivial slight as an ego threat. As such, the addict's stress glass is always full, and the slightest disruption will cause an exaggerated stress response. Unfortunately, addicts are prone to volatile emotional responses to stress, and resort to escape/avoidance behavior to cope.

When we return to life in recovery, we deserve to be happy, and learning to keep our stress glass low or empty is a requisite for happiness and peace of mind. After all, we all live better, happier lives when we have resilience – the ability to maintain our serenity and "roll with the punches" regardless of what's going on around us. When our mind is full of unresolved stress, we have difficulty with other functions of the mind. We tend to be unhappy, and our mind is filled with conflict and worry rather than peace.

Remember, too, that there are other forms of escape/avoidance coping that we should watch for in recovery, lest we switch to another dysfunctional behavior. These include "process addictions" (such as compulsive gambling, compulsive shopping, video game addiction, and sex or porn addiction), involvement in co-dependent relationships, and even isolating and watching movies or reading for prolonged periods to escape reality. Some of these are legitimate ways to relax and de-stress, but we should have balance; when we cross the line from de-stressing to escaping reality the activities become excessive and interfere with our function.

Stress in general is terrible for our overall health. It's normal to feel stress in a moment of emergency, such as if we were to trip and almost fall down the stairs. In such situations, the body's stress response provides a burst of energy so that we can act fast and deal with the problem by grabbing onto something and preventing disaster. Our heart beats faster, our blood pressure spikes, we breath faster, and we have heightened awareness, all so we can react quickly and save ourselves from danger. However, as soon as the threat passes, the stress response stands down and everything in our body returns to normal.

When we're chronically stressed, however, the stress response continues to work, sometimes all day and all night. This even happens with chronic low-level stress. The hormones that create the stress response – such as epinephrine (also known as adrenaline) and cortisol (known as the stress hormone) – continue to be released and don't back down. So, our body and mind end up like a car engine idling dangerously fast with a stuck gas pedal.

The stress hormone cortisol is detrimental to our physical and mental health when it's released on a continuing basis. It causes blood sugar to elevate, and promotes the build-up of body fat. Together, these can lead to the development of obesity and diabetes. Cortisol also impairs the immune system, making individuals more likely to get sick and stay sick. Epinephrine, also continually released in chronic stress, produces elevated blood pressure and rapid heart rate, both of which can damage the heart and blood vessels and elevate the risk of heart attack and stroke. The stress-related hormones together also disrupt sleep and impair memory and concentration. These factors can make people less able to handle the stress they're facing; in other words, the continual release of stress hormones makes people less able to handle stress. You can see how a vicious cycle develops when we're over-stressed.

Studies have shown – and common sense tells us – that self-care activities improve our ability to tolerate stress, decrease the health-defeating effects, and improve our function. These "health promotion activities" aren't time-consuming, expensive, fancy interventions; we're talking about eating nutritionally balanced meals, getting restorative sleep, and engaging in even minimal physical activity. These provide a healthy basis for better stress tolerance, and there are other ways to build on this.

The medical and scientific communities have long recognized the positive effects of meditation, and there's been much empirical study on the impact of meditation on health and well-being. Research studies have shown meditative practice to be particularly effective for reducing stress hormone levels and improving a number of domains of health and wellness; it's a great way to keep our stress glass empty.

Something as simple as social contact is also a proven de-stressing strategy. Rather than holing up inside ourselves, it's much healthier to get outside ourselves by connecting with others in times of stress, and sharing our struggles. We don't have to share our secrets with everyone, but we all should have someone we can talk to about our struggles.

Humans are social beings, and cues for social interaction are built right into our genes. We need social contact to develop and thrive. Humans rely on interaction with others, and we cannot properly develop without it. Infants are born to learn, but their developing brain circuits rely entirely on input from social interactions. Our brain's higher functions won't develop properly or even at all without this interaction. Contact with people outside ourselves is a primal human need, not just a nicety.

Our ancient ancestors were only able to survive by banding together. They needed each other for protection, gathering food, hunting, and propagating the species. Those who formed close connections with others were more likely to survive, especially when faced with adversity or danger. Now, that need for connection continues, deeply embedded in our DNA and most basic instincts. Connection with others makes us feel empowered and less anxious. Connection, especially transcendent connection (i.e., to something larger than ourselves), is an antidote to stress and hardship. If you ever observe people who've just experienced a traumatic event, they're hugging each other and seeking connection; they sense that they need the connection to feel better and not feel anxious or out of control. It's part of our survival instinct to seek connection when we feel stress or danger. Being alone may feel like a safe place, but it's not a healthy or healing place.

The effect we get from connections with others can be strengthened by a connection with a power greater than ourselves. Those who have a faith or belong to a religious group may find availing themselves of these connections an excellent coping mechanism. The higher power attachment stays with us, and we can draw on that association anytime, anywhere, even if we're alone. An awareness of this connection helps us to stay focused as we face stressful situations. This helps stave off the alarms that go off in our mind when we face danger or adversity alone. Many people enjoy some kind of an awareness or a connection with a higher power who's not named

"God." Nature, the cosmos, fate, a group of people, or any meaningful thing that's greater than ourselves works. Some people don't even know what it is; they just know they're not the most powerful thing in the universe. Feeling a bond to something larger than ourselves overrides our immediate panicky, emotional, and selfish reactions. Connection with other people, the world around us, and – for some – some sort of a higher power – is what I refer to as "spirituality." Thus, a need for spiritual ties is a deep-rooted human need, and restoring and improving these connections is of great therapeutic value when we've lost these bonds.

The absence of social connection is a cruelty. Social isolation is used as a form of punishment, and even torture. Social isolation drives people crazy, literally. The effects of social connections on mental and physical health are well documented, and people who're socially connected are healthier and live longer than those who are not. In fact, it was proven in the 1980s and confirmed by numerous clinical studies since that social isolation is as bad a risk factor for physical illness and premature death as are the worst biological risk factors: smoking, obesity, sedentary lifestyle, and high blood pressure. Given that these are the things that kill the vast majority of people, social connectedness is a crucial aspect of good health and function, not just a simple nice-to-have. For people who need to escape the powerful grasp of intolerable stress, it's an absolute must-have.

However, if you're not a social butterfly who can juggle hundreds of close friends, fear not! Studies have shown that the health benefits of social connectedness depend on our *perceived* social connectedness. So, if we're fulfilled with a few good friends and have quality, supportive, and meaningful contact with them, our health is just as safe as it is for the social butterflies. The risk for mental, cognitive, and physical problems lies with those who feel isolated and lack quality interpersonal attachments.

*   *   *

Just about every addict can trigger on poorly-handled stress. However, success in recovery isn't about trying to get a stress-free life;

rather, it's about learning how to handle stress in a healthy way when it does arise, as it inevitably will. One of the reasons that some people get so stressed when complications arise is that they have unrealistic expectations of life. The human mind is often preoccupied with fears of things going wrong, problems arising, and things not turning out well. But those fears are based on unreasonable expectations that everything must go just right for us and that we must get what we want for life to be good. But life will never go just right and be problem-free for anybody, no matter who they are. We must accept that not everything will go our way. Yes, it's disappointing when things don't go well, but we can either drive ourselves crazy worrying and fretting over it, or we can decide to be happy within ourselves rather than allow our happiness to be determined by what's going on in our life at that particular moment.

There are things in life that will go wrong that we have no control over. What we do have control over is how we respond to them. We can derive meaning from adverse experiences by how we handle adversity. If we fall apart and give in to the poor me's, we're allowing external events to control us. If we maintain our composure and dignity, and respond in an admirable way – accepting things that are beyond our control rather than grumbling about them, and helping others rather than feeling sorry for ourselves and taking from others to make ourselves feel better – then we're choosing to not allow external events corrupt our principles. Rather than expecting that everything will always go just fine, we can choose to adopt a different mindset, an attitude about life and its inevitable ups and downs. Life isn't about never *facing* hardship; rather, it's about how we *endure* hardship. When times are tough, it helps to remember a couple of simple mantras: *this, too, shall pass*, and: *the sun sets on every day*.

Acceptance of life's disappointments isn't something that comes naturally to humans. Strangely, we like to feel and act like victims, we like other people's pity, we like to complain and get angry, and we loathe accepting things that aren't how we want them to be. Acceptance is definitely an acquired trait, and one that takes some practice and presence of mind.

For addicts, this perspective and approach to life's stressors is a matter of life and death. Addicts are people who – in the past – reacted to stress by reaching for the bottle or needle, so they need a better way to handle life on life's terms.

Personally, I refuse to allow other people or things get under my skin and take my happiness and peace of mind from me. I worked too hard to overcome my addiction and heal my mind, so I refuse to allow people and things to undermine that. If other people had a similar attitude, we'd have a lot fewer angry and unhappy people in the world. Making up your mind to protect your happiness and peace of mind from stress is up to you.

*   *   *

Another technique for keeping our stress glass low is by protecting ourselves from being overwhelmed by life and its challenges. When we feel overwhelmed, we may succumb to stress and just shut down, or sacrifice self-care to try to handle everything. But let me ask you a question: how do you eat an elephant? The answer: one bite at a time! When stress mounts because we have too much on our plate, it's helpful to break down overwhelming problems and tasks. In other words, to take life, tasks, and problems one bite at a time. Psychologists refer to this as *chunking*.

Chunking involves breaking down otherwise overwhelming problems and tasks into bite-sized chunks, rather than looking at the problem as a whole. This helps us avoid feeling overwhelmed by information overload, or by the size of the task or problem. For example, if a person needs to buy a car that costs $20,000, paying that amount up front may be overwhelming and impossible. However, a financing option would allow the person to buy the car and make manageable monthly payments so that the cost is no longer overwhelming. Over time, the small loan payments add up, and the car gets paid off. Similarly, we can break down our problems and tasks into manageable chunks and focus on taking care of one chunk at a time. When we focus on the bite-sized chunk we have before us, we can let go of worry about the rest of the task, safe in the knowledge that we'll take care of each chunk as it comes, one at a time.

Chunking is supported by considerable research and is even used by the U.S. Navy SEALs as a tool for facing the most daunting tasks. The Navy SEALs – famous for their mental toughness and ability to endure any hardship – employ chunking as a mental technique to help them get through physically or mentally demanding situations. For example, during their BUD/S training (considered to be the most grueling military training in the world), Navy SEALs trainees don't focus on completing the six months of hell that they must endure, or they'd feel overwhelmed and fearful and may doubt their ability to get through it. Instead, they focus on getting through the particular task they're confronted with right now. If they're facing their notoriously punishing obstacle course, they focus on getting through it and giving their best effort. They forget everything else; they concentrate all their resources on that particular task. If even that seems overwhelming, they further break it into chunks, such as each individual obstacle, one obstacle at a time.

The Twelve Step program employs chunking with its focus on staying sober "one day at a time." Rather than becoming overwhelmed by having to keep clean and sober for months or years, addicts are encouraged to break down sobriety into bite-sized chunks – one day at a time. If the day is tough, then break it down into one hour at a time. The program also uses the same concept to help addicts in recovery cope with life when they feel overwhelmed. Rather than focusing on dealing with all their problems, they break them down to what they can do to help their problems today, and let go of worrying about the rest. Like the U.S. Navy SEALs, recovering addicts can use chunking to overcome sobriety's difficulties and life's challenges.

*   *   *

I want to share a passage from the story of one alcoholic who recognized that we cannot allow outside events or people determine our success in recovery: *...I realized that I had to separate my sobriety from everything else that was going on in my life. No matter what* *happened or didn't happen, I couldn't drink…. The tides of life flow endlessly for better or worse, both good and bad, and I cannot allow my sobriety to become dependent on these ups and downs of living. Sobriety must live a life of its own (Alcoholics Anonymous*, pages 450-1).

Positive Self-Efficacy

An external locus of control and learned helplessness are especially toxic because they destroy self-efficacy. Self-efficacy has come up a few times in past chapters – it's the term psychologists use to describe our belief in our ability to accomplish a particular goal. Addicts have extremely low self-efficacy beliefs about their ability to get sober and straighten out their life, largely because they've already tried and failed many times. This lack of self-efficacy is a serious barrier to recovery, and must be corrected if anyone is to make the commitment and put forward the effort required to beat their addiction. After all, what's the point of trying if you don't believe you're capable, *right?*

The most effective way of establishing self-efficacy for recovery and life in general is through vicarious experience. As we discussed earlier, vicarious experience is where we hear or read the stories of people we can identify with – in this case, addicts who've succeeded in recovery. Vicarious experiences model and motivate recovery, but best of all they increase self-efficacy beliefs. I've spoken with a number of addicts in recovery who told me that vicarious experience was the turning point in their recovery.

Self-efficacy beliefs also increase when we experience small successes, and a pattern of success helps us realize that we have some control over how our life goes, after all. One of the advantages of chunking is that as we accomplish each small piece that leads to our goal, we gain positive self-efficacy beliefs as we go, increasing with each chunk. Psychologists refer to these small accomplishments as *mastery experiences*. As we build positive self-efficacy beliefs, we can take on bigger and bigger challenges, and our mastery experiences become more and more significant. The external locus of control, learned helplessness, and lack of self-efficacy melt away.

The transformative power of mastery experiences is one of the reasons that I encourage addicts in early recovery to take it easy. I find that addicts new to recovery tend to want it all right away – they want to be ten years sober, have a great job, a romantic relationship, a new apartment, and all their problems sorted out... right away. But by building mastery experiences by first focusing on their recovery one day at a time and then slowly taking on small mastery experiences by biting off one chunk at a time, they can avoid overwhelming themselves and setting themselves up for failure. This allows for increasingly bigger mastery experiences, versus certain failure if they try to change their whole world in a week.

Another excellent path to improved self-efficacy is through positive self-talk. The harsh inner critic of the addicted mind will convince us that we're going to fail, and it may become a self-fulfilling prophecy if we don't shut it down. Replacing the inner critic with positive, affirming self-talk is a potent way to improved self-efficacy.

Honesty

The psychological turn-around we seek in recovery begins with opening up – getting stuff off our chest. I know from my research interviews (and my personal experience) that once we take the leap of faith and finally let go of the secrecy and tell our story, it's almost magically therapeutic. BUT... to fully benefit, we must be entirely honest; telling our story begins the healing, but it must be the whole story. It's much easier to open up and get our secrets off our shoulders when we do this with people who understand, won't be judgmental, and can identify with us. That's why beginning with fellow addicts at a treatment center or recovery support group is the perfect place. They understand the things we've done because they've been there too.

Opening up requires admitting we have a problem. Denial is a core symptom of addiction, but finally letting go of the rationalization and denial and blamefulness is a necessary part of recovery. After all, if we don't truly believe we have a problem, why should we put all the effort into recovery? The problem I'm talking about is this: we are people who cannot control our substance use. Similarly, if we don't continue to acknowledge our problem during recovery, we're at considerable risk for relapse. It's been years since I've had a drink or drug, and the cravings, urges, and thoughts of using are long gone, but I don't forget that I have a problem: I'm an addict, and I cannot control my substance use. As soon as I stop acknowledging my problem, my addict's brain will slowly work its way back into my thoughts, and I'll try drinking or using again. I know this because I've interviewed a lot of people who've had exactly that happen to them.

Once we have an open mind and we're willing to let go of our secrets, we can start addressing the guilt, self-loathing, and other negative feelings, and the overwhelming cognitive dissonance that plays such a big part in driving substance use. But our mind will not release us from guilt unless we've come clean about the stuff we feel guilty about. The Twelve Step program describes itself as a "program of rigorous honesty" because they know that no one heals without letting go of their secrets. Secrets keep us sick.

As a caveat, we should be careful about who we come clean with. We should avoid coming clean with someone we would hurt with the truth, and we should avoid situations where we may get ourselves into trouble with the truth. Generally, a neutral person with a commitment to confidentiality, such as a recovery sponsor, a fellow addict in recovery, a counselor, or a member of the clergy may be a good place to start.

Focus on the Here and Now

The human mind – and the addicted mind in particular – has a penchant for scaring itself by projecting problems into the future. This generates fear because we tend to blow things out of proportion, thinking up the worst possible outcome. Some people go through life ruminating about things that'll never happen, which manufactures fear and anxiety. They worry, dread, and fear what hasn't happened and probably never will, putting themselves through torture for naught. Often they'll lay awake at night and allow themselves to be consumed by anxieties of the future. In the dark of night, the mind can dream up terrible things, anticipating the cruelest of evils. They suffer intense fear from their imagination, rather than anything real. Psychologists refer to these fears about things that aren't present or don't exist as *anticipatory anxiety*. In short, people are afraid because they imagine what might happen.

Anyone who finds themself worrying about problems and how they may play out may wish to try the "one day at a time" attitude. The idea is that every morning we get up and resolve to do what we can on that day to help our problems, and we let tomorrow take care of itself. We can plan for the future, but it's counter-productive to plan the outcome, wasting brain-power on the "what-ifs" of tomorrow. Projecting our problems and worries into the future is counter-productive, wasted brain-power, and self-manufactured artificial stress. Don't sell your hard-earned serenity and peace of mind for cheap!

Similarly, the addicted mind obsesses terribly about the past, ruminating on regrets, and "what-ifs," and *why did this happen to me?* When we ruminate about the past, our inner critical voice becomes active and tears us apart. Our self-esteem doesn't stand a chance. To let go of the past, we can look at our perceived shortcomings or mistakes with an objective scientific viewpoint. What can I learn from the experience? Analyze it once, take a lesson from it, use it to improve ourselves, and then move on and let it go. We can make a statement of action, such as: *in the future, I commit to* _____ ... and then drop the matter. Any further discussion with our inner critic will only do us harm.

People in recovery can use their metacognition skills to interrupt and change the channel when their mind tries to obsess about the past or the future. The problems we can do nothing about, we should accept. Likewise, we should practice acceptance of what has happened in the past because we cannot change it.

Coping with Toxic Emotions

Just as it's important to learn to handle stress in a healthy way, keeping the mind healthy in recovery requires strategies for coping with toxic emotions. These emotions have already come up in our discussions – anger, resentment, guilt, self-pity, depressed mood, jealousy, and so on. These emotions are a powerful driver of substance use during active addiction, and can also be a powerful driver of relapse.

It may sound odd, but the mind in recovery needs to be able to handle the highs of positive emotions, too – celebrating high emotions are a relapse trigger for some people.

Coping with negative (and positive) emotions isn't much different from the healthy coping strategies we've discussed in this chapter. Perhaps the most important part is learning not to bottle up our emotions, and to seek out social support and a supportive listener when we're hurting or feel that we may be in trouble.

*   *   *

I suggest some healthy attitudes and practices that contribute to a mindset consistent with recovery and good function:

- Establishing daily recovery habits, such as reading about recovery, maintaining contact with others in recovery, and participating in a recovery support group,
- Accepting that life may not always go well or as planned; ups and downs and surprises are simply a normal part of life,
- Learning to stop ruminating and obsessing over the past or blowing problems out of proportion by projecting them into the future,
- Correcting low self-esteem by bringing together the ideal and actual self,
- Self-forgiveness, thereby ending the guilt, regret, remorse, and self-criticism that create constant low-grade stress,
- Establishing self-efficacy for recovery and life in general through vicarious experiences,

- Establishing a stress support system through recovery meetings, connecting with others in recovery, a recovery sponsor, and maintaining a social support system of family and friends,
- Self-care, including a healthy diet, physical activity, proper sleep, and proper medical and psychiatric care,
- Developing a self-identity as a person in recovery,
- Altruism,
- Anger management, and
- Becoming a helpful and productive member of the family unit and society.

Addiction treatment programs do their best to help addicts learn and live a new, healthy mindset. However, their time is short, and they seldom accomplish even close to what most of us need. As such, I encourage anyone new to recovery to seek the healing and recovery supports they need after they're discharged from treatment.

A common pitfall I see is when addicts complete a treatment program and return home with no plan for their ongoing recovery. Many "parachute" back into their old life again and carry on as if nothing had happened, with no plan or resources in place to support their recovery. Some treatment facilities have "aftercare" programs that involve a weekly meeting for 6-12 months at the facility. However, the dropout rate is high. Usually, there's too much travel involved to get to the weekly meetings. As the weeks pass, individuals see fewer and fewer of their friends from the same treatment cohort, so the social aspect of the meetings falls away and they lose interest. Besides, 6-12 months of aftercare isn't nearly enough; recovery activities must be in place for a lifetime. Addicts who come home from treatment with no plan for ongoing recovery activities are treating their addiction as if it was cured. Sadly, my experience has been that they often find out the hard way that it wasn't.

I highly recommend joining a Twelve Step group for ongoing healing, recovery support, and relapse prevention. The program has all the tools needed and provides an excellent basis for all the recovery-oriented mindsets we discussed in this chapter. For those with serious lingering issues, especially mental health struggles, after-effects of past traumatic events, or prolonged severe addiction, additional supports – such as outside counseling, medical support, or a stay in a sober living house – may be well-advised. If you're struggling, don't be a hero – let others in. Don't try to do it on your own.

7

What Happens in Relapse

Understanding how relapse happens allows us to recognize the process in ourselves and engage our relapse prevention "tools" when we mindfully see ourselves headed that way. My recovery sponsor is an older guy with many years of sobriety and a lot of experience in helping newcomers. He amazes me by how he can almost smell relapse in people. Many times, he's whispered in my ear at a meeting: *see that guy over there? He's going to relapse in the next couple of weeks.* Honestly, I've never known him to be wrong. Some people can really sense when someone's on the path to relapse. And that brings up the most important thing to know about relapse: it's almost always a process, not a spontaneous event.

One study found that relapse usually develops over a period of at least three weeks, sometimes longer. So, using our metacognition skills to recognize and arrest the process before it plays out is a cornerstone of relapse prevention. In this chapter, we'll discuss exactly how to do that, and how these actions can be planned out and practiced in advance as part of a relapse prevention strategy.

*   *   *

The research literature breaks down the relapse process into three distinct stages:

Stage 1 – Emotional relapse – at this stage, the person isn't thinking about returning to substance use, and they don't want to relapse. However, their emotions and behaviors are funneling them toward relapse. During treatment, addicts are taught to self-monitor for the red flags of emotional relapse – these are represented by the acronym HALT (hungry, angry, lonely, tired) – so they can recognize trouble brewing and engage their recovery tools. The emotional relapse stage should be suspected when the recovering addict begins:

- Engaging in denial,
- Bottling up emotions,
- Not attending recovery meetings, and not sharing at meetings,
- Self-isolating,
- Neglecting self-care,
- Feeling restless, irritable, and discontent, and
- Experiencing thoughts of substance use to escape stress and bottled-up negative feelings.

Stage 2 – Mental relapse – in this stage, motivation for recovery and efforts at recovery activities erode, and the individual becomes increasingly attracted to the idea of returning to substance use. This stage of relapse is characterized by:

- Bargaining (thinking up scenarios where substance use would be OK, rationalizing going to high-risk environments (such as parties with old drinking/using buddies), justifying relapse by committing to only "occasional" substance use, or by switching to a different addictive substance),

- Cravings and pervasive thoughts about substance use,
- Glamorizing or engaging in fond memories of past substance use,
- Rationalizing connecting with people, places, and things associated with past substance use,
- Downplaying the consequences of using,
- Lying (this is a major red flag),
- Convincing oneself of the viability of ways to control substance use, contrary to past experiences,
- Seeking out opportunities where relapse would be possible, and
- Full-out planning a relapse.

Occasional thoughts of drinking or using in recovery are common and aren't in themselves an indication of mental relapse. You'll notice that the word "rationalizing" appears several times in the description of mental relapse, as well as the word "bargaining." These are the "cognitive bias" of the addicted mind – where the mind will bend the truth, warp facts, and ignore contradictory information to support what it wants to believe – beginning to reassert itself. This begins happening in mental relapse, as individuals ignore facts about the peril of relapse and convince themselves that: **this** time it'll be different, **this** time I'll be careful, **this** time I'll control it. Rationalizing substance use and downplaying the consequences indicates that an individual is well on the road to relapse.

Stage 3 – Physical relapse – this is where the individual begins using substances again, in lapses and/or relapses. Addicts usually engage in physical relapse after they've had time to convince themselves that it's OK to drink or use again during mental relapse, and they've had some time to get used to the idea. They'll often plan ahead for the exact moment they'll relapse, usually during a window of opportunity during which they believe they won't get caught. I've seen lots of people carry on the charade that they're still in recovery long after they've physically relapsed. Often, they'll even continue going to recovery support group meetings, but they seldom fool anybody for long.

134

The earlier on in the relapse cascade that individuals recognize and take action to interrupt the process, the higher the likelihood of averting disaster. We'll discuss relapse action plans shortly, but often all it takes is a simple phone call to a sponsor or another addict in recovery and a little bit of honesty to derail the entire relapse cascade. Sadly, many people returning from relapse report that they recognized very clearly that they were in the process of relapsing, but did nothing to interrupt it, even though they knew better.

*   *   *

There are certain indicators that allow us to recognize that we may be vulnerable to relapse, or perhaps on the road to relapse. These are all symptoms of the addicted brain and mind re-asserting themselves, and should therefore flag us to engage our relapse prevention tools:

- Feeling hungry, angry, lonely, and/or tired (HALT): we've already discussed the HALT acronym as an indicator of emotional relapse, stage 1 of the relapse process. These are all self-care issues, so HALT should cue individuals to HALT what they're doing and take a moment to care for themselves. The HALT acronym represents being Hungry (not eating properly), Angry (irritable, edgy, mood swings, defensiveness), Lonely (self-isolating, being secretive, making excuses not to socialize, not asking for help), or Tired (not getting enough rest, overworking),
- Handling stress poorly, elevated stress reactions,
- Experiencing mental illness symptoms,
- Not participating in a recovery program, bad-mouthing recovery activities, showing contempt for recovery, denying a need for recovery activities, or feeling over-confident in recovery. These indicate a change in attitude and motivation,
- Reactivation of denial,
- Reactivation of avoidance,
- Irresponsible behavior (such as skipping school or work),
- Changes in routine,
- Lying, deceiving, becoming defensive,

- Re-engaging with or even thinking about dubious people, places, and things related to past substance use, and
- Glamorizing, thinking positively about, or talking about substance use.

I encourage addicts in recovery to involve their family and friends in their recovery. People who know us well can sense when something isn't right with us. They just know something's "off," and they have concerns. If you've made your loved ones part of your "red flag team," they can watch out for your well-being and know how to back you up when you're in trouble. When addicts are in trouble, they may become defensive and secretive, and loved ones can help snap them out of it. In my book *Understanding and Helping an Addict*, I explain to family members how they can support your recovery without becoming overbearing or taking on the role of "recovery police." I strongly encourage people in recovery to give permission to their loved ones to contact their sponsor or counselor early in recovery and when needed, and to keep that contact line open. Now is the time to use that privilege. My family called my sponsor once in a while so they all knew each other (with my permission, not behind my back), so the lines of communication were easy. They often called him with questions, not necessarily because they had concerns. Recovery sponsors are used to that.

Many detox facilities have a relapse prevention program, where people in recovery who fear they may relapse can be admitted for a few days to remove themselves from their situation, get some time with a counselor, and re-invigorate their recovery. I've seen lots of recovering addicts check themselves in for relapse prevention during a moment of vulnerability or a crisis, always with good effect. Even just going to a recovery group meeting and opening up about our concerns is usually enough to derail relapse. In my experience, an addict in recovery who's in trouble avoids relapse if they simply tell someone about it – either a sponsor, counselor, trusted friend, someone else in recovery, or a family member. Even a phone call will do it. If the individual cares enough to come forward and be honest about their thoughts of relapse, they care enough to respond to help. That's all it takes.

Some addicts reach a point where they've made up their mind that they're going to relapse, and there's nothing that'll stop them. They'll be defensive and aggressive, and remove themselves from help. They'll run away when confronted, not answer the phone when their sponsor tries to contact them, and disappear so that anyone who tries to help can't find them. When this happens, the old laser-focused addicted mind has taken over, and nothing will stop them. Remember, it takes some addicts several tries (or more) before they make it. Some relapses are brief, others are not. Sometimes it takes a relapse to shake us up to a deeper commitment to recovery. After all, even a brief relapse causes untold misery. I've interviewed hundreds of addicts who've just come back from a relapse, and they're a miserable lot, even if their relapse only lasted a few days. Never once have I heard one of them say: *that was awesome!*

*   *   *

Having a relapse prevention action plan is quite simple, and it should be put together right away in early recovery. The number one action is to reach out and not keep it inside, and this is often all it takes. I've observed two factors that seem to propel recovering addicts to keep their concerns about relapse to themselves, even though they know better: feelings of guilt, and a latent desire to relapse. In such cases, they usually put on an outward appearance that all is well, resorting to the addicted mind's penchant for being the actor. When someone recognizes this through their metacognition, they should immediately apply their relapse prevention plan.

Besides the two mainstays of relapse prevention – picking up the phone and/or going to a meeting – addiction counselors teach "The Big Three" tools for derailing a relapse. These tools – all three are borrowed from the Twelve Step program – are designed to interrupt the dysfunctional thinking that drives the progression to relapse. They're simple, but they work:

Remember when – when the addicted mind starts trying to convince the addict that drinking or using was fun and a great escape from reality, addicts are encouraged to pause and think back to all the misery, sickness, pain, loss, and regret that their substance use caused them, how badly they wanted to stop, and how difficult it was to stop. Remembering specific situations that were especially painful is helpful; most addicts have a few specific memories they use for their "remember when,"

Follow the tape through to the end – when the addicted mind becomes obsessed with relapse, it focuses on "the party." "Playing the tape through to the end" is a mental cue to follow through in our mind and think about what happens *after* the party, the next day – the inevitable guilt, shame, disappointment, sickness, and renewed obsession with substance use that will inevitably follow "the party," and

Actively avoid high-risk situations – it's true of any temptation that it's much easier to say no at the beginning than at the end. Addicts are taught to cut off high-risk situations as soon as they recognize them developing, rather than waiting and allowing the situation to progress. I've seen many relapses occur after addicts allowed themselves to get into a situation that they knew damn well was high-risk, and they knew perfectly well that they shouldn't be there... but they did it anyway. Recognizing and actively avoiding these situations is a must-do.

I advise a simple action plan, very simple. When addicts feel they may be on the path to relapse, they should do all of the following, in order:

- Get to a safe place away from the relapse situation or trigger,
- Call their sponsor, or another addict in recovery, or their addiction counselor, or a family member or friend, and be honest,
- Practice "The Big Three," and

138

- Go to a meeting and be honest.

*   *   *

What makes people relapse after all the work they've done to get sober? Surveys of people who've relapsed showed the following common reasons: stress, negative mood, anxiety, drug-related cues, temptations, boredom, and lack of positive supports (e.g., job, family relationships, and recovery supports).

Metacognition is an effective measure for relapse prevention, so being aware of high-risk situations is an effective technique taught by addiction counselors. The U.S. National Institute on Drug Abuse (NIDA) lists the ten most common dangers that lead to relapse:

- Being around familiar drugs, drug users, or drug-related settings (i.e., people, places, and things),
- Experiencing negative feelings,
- Celebrating positive feelings,
- Experiencing boredom,
- Getting high on *any* mood-altering substance,
- Experiencing physical pain,
- Focusing on getting high,
- Having a lot of money all of a sudden,
- Taking prescription medications that cause a high, and
- Believing that occasional substance use is possible.

These are generalities, and some may be more dangerous than others for different people. As well, other factors can trigger relapse, such as feeling lonely, experiencing stress, and untreated mental health symptoms. Each person in recovery should reflect on what their own triggers are. This allows us to take measures as part of our relapse prevention plan to avoid our specific triggers. For example, my big triggers are stress and boredom. This meant that I needed to ensure that these factors were minimized in my life in recovery. Fortunately, the Twelve Step process – which I completed in early recovery – gave me the ability to handle stress in a much better and healthier way than

I ever could before. I also took a graduated approach to returning to work and life in general, rather than rushing back into a full-stress routine. *Easy does it* guided my early sobriety, and I still repeat that to myself if I try to take on too much. As well, since boredom is a relapse trigger for me, I make sure that I always have a list of things on hand that I can do in moments when I'm alone with nothing going on. I've started a couple of hobbies, I always have a reading list I'm working through, I take courses, and I have workout goals. If I don't feel like doing a particular activity, others are always on hand. Other factors aren't triggers for me, so I haven't had to worry about addressing them. For example, celebrating a success or having positive feelings aren't really triggers for me, nor is having money in my bank account (which happens occasionally). However, for some people those are triggers, and if so they're well advised to take care in advance to ensure that they have measures in place to counter the effects should they arise. It's yet another tool for countering the addicted mind.

*   *   *

Not all relapses occur on the same scale. Some individuals can re-establish their recovery early after a relapse, while others may continue for months or years. To this end, the medical literature makes distinctions about a return to substance use based on how it plays out:

- **Lapse** – the return to substance use is brief and not at the previous levels; this is usually in the context of drinking or using again and instantly regretting the decision and returning to recovery, and
- **Relapse** – re-activation of the addiction; a return to previous levels of use and behaviors.

I've heard addicts refer to a "lapse" as a "slip." I generally don't use the terms "lapse" or "slip" for a couple of reasons. First, I don't like minimizing the impact of a return to substance use on any scale. The risk of overdose death is very high during relapse, and even a "lapse" can prove fatal. This is primarily because addicts in recovery commonly return to the same high doses as before, but their tolerance is now much lower, so their previous dosing levels may now be fatal. As well, even a single use of drugs is dangerous because nowadays addicts have no way of knowing exactly what's in their drugs; the fiendish presence of the ultra-high potency opioids that now adulterate drugs has become the norm.

The other reason I don't use the terms "lapse" or "slip" is because regardless of how long the return to substance use lasted, there was still a mental process to get there, and obviously something's going wrong with the person's recovery. As such, I don't like making it appear that it was but a momentary lapse in judgment. Something went wrong that brought the individual to a place where there are drugs or alcohol, and induced them to put the toxic life-wrecking substance in their body. To write it off as a "slip" is to squander an opportunity to correct something that's not right. Instead, I use the term "brief relapse" if the relapse was… well… brief.

I've definitely seen cases where a relapse was brief. This usually happens with alcohol; I haven't seen it happen quite so much with opioids and stimulants. I recently interviewed a guy who was three years into recovery from drugs and alcohol, but experienced a brief relapse. He'd gotten into a bitter argument and immediately marched down to the bar. He ordered a beer and took a few sips, immediately regretted it, and then walked away. I know he was being truthful because I see him regularly and I know that he hadn't been out on a full-out relapse. Brief relapses (or "lapses") do occur.

One thing that stands out about relapse is how incredibly rapidly people with even years of recovery return to their previous levels of substance use, the same behaviors, and the same mental state. It's often a matter of a day or two before they're right back where they were before. I've heard many say the same thing: *I picked up right where I left off.*

Another guy I interviewed – Tyler – wrecked his six years of recovery with a three-day drinking binge after agreeing to go out for "a beer" with a friend. That "a beer" triggered an immediate full-out relapse that, fortunately, only lasted three days before he checked himself into a detox facility. The evening that Tyler went out for "a beer," he went home drunk, and his wife did the: *I'm not going through this again!* thing and kicked him out. He had very little money with him, and his wife (wisely) called the bank to shut down his bank card and credit card, so he quickly ran out of cash and ended up drinking mouthwash and sleeping on a park bench. When I saw him in detox he looked trashed, and he was ashamed and disappointed in himself (his breath smelled great, though). He definitely wasn't saying: *that relapse was awesome!*

Tyler's case illustrates how quickly a "slip" or "lapse" can progress to a full-blast relapse, but it also illustrates a couple of other points that are important to understanding relapse. This guy had been sober for more than six years when he relapsed. When I asked him why he thought he'd relapsed, he immediately answered that it was because he'd stopped all his recovery activities. About eight or ten months earlier, he'd stopped going to meetings, ceased contact with his sponsor, and given up on his other recovery practices. *Why?* I asked him. *Life got busy*, he said. *Besides, I was six years sober, so I thought I was good*. Without his recovery activities, life began getting to him, and he lost touch with the recovery frame of mind. In the absence of doing the things he needed to do to stay sober, his addicted mind began re-asserting itself. In hindsight, he said he was getting quicker to anger, wasn't as good at handling stress, and began thinking about drinking again. He believed "going out for a beer" would be harmless because he'd limit himself to one or two and then go straight home. Famous last words. Unfortunately, his story is far from uncommon. So, as we can see from Tyler's story, the relapse process often begins with the decision to let go of recovery activities, especially ongoing participation in a recovery support group.

The other important point that Tyler's story illustrates is how quickly the old addiction brain circuitry can be re-activated following exposure to even one episode of substance use.

*   *   *

It's often said (not by me) that relapse is a normal part of recovery, and I've heard addiction counselors say that. I believe the reason behind this odd statement is to encourage individuals to return after relapse by reassuring them that relapse is "normal." Fair enough. After all, the shame of relapsing keeps many from returning to their recovery support groups or being truthful about what happened. However, I've never liked the idea of teaching addicts that relapse is "normal."

This view of relapse may end up enabling alcohol and drug use by giving the addicted mind an opening. The tipping point in relapse is often the search for any reason to substantiate a bad decision, and the view of relapse as "normal" can be fodder for the addicted mind.

I believe it's more appropriate to look at it this way: *relapse may happen and often does, but doesn't have to happen.* It should be everyone's goal in recovery to never relapse. Personally, I've never said to anyone that relapse is a normal part of recovery.

However... if relapse does happen, it's important to remember that relapse isn't the end of recovery. Relapse doesn't mean that treatment isn't working, or the person isn't trying, or the person will never be able to succeed at recovery. Some people relapse many times before they finally get recovery, and some go to treatment more than a few times. What's important is to never give up. I've met lots of people with a long and healthy recovery who were in treatment three or four times (or more) before they finally "got it." Every person is worth another effort. **Relapse must never be allowed to be the final defeat.**

The biggest psychological barrier to returning to the recovery support group following relapse is shame. However, addicts should note that many people in their recovery support group (perhaps even their sponsor) have relapsed in the past, but they all came back to pick up their recovery. Even relapse can have a silver lining if we learn from the experience to strengthen our recovery.

When addicts relapse, it may be some time before they're ready to come back to recovery. In Tyler's case, he checked himself into detox – of his own accord – after three days of a full-blown relapse. In Liam's case (I told you about Liam back in chapter 5) it was after eight months. I've seen addicts come back after a "lapse" – a few sips of beer, or taking some pills, or doing a line of powder cocaine at a party. Some have to go through the same mental process to become ready to accept help as they did the first time around, but I've observed that they tend to do so much more quickly than before; probably because they already know that recovery is possible (i.e., they have self-efficacy) and they know how it works and what to do. For them, getting back into recovery may be a matter of picking up the recovery tools that lay, unused, at their feet.

*   *   *

A recurrent theme about relapse that emerges from Tyler's and Liam's stories is that the gradual progression to relapse often begins when people let go of their recovery activities, even if they have significant recovery time under their belt. Let's talk about that for a moment.

Certainly, not every individual needs to participate in ongoing, long-term recovery activities to maintain abstinence. However, it's very common to see people who've given up their recovery activities revert to old ways and begin the downward mental spiral to relapse. I see it a lot. Remember that our disease is always out in the parking lot doing push-ups, waiting for us to let our guard down. I suggest that to abandon recovery activities is to tempt fate with a potentially fatal disease.

We've talked about these "recovery activities," but let's quickly review them. The primary and most important is continuing involvement with a recovery support group, including regularly attending meetings. Other activities include reading recovery literature provided by your support group, learning about addiction and recovery, maintaining contact with other people in recovery, regular contact with a sponsor or recovery mentor, putting together a relapse prevention action plan, establishing healthy relationships and social supports, and practicing healthy coping skills.

The cost is too high when addicts wander away from doing what they need to do to stay sober. Based on Liam's and Tyler's experience – which is far from unique – I suggest committing to a lifetime of recovery activities. Of course, as addicts progress in their recovery they usually

144

require less and less time for these activities, but they should always keep in touch with them.

Many addiction counselors recommend that addicts attend ninety recovery meetings in their first ninety days after treatment. When the counselors told me that, I thought they were crazy: *no way can I do ninety meetings in ninety days!* I ended up doing 172 meetings in my first ninety days. Why? Because I absolutely loved the meetings. After being sick and miserable for so long, I could sense that the way out would be among these people, and I loved the healing. I was learning about myself, and I was learning how to be healthy and never go back to that miserable existence. My family began to trust me again, because they saw me going to meetings and doing my recovery work. After years of hearing my repeated empty promises, my actions meant something.

Before I saw them for myself, I thought Twelve Step groups were a bunch of drunks and junkies sitting in a circle whining to each other about how they can't get sober. However, the meetings are nothing like that. They consist of lots of people with significant sobriety – many with decades of abstinent recovery – who're there to help others as well as themselves. There's a rich air of positivity, and an altruistic attitude whereby they'll go well out of their way to help another addict in need. Their primary focus is on newcomers.

Of course, the Twelve Step program works best when individuals actually do the Steps. Indeed, the recovery success rate skyrockets in people who do the Steps. Although most addiction treatment programs are Twelve Step based, many only address the first three Steps, meaning that graduates of these programs must pick up on their Step-work after returning home. The meat of the healing occurs in Steps four through nine, and much of the relapse prevention skills are derived from Steps ten through twelve. Addicts who only do the first three Steps miss out on all that healing and growth. Of course, the Twelve Step groups aren't the only option out there for recovery support. I suggest the best choice is whatever group or program works for *you*.

Another valuable resource for relapse prevention in early recovery is sober living houses. Returning to an unsafe place to live –

i.e., an environment with easy access to drugs or alcohol, or with many cues and triggers around – makes maintaining sobriety much more difficult, and an unsafe environment is a major risk factor for relapse. Sober living homes offer a chance to re-integrate safely into society, and to live a structured lifestyle. It gives addicts time to get into a routine consistent with ongoing recovery and life success, and to arrange for safer accommodations after the sober living home. Most sober living homes offer inexpensive accommodations for up to a year, and provide programs for relapse prevention, such as support groups, on-site counselors, medication support, and relapse prevention training. My experience with sober living homes is that they're well-liked and provide an excellent start for a lifetime of recovery. I highly recommend sober living homes for early recovery.

*   *   *

So, what if relapse occurs? Well, it could very well happen. According to the U.S. National Institute on Drug Abuse (NIDA), the relapse rate for substance use disorders is 40-60%. However, I would like to qualify that statistic. That number encompasses *all* addicts, regardless of what their recovery looks like. My experience has been that the relapse rates are much lower in individuals who're intrinsically motivated for recovery (i.e., they attend treatment willingly, are enthusiastic about recovery, and are engaged in the treatment and recovery process) versus those who're there for extrinsic motivations (i.e., because of a court order, to please a family member, or to keep their job). As well, those who engage in ongoing recovery activities (attend meetings, complete the Twelve Steps, maintain regular contact with a sponsor, etc.) have a far better chance of success than those who carry on in recovery without those crucial supports. Other factors further lower the risk of relapse, such as getting proper medical care for co-occurring mental illness, and having a social support system. So, as scary as the 40-60% relapse rate sounds, it cannot be applied to every individual.

For some, the misery of a relapse may be the learning experience needed to take recovery more seriously. Some addicts relapse several

146

times or more before they finally get recovery right. I watched a friend of mine progressively destroy his life with cocaine and alcohol as he repeatedly failed to get sober. He would check into a detox center and get a few months of sobriety under his belt, but would then relapse. I watched as he cycled through this process at least a dozen times, but I always held out hope for him. During his short bouts of sobriety he would attend Twelve Step meetings and say all the right things, but then he would drop off and disappear. Finally, he "got it." Something clicked in his mind, and rather than simply attending meetings, he got himself a good sponsor, did the Twelve Steps (for the first time), and applied himself to all the program has to offer. I'm pleased to say that he recently celebrated three years of strong and stable recovery, his family is back together again, and he's a happy and productive guy again. In fact, he's helped many other people find their way to recovery. He's a perfect example that relapse – even multiple relapses – isn't necessarily the end of the story.

I suggest that addicts who relapse keep in mind a few things: 1) addiction is a disease with a high relapse rate, 2) relapse often provides addicts with the lesson they need to succeed next time around, and 3) relapse must never be allowed to be the final defeat.

*   *   *

So ends our study of the science of addiction and recovery. After reading this book and experiencing addiction yourself, you probably know more about addiction than does your doctor. So, what do we do with this information? If you have problems with alcohol or drugs or addictive behaviors, I hope you'll use the information to help you in your recovery, and to help others in theirs, if you choose to do so. If you're not in recovery, I hope this information might bring you closer to finding out for yourself that recovery is its own reward, and more than worth every effort. I hope this information will help you recognize other people in your life who may be troubled by substance use or other mental health struggles. If you have children in your life, I hope this information may empower you to provide them with more informed awareness about the dangers of drugs and other temptations that are far too prevalent among young people.

In the end, those of us in recovery are all in this together, and we need each other. I know I need you, because I do not do recovery alone. If you have any comments or suggestions or pearls of wisdom you'd care to pass on, or if you just want to share your story, I'd love to hear from you. Please feel free to email me at alcoholism.addiction@gmail.com.

Well-fed dogs always return to their master. Let's stay healthy and self-aware, and never let our guard down and return to dark paths we've tread in the past.

Appendix

The Stages of Addiction and Readiness for Recovery

In my work and research, I've noticed that people with addictions follow a strikingly similar path as they go from obstinate denial and refusal of help to complete readiness to give themselves honestly and wholeheartedly to the help they need. Of course, every individual is different, and some will seek help much sooner than others. Nevertheless, I've observed four different stages of mental readiness for recovery. These are:

Stage 1 – addiction begins taking its toll. This starts when individuals realize that their substance use has been escalating, and they're seeing the beginnings of adverse effects on their health, family, finances, job, and well-being. They start having arguments at home over their drinking or using and their behaviors while intoxicated or hung over (i.e., in withdrawal). They begin covering up for their substance-related misbehaviors or neglected responsibilities. They're increasingly calling in sick at work or missing school or other responsibilities. People who're not addicts will usually stop or significantly cut back their substance use by this point.

At this stage, they're not willing or wanting to stop their drinking or using, even if they could. They become annoyed and defensive when people talk about their substance use. They try to get "naggers" off their back by hiding their substance use and promising they'll stop, even though they have no serious intention of doing so. They become good at making excuses for their substance use (*I'm just going through a rough time*) and for their behaviors while intoxicated or hung over (*I was feeling sick, I think I'm coming down with the flu*). They start avoiding "naggers" and socially isolating, which is a major red flag for addiction.

They're already starting to choose their substance use over people and things, and are willing to endure frayed relationships, sagging job performance, loss of hobbies and activities, and material loss for their substance use. They're developing tolerance to their substance of choice, and are therefore using larger amounts and more often. They may begin experimenting with other substances as they "chase the high." They begin changing their friends and hangouts in favor of other people and places that support their substance use. They're often out on prolonged, unexplained outings.

They're getting physically sick from their substance use. Cognitive dissonance is getting noticeably uncomfortable. Their daily thoughts are becoming increasingly focused on substance use and worry over ensuring they have an adequate supply. They sense they're somehow becoming different, doing things they previously would've considered selfish and stupid. They may not understand what's happening to them.

Stage 2 – full-out addiction. This stage begins when addicts reach the point where they want to stop, but they stubbornly insist they can do it on their own. *I got this*, and *I can stop: I've done it before*, and *as of Monday I'll stop* becomes their mantra to concerned family and friends. They sincerely mean it and believe it when they say they'll stop. They believe their willpower will do it. Everything becomes "tomorrow." *Tomorrow* is when they'll deal with the bank problem, fix the broken garage door, have that talk with their boss, or take the kids to the movies. And they believe it every time they say it.

Even though addicts in this stage are going to great lengths to conceal their alcohol or drug use, they aren't fooling anyone. Family and friends are worried sick, and are repeatedly trying to get them to talk to a doctor, go to rehab, or go to A.A., but the addicts come up with every excuse not to. Their denial is in full swing, and they try to downplay the extent of their problem to their family and friends, their doctor, and anyone else who tries to help. They need to be in control. They want to stop but still don't believe they need help. If they accept help, it'll only be bits and pieces of their choosing, and they won't fully commit. They may even pretend to seek help just to get the "naggers" off their back.

Their false pride and substance-disordered thinking are in full swing. All the behaviors and thought processes we discussed are present. They're angry, resentful, self-pitying, selfish, and blameful.

At this point, they're probably trying – over and over and over again – to control or stop their drinking or using. But it always has to be their way: on their own with them in control. They're seeking what the Twelve Step program refers to as "the easier, softer way:" *I'll just use on weekends*, or: *I'll switch to beer or weed*, or: *I won't drink or use until after work*, are the plan, but it never works out. They may attempt the famous "geographical cure" by moving to a new city to escape their problems, but this never works; they may have many problems in a certain place, but the place isn't the problem.

Each new low (an impaired driving charge, ending up in jail, losing their job, etc.) makes them swear off the drugs or alcohol, and they mean it. Sometimes they do stop. It'll last a day or two, sometimes a week or more, but they always end up right back where they started because nothing has changed in their substance-soaked mind. Despite all their failures, they still cling to the belief that they can stop on their own. They're not ready to commit to what it takes to beat addiction.

They're seeing serious losses from their substance use: marriage, job, money, house, driver's license, access to their children, their health.

If they don't get out of this "not yet ready" stage they'll end up homeless, edging toward jails, institutions, and death. They're having serious health problems. They're sick all the time. But the substance use continues and accelerates.

Stage 3 – readiness to surrender. Those lucky enough will enter this stage of readiness before they've lost too much, including life itself. This is the stage where they're finally desperate enough to seek and accept help. This is what the Twelve Step program refers to as "hitting their bottom." This is when the essential ingredient for recovery comes into play: a complete willingness to give up their need for control and do what they need to do to beat their addiction. This means giving up on the need to do things their way; after all, their best thinking and doing things their way has gotten them into this mess. They're ready to "surrender" their need for control and secrecy.

At this point they may express a sense of relief that all the lying, deception, and running around are finally over. They may become much more honest about things and begin revealing the true extent of their substance use and what they were doing to obtain their drug. The details may be shocking, even to those who thought they knew what the addict was up to.

Stage 4 – terminal addiction. This stage only happens to those who never reach stage 3, or who did, but relapsed and gave up trying. They may have tried rehab and other programs numerous times but have always found themselves back drowning in their substance use. Some may have honestly tried in their recovery efforts, while others may not have fully committed. In most cases, these are people who didn't continue with recovery activities after attending treatment, which they may have done multiple times.

This stage begins when addicts finally give up and accept that they'll ride their addiction to the end. This is where we find serious physical and mental consequences of chronic substance use (such as Wernicke-Korsakoff syndrome, advanced liver cirrhosis, and/or alcoholic cardiomyopathy in alcohol users).

People in this stage usually live on the fringes of society, and look and act like outcasts. This stage of addiction will almost certainly be fatal. However, some still escape the grave and find sobriety if they finally become willing to commit to recovery, as in stage 3.

Works Cited and Consulted

Adler, N., Glymour, M., & Fielding, J. (2016). Addressing social determinants of health and health inequalities. *JAMA, 316(16),* 1641-1642. https://cdn.ymaws.com/hpaapta.site-ym.com/resource/resmgr/Resource/social_Determinants_Adler_20.pdf

Ajzen, I. (1985). From intentions to actions: A theory of planned behavior. In J. Kuhl & J. Beckmann (Eds.), *Action control: From cognition to behavior* (pp. 11-39). Springer-Verlag.

Ajzen, I. (1991). The theory of planned behavior. *Organizational Behavior and Human Decision Processes, 50,* 179-211.

Alavi, H.R. (2011). The role of self-esteem in tendency towards drugs, theft, and prostitution. *Addiction & Health, 3(3-4),* 119-124.

Albrecht, Karl. (2015). The paradoxical power of humility [Web log post]. *Psychology Today.* www.psychologytoday.com/blog/brainsnacks/201501/the-paradoxical-power-humility

Alcoholics Anonymous World Services. (1939/2001). *Alcoholics Anonymous: the story of how many thousands of men and women have recovered from alcoholism* (4th ed.). Author.

Alcoholics Anonymous World Services. (2014/1975). *Living sober.* Author.

Alcoholics Anonymous World Services. (1953/2014). *Twelve steps and twelve traditions* (80th ed.). Author.

Alden, L.E., & Trew, J.L. (2013). If it makes you happy: Engaging in kind acts increases positive affect in socially anxious individuals. *Emotion, 13(1),* 64–75. https://doi.org/10.1037/a0027761

Alderson-Day, B., & Fernyhough, C. (2015). Inner speech: Development, cognitive functions, phenomenology, and neurobiology. *Psychological Bulletin, 141(5),* 931–965. https://doi.org/10.1037/bul0000021

Alfonso, J., Caracuel, A., Delgado-Pastor, L., & Verdejo-García, A. (2011). Combined goal management training and mindfulness meditation improve executive functions and decision-making performance in abstinent polysubstance abusers. *Drug and Alcohol Dependence, 117(1),* 78–81. doi:10.1016/j.drugalcdep.2010.12.025

American Psychiatric Association (APA). (2013). *Diagnostic and statistical manual of mental disorders* (5th ed.). Author.

American Psychological Association. (2012). *What you need to know about willpower: The psychological science of self-control.* http://www.apa.org/helpcenter/willpower

Amodeo, J. (2015). Why pride is nothing to be proud of [Web log post]. *Psychology Today.* https://www.psychologytoday.com/ca/blog/intimacy-path-toward-spirituality/201506/why-pride-is-nothing-be-proud

Anderson, B. (2016). What is abnormal about addiction-related attentional biases? *Drug and Alcohol Dependence, 167,* 8-14. http://dx.doi.org/10.1016/j.drugalcdep.2016.08.002

Andersson, H.W., Wenass, M., & Nordfjærn, T. (2019). Relapse after inpatient substance use treatment: A prospective cohort study among users of illicit substances. *Addictive Behaviors, 90,* 222-228. https://doi.org/10.1016/j.addbeh.2018.11.008

Arigo, D., Suls, J., & Smyth, J.M. (2012). Social comparisons and chronic illness: Research synthesis and clinical implications. *Health Psychology Review, 8(2),* 154-214. DOI: 10.1080/17437199.2011.634572

Armitage, C.J., Harris, P.R, & Arden, M.A. (2011). Evidence that self-affirmation reduces alcohol consumption: Randomized exploratory trial with a new, brief means of self-affirming. *Health Psychology, 30(5),* 633-641. DOI: 10.1037/a0023738

Aronson, E., Wilson, T.D., Fehr, B., & Akert, R.M. (2013). *Social psychology* (5th Canadian ed.). Pearson.

Arts, N.J., Walvoort, S.J., & Kessels, R.P. (2017). Korsakoff's syndrome: A critical review. *Neuropsychiatric Disease and Treatment, 13,* 2875–2890. https://doi.org/10.2147/NDT.S130078

Ashim, K., & Tridip, C. (2017). Stress and its vulnerability to addiction. *Global Journal of Intellectual & Developmental Disabilities, 3(5).* DOI: 10.19080/GJIDD.2017.03.555623

Ashwini, U.R., & Indumathy, J. (2018). Altruism and general well-being among adults. *International Journal of Research in Social Sciences, 8(4),* 528-540.

Aspinwall, L.G. & Tedeschi, R.G. (2010). The value of positive psychology for health psychology: Progress and pitfalls in examining the relation of positive phenomena to health. *Annals of Behavioral Medicine, 39*, 4-12.

Aten, J. (2019). Humility and resilience [Web log post]. *Psychology Today.* https://www.psychologytoday.com/intl/blog/heal-and-carry/201901/resilience-and-humility

Atkinson, R.C., & Shiffrin, R.M. (1968). Human memory: A proposed system and its control processes. In K.W. Spence & J.T. Spence (Eds.). *The psychology of learning and motivation* (pp. 89–195). Academic Press.

Austin, Michael W. (2012). Humility [Web log post]. *Psychology Today.* www.psychologytoday.com/blog/ethics-everyone/201206/humility

Baler, R., & Volkow, N. (2006). Drug addiction: The neurobiology of disrupted self-control. *Trends in Molecular Medicine, 12(12),* 559–66. doi: 10.1016/j.molmed.2006.10.005

Balhara, Y.P., Kuppili, P.P., Gupta, R. (2017). Neurobiology of comorbid substance use disorders and psychiatric disorders. *Journal of Addictions Nursing. 28(1),* 11-26. doi: 10.1097/JAN.0000000000000155

Bandura, A. (1994). Self-efficacy. In V. S. Ramachaudran (Ed.), *Encyclopedia of human behavior* (Vol. 4) (pp. 71-81). Academic Press. (Reprinted in H. Friedman [Ed.]. (1998). *Encyclopedia of mental health*. Academic Press).

Bandura A. (1977a). Self-efficacy: Toward a unifying theory of behavioral change. *Psychological Review, 84(2),* 191–215. https://doi.org/10.1037/0033-295X.84.2.191

Bandura, A., & Locke, E.A. (2003). Negative self-efficacy and goal effects revisited. *Journal of Applied Psychology, 88(1),* 87–99. DOI: 10.1037/0021-9010.88.1.87

Banks, S., Eddy, K., Angstadt, M., Nathan, P., & Phan, K. (2007). Amygdala-frontal connectivity during emotion regulation. *Social Cognitive and Affective Neuroscience, 2(4),* 303–312. https://doi.org/10.1093/scan/nsm029

Baranowski, T. (1990). Reciprocal determinism at the stages of behavior change: An Integration of community, personal and behavioral perspectives. *International Quarterly of Community Health Education, 10(4),* 297–327. https://doi.org/10.2190/NKBY-UVD6-K542-1QVR

Bartone, P., Hystad, S., Eid, J., & Brevik, J. (2012). Psychological hardiness and coping style as risk/resilience factors for alcohol abuse. *Military Medicine, 177(5),* 517-524. https://watermark.silverchair.com/milmed-d-11-00200.pdf

Baskin-Sommers, A., & Sommers, I. (2006). The co-occurrence of substance use and high-risk behaviors. *The Journal of Adolescent Health, 38*(5), 609–611. https://doi.org/10.1016/j.jadohealth.2005.07.010

Batho, D. (2017). Addiction as powerlessness? Choice, compulsion, and 12-Step programmes green paper (November 2017). *University of Essex.* Doi: 10.13140/RG.2.2.20695.16809. p.12.

Baumeister, R.F. (1982). Self-esteem, self-presentation, and future interaction: A dilemma of reputation. *Journal of Personality, 50(1)*, 29-45.

Bayer, R., & Spitzer, R.L. (1982). Edited correspondence on the status of homosexuality in DSM-III. *Journal of the History of Behavioral Science, 18(1)*, 32–52.

Bechara, A. (2005). Decision making, impulse control and loss of willpower to resist drugs: A neurocognitive perspective. *Nature Neuroscience, 8*, 1458-1463. https://doi.org/10.1038/nn1584

Bechara, A. (2004). Disturbances of emotion regulation after focal brain lesions. *International Review of Neurobiology, 62*, 159-193.

Bechara, A., Nader, K., & van der Kooy, D. (1998). A two-separate-motivational systems hypothesis of opioid addiction. *Pharmacology, Biochemistry, and Behavior, 59(1)*, 1–17. doi: 10.1016/S0091-3057(97)00047-6

Becker-Phelps, L. (2010). The secret of success: Lower your expectations [Web log post]. *Psychology Today.* https://www.psychologytoday.com/ca/blog/making-change/201007/the-secret-success-lower-your-expectations

Belludi, N. (2014). *Feed the right wolf: An American-Indian parable on cultivating the right attitudes* [Web log post]. https://www.rightattitudes.com/2014/01/15/the-two-wolves/

Bem, D.J. (1972). Self-perception theory. *Advances in Experimental Psychology, 6*, 1-62.

Bergland, C. (2012). The neurochemicals of happiness. *Psychology Today.* https://www.psychologytoday.com/ca/blog/the-athletes-way/201211/the-neurochemicals-happiness

Berman, M., Misic, B., Buschkuehl, M., Kross, E., Deldin, P., Peltier, S., et al. (2014). Does resting-state connectivity reflect depressive rumination? A tale of two analyses. *NeuroImage, 103*, 267–279. doi: 10.1016/J.NEUROIMAGE.2014.09.027

Bernhard, J. (2016). A sure-fire way to silence your inner critic [Web log post]. *Psychology Today.* https://www.psychologytoday.com/ca/blog/turning-straw-gold/201604/sure-fire-way-silence-your-inner-critic

Bevilacqua, L., & Goldman, D. (2009). Genes and addictions. *Clinical Pharmacology and Therapeutics, 85(4),* 359–361. https://doi.org/10.1038/clpt.2009.6

Bhat, P.S., Ryali, V., Srivastava, K., Kumar, S. R., Prakash, J., & Singal, A. (2012). Alcoholic hallucinosis. *Industrial Psychiatry Journal, 21(2),* 155–157. https://doi.org/10.4103/0972-6748.119646

Bigler, M., Neimeyer, G.J., & Brown, E. (2001). The divided self revisited: Effects of self-concept clarity and self-concept differentiation on psychological adjustment. *Journal of Social and Clinical Psychology, 20(3),* 396-415.

Bishop, S. (2009). Trait anxiety and impoverished prefrontal control of attention. *Nature Neuroscience, 12,* 92-98. doi: 10.1038/nn.2242

Bishop, S.R., Lau, M., Shapiro, S., Carlson, L., Anderson, N.D., Carmody, J., et al. (2004). Mindfulness: A proposed operational definition. *Clinical Psychology: Science and Practice, 11(3),* 230-241. doi:10.1093/clipsy.bph077

Black, J. & Enns, G. (1997). *Better boundaries: Owning and treasuring your life.* Raincoast Books.

Blanchard, M., & Farber, B. (2015). Lying in psychotherapy: Why and what clients don't tell their therapist about therapy and their relationship. *Counselling Psychology Quarterly, 29(1),* 90-112. https://doi.org/10.1080/09515070.2015.1085365

Bliss, T.V., & Collingridge, G.L. (1993). A synaptic model of memory: Long-term potentiation in the hippocampus. *Nature, 361,* 31-39. doi:10.1038/361031a0. PMID 8421494.

Blum, D. (2010, Feb 19). The chemist's war. *Slate Medical Examiner.* http://www.slate.com/articles/health_and_science/medical_examiner/2010/02/the_chemists_war.single.html

Bluth, K., & Neff, K. (2018). New frontiers in understanding the benefits of self-compassion. *Self and Identity, 17(6),* 605-608. https://doi.org/10.1080/15298868.2018.1508494

Boening J. A. (2001). Neurobiology of an addiction memory. *Journal of Neural Transmission, 108(6),* 755–765. https://doi.org/10.1007/s007020170050

Bogenschutz, M.P., Tonigan, J.S., & Miller, W.R. (2006). Examining the effects of alcoholism typology and AA attendance on self-efficacy as a mechanism of change. *Journal of Studies on Alcohol, 67(4),* 562-567. https://doi.org/10.15288/jsa.2006.67.562

Bollinger, R.A., & Hill, P.C. (2012). Humility. In T.G. Plante (Ed.), *Religion, spirituality, and positive psychology: Understanding the psychological fruits of faith* (pp. 31–48). Praeger.

Boney-McCoy, S., Gibbons, F.X., & Gerrard, M. (1999). Self-esteem, compensatory self-enhancement, and the consideration of health risk. *Personality And Social Psychology Bulletin, 25(8)*, 954-965.

Bourg-Carter, S. (2014). Helper's high: The benefits (and risks) of altruism [Web log Post]. *Psychology Today.* www.psychologytoday.com/blog/high-octane-women/201409/helpers-high-the-benefits-and-risks-altruism

Bowler, J., Bowler, M., & James, L. (2011). The cognitive underpinnings of addiction. *Substance Use and Misuse, 46,* 1060-1071. DOI: 10.3109/10826084.2011.552934

Bremner, R.H., Koole, S.L., & Bushman, B.J. (2011). "Pray for those who mistreat you:" Effects of prayer on anger and aggression. *Personality and Social Psychology Bulletin, 20(10),* 1-8. DOI: 10.1177/0146167211402215

Brown, A. (1987). Metacognition, executive control, self-regulation and other more mysterious mechanisms. In F. Weinert, & R. Kluwe (Eds.). *Metacognition, motivation, and understanding* (pp. 65– 116). Erlbaum.

Brown, G.W., Bifulco, A.T., & Andrews, B. (1990). Self-esteem and depression: III. Aetiological issues. *Social Psychiatry and Psychiatric Epidemiology: The International Journal for Research in Social and Genetic Epidemiology and Mental Health Services, 25(5),* 235– 243. https://doi.org/10.1007/BF00788644

Brown, S.L., Nesse, R.M., Vinokur, A.D. & Smith, D.M. (2003). Providing social support may be more beneficial than receiving it: Results from a prospective study of mortality. *Psychological Science, 14(4),* 320–327.

Buchanan, K.E., & Bardi, A. (2010). Acts of kindness and acts of novelty affect life satisfaction. *The Journal of Social Psychology, 150*(3), 235–237. https://doi.org/10.1080/00224540903365554

Buri, J. R. (1988). The nature of humankind, authoritarianism, and self-esteem. *Journal of Psychology and Christianity, 7*, 32–38.

Burkhouse, K., Jacobs, R., Peters, A., Ajilore, O., Watkins, E., & Langenecker, S. (2017). Neural correlates of rumination in adolescents with remitted major depressive disorder and healthy controls. *Cognitive, Affective, & Behavioral Neuroscience, 17,* 394–405. doi: 10.3758/s13415-016-0486-4

Buss, D. (Ed.). (2016). *Handbook of evolutionary psychology* (2nd ed.). John Wiley & Sons.

Butler R. & Bauld L. (2005) The parents' experience: Coping with drug use in the family. *Drugs, Education, Prevention and Policy, 12(1),* 35–45.

Buunk, B.P., & Ybema, J.F. (1997). Social comparison and occupational stress: The identification-contrast model. In B.P. Buunk, & F.X. Gibbons (Eds.). *Health, coping, and well-being: Perspectives from social comparison theory* (pp. 359-388). Erlbaum.

Cacioppo, J., Reis, H., & Zautra, A. (2011). Social resilience: The value of social fitness with an application to the military. *American Psychologist, 66(1),* 43-51. http://dx.doi.org/10.1037/a0021419

Campbell, J.D. (1990). Self-esteem and clarity of the self-concept. *Journal of Personality and Social Psychology, 59(3),* 538-49.

Campbell, J.D., Chew, B., & Scratchley, L.S. (1991). Cognitive and emotional reactions to daily events: The effects of self-esteem and self-complexity. *Journal of Personality, 59(3),* 473–505. https://doi.org/10.1111/j.1467-6494.1991.tb00257.x

Campbell, J.D., Trapnell, P.D., Heine, S.J., Katz, I.M., Lavallee, L.F., & Lehman, D.R. (1996). Self-concept clarity: Measurement, personality correlates, and cultural boundaries. *Journal of Personality and Social Psychology, 70(1),* 141–156. https://doi.org/10.1037/0022-3514.70.1.141

Cardinal, R.N., Parkinson, J.A., Hall, J., & Everitt, B.J. (2002). Emotion and motivation: The role of the amygdala, ventral striatum, and prefrontal cortex. *Neuroscience and Biobehavioral Reviews, 26,* 321-352

Carlson, B., & Larkin, H. (2009). Meditation as a coping intervention for treatment of addiction. *Journal of Religion & Spirituality in Social Work, 28,* 379-392. DOI: 10.1080/15426430903263260

Carmody, J., Reed, G., Kristeller, J., & Merriam, P. (2008). Mindfulness, spirituality, and health-related symptoms. *Journal of Psychosomatic Research, 64(4),* 393-403. https://doi.org/10.1016/j.jpsychores.2007.06.015

Cartwright-Hatton, S., & Wells, A. (1997). Beliefs about worry and intrusions: The meta-cognitions questionnaire and its correlates. *Journal of Anxiety Disorders, 11(3),* 279-96. DOI:10.1016/s0887-6185(97)00011-x

Carver, C.S., & Johnson, S.L. (2010). Authentic and hubristic pride: Differential relations to aspects of goal regulation, affect, and self-control. *Journal of Research in Personality, 44(6),* 698–703. https://doi.org/10.1016/j.jrp.2010.09.004

Caselli, G., Bortolai, C., Leoni, M., Rovetto, F., & Spada, M.M. (2008). Rumination in problem drinkers. *Addiction Research & Theory, 16(6),* 564-571. https://doi.org/10.1080/16066350802100822

Caselli, G., Ferretti, C., Leoni, M., Rebecchi, D., Rovetto, F., & Spada, M.M. (2010). Rumination as a predictor of drinking behaviour in alcohol abusers: A prospective study. *Addiction, 105,* 1041-1048. doi:10.1111/j.1360-0443.2010.02912.x

Caselli, G., Martino, F., Spada, M., & Wells, A. (2018). Metacognitive therapy for alcohol use disorder: A systematic case series. *Frontiers in Psychology.* https://doi.org/10.3389/fpsyg.2018.02619

Center for Substance Abuse Treatment. (2005). Substance-induced disorders. Substance Abuse Treatment for Persons With Co-Occurring Disorders. *Treatment Improvement Protocol (TIP) Series, No. 42.* https://www.ncbi.nlm.nih.gov/books/NBK64178/

Centers for Disease Control and Prevention (CDC). (2019). *2019 Annual surveillance report of drug-related risks and outcomes.* https://www.cdc.gov/drugoverdose/pdf/pubs/2019-cdc-drug-surveillance-report.pdf

Centers for Disease Control and Prevention (CDC). (2020). *CDC Drug Overdose Surveillance and Epidemiology (DOSE) System.* https://www.cdc.gov/drugoverdose/data/nonfatal/case.html

Centers for Disease Control and Prevention (CDC). (2020). *CDC WONDER.* https://wonder.cdc.gov/

Centers for Disease Control and Prevention (CDC). (2020). *Drug overdose deaths.* https://www.cdc.gov/drugoverdose/data/statedeaths.html

Centers for Disease Control and Prevention (CDC). (2019). *Prescribing practices.* https://www.cdc.gov/drugoverdose/data/prescribing/prescribing-practices.html

Centers for Disease Control and Prevention (CDC). (2020). *Synthetic opioid overdose deaths.* https://www.cdc.gov/drugoverdose/data/fentanyl.html

Centers for Disease Control and Prevention (CDC). (2020). *U.S. opioid prescribing rate maps.* https://www.cdc.gov/drugoverdose/maps/rxrate-maps.html

Centers for Disease Control and Prevention (CDC). (2017). Vital Signs: Changes in opioid prescribing in the United States, 2006–2015. *MMWR, 66(26),* 697-704. https://www.cdc.gov/mmwr/volumes/66/wr/mm6626a4.htm

Centers for Disease Control and Prevention (CDC). (2020). *Youth Risk Behavior Surveillance System (YRBSS).* https://www.cdc.gov/healthyyouth/data/yrbs/index.htm

Chartrand, T.L., & Bargh, J.A. (1999). The chameleon effect: The perception–behavior link and social interaction. *Journal of Personality and Social Psychology, 76(6),* 893–910. https://doi.org/10.1037/0022-3514.76.6.893

Cheng, J.T., Tracy, J.L., & Henrich, J. (2010). Pride, personality, and the evolutionary foundations of human social status. *Evolution and Human Behavior, 31,* 334–347. doi:10.1016/j.evolhumbehav.2010.02.004

Ciccarone D. (2011). Stimulant abuse: Pharmacology, cocaine, methamphetamine, treatment, attempts at pharmacotherapy. *Primary care, 38(1),* 41–58. https://doi.org/10.1016/j.pop.2010.11.004

Cinoğlu, H., & Arıkan, Y. (2012). Self, identity and identity formation: From the perspectives of three major theories. *Journal of Human Sciences, 9(2),* 1114-1131. https://www.j-humansciences.com/ojs/index.php/IJHS/article/view/2429/972

Cicei, C.C. (2012). Examining the association between self-concept clarity and self-esteem on a sample of Romanian medical students. *Procedia – Social and Behavioral Sciences, 46,* 4345-4348. https://doi.org/10.1016/j.sbspro.2012.06.252

Collier, L. (2016). Growth after trauma. *American Psychological Association Monitor on Psychology, 47(10),* 48. https://www.apa.org/monitor/2016/11/growth-trauma

Cooke, S.F., & Bliss, T.V. (2006). Plasticity in the human central nervous system. *Brain, 129(7),* 1659–1673. doi:10.1093/brain/awl082

Cooney, R., Joormann, J., Eugène, F., Dennis, E., and Gotlib, I. (2010). Neural correlates of rumination in depression. *Cognitive, Affective, & Behavioral Neuroscience, 10,* 470–478. doi: 10.3758/CABN.10.4.470

Craig, A.D. (2009). How do you feel — now? The anterior insula and human awareness. *Nature Review Neuroscience, 10,* 59–70. https://doi.org/10.1038/nrn2555

Creswell, J.D., Welch, W., Taylor, S.E., Sherman, D.K., Gruenewald, T., & Mann, T. (2005). Affirmation of personal values buffers neuroendocrine and psychological stress responses. *Psychological Science, 16,* 846-851. DOI: 10.1111/j.1467-9280.2005.01624.x

Crews, F., & Vetreno, R. (2014). Neuroimmune basis of alcoholic brain damage. *International Review of Neurobiology, 118,* 315-57. doi: 10.1016/B978-0-12-801284-0.00010-5

Cristea, I., Kok, R., & Cuijpers, P. (2016). The effectiveness of cognitive bias modification interventions for substance addictions: A metaanalysis. *PLoS ONE 11(9)*, e0162226. doi:10.1371/ journal.pone.0162226

Crocker, J., Canevello, A., & Brown, A. (2016). Social motivation: Costs and benefits of selfishness and otherishness. *Annual Review of Psychology, 68,* 299-325. https://doi.org/10.1146/annurev-psych-010416-044145

Cui, C., Shurtleff, D., & Harris, R.A. (2014). Neuroimmune mechanisms of alcohol and drug addiction. *International Review of Neurobiology, 118*, 1–12. https://doi.org/10.1016/B978-0-12-801284-0.00001-4

Curry, O.S., Rowland, L.A., Van Lissa, C.J., Zlotowitz, S., McAlaney, J., & Whitehouse, H. (2018). Happy to help? A systematic review and meta-analysis of the effects of performing acts of kindness on the well-being of the actor. *Journal of Experimental Social Psychology, 76,* 320-329. https://doi.org/10.1016/j.jesp.2018.02.014

Cicero, T.J., Ellis, M.S., & Kasper, Z.A. (2020). Polysubstance use: A broader understanding of substance use during the opioid crisis. *American Journal of Public Health, 110*, 244-250. https://doi.org/10.2105/AJPH.2019.305412

Crummy, E.A., O'Neal, T.J., Baskin, B.M., & Ferguson, S.M. (2020). One is not enough: Understanding and modeling polysubstance use. *Frontiers in Neuroscience, 14*, 569. https://doi.org/10.3389/fnins.2020.00569

Culpepper, L. (2016). Positive psychology and spirituality. *Journal of Psychology and Clinical Psychiatry, 6(7)*, 00407. DOI: 10.15406/jpcpy.2016.06.00407

Dale, S. (2015). Heuristics and biases: The science of decision-making. *Business Information Review, 32(2)*, 93–99. DOI: 10.1177/0266382115592536

Daley, D.C., & Marlatt, G.A. (1997). *Managing your drug or alcohol problem: Therapist guide.* Oxford university Press.

Darke, S., Larney, S., and Farrell, M. (2017). Yes, people can die from opiate withdrawal. *Addiction, 112(2)*, 199–200. doi: 10.1111/add.13512.

David, A.S. (1990). Insight and psychosis. *British Journal of Psychiatry, 156*, 798-808. DOI: 10.1192/bjp.156.6.798

David, V., Beracochea, D., & Walton, M. (2018). Editorial: Memory systems of the addicted brain: The underestimated role of cognitive biases in addiction and its treatment. *Frontiers in Psychology.* https://doi.org/10.3389/fpsyt.2018.00030

Davidson, R., Kabat-Zinn, J., Schumacher, J., Rosenkranz, M., Muller, D., Santorelli, S., et al. (2003). Alterations in brain and immune function produced by mindfulness meditation. *Psychosomatic Medicine, 65 (4)*, 564–570. doi: 10.1097/01.PSY.0000077505.67574.E3).

Davis, D.E., Worthington, E.L., & Hook, J.N. (2010). Humility: Review of measurement strategies and conceptualization as personality judgment. *The Journal of Positive Psychology, 5(4)*, 243–252. https://doi.org/10.1080/17439761003791672

Davison, G.C., & Best, J.L. (2003). Think-aloud techniques. In W. O'Donohue, J.E. Fisher, & S. Hayes (Eds.), *Cognitive behavioral therapy: Applying empirically supported techniques in your practice* (pp. 423-427). John Wiley & Sons.

Deci, E.L., Ryan, R.M., & Koestner, R. (1999). A meta-analytic review of experiments examining the effects of extrinsic rewards on intrinsic motivation. *Psychological Bulletin, 125(6)*, 627-668.

Diamond, S. (2008). The psychology of spirituality [Web log post]. *Psychology Today*. https://www.psychologytoday.com/blog/evil-deeds/200812/the-psychology-spirituality

Diaper, A.M., Law, F.D., & Melichar, J.K. (2014). Pharmacological strategies for detoxification. *British Journal of Clinical Pharmacology, 77(2)*, 302–314. https://doi.org/10.1111/bcp.12245

Dillon, M.M. (2009). Is it good to do good? Altruism and health. *The University Dialogue, 48.* https://scholars.unh.edu/discovery_ud/48

Dolan, S.L., Martin, R.A., & Rohsenow, D.J. (2008). Self-efficacy for cocaine abstinence: Pretreatment correlates and relationship to outcomes. *Addictive Behaviors, 33(5)*, 675–688. https://doi.org/10.1016/j.addbeh.2007.12.001

Domeier, M., Sachse, P., & Schafer, B. (2018). Motivational reasons for biased decisions: The sunk-cost effect's instrumental rationality. *Frontiers in Psychology*. https://doi.org/10.3389/fpsyg.2018.00815

Dominguez-Salas, S., Diaz-Batanero, C., Lozano-Rojas, O., & Verdejo-Garcia, A. (2016). Impact of general cognition and executive function deficits on addiction treatment outcomes: Systematic review and discussion of neurocognitive pathways. *Neuroscience & Biobehavioral Reviews, 71*, 772-801.

Dong, Y., Taylor, J.R., Wolf, M.E., & Shaham, Y. (2017). Circuit and synaptic plasticity mechanisms of drug relapse. *The Journal of Neuroscience, 37(45)*, 10867–10876. https://doi.org/10.1523/JNEUROSCI.1821-17.2017

Donovan, D., Ingalsbe, M., Benbow, J., & Daley, D. (2013). 12-step interventions and mutual support programs for substance use disorders: An overview. *Social Work in Public Health, 28(3-4)*, 313–332. doi:10.1080/19371918.2013.774663 dos Santos, J.C., Barros, S., & Huxley, P.J. (2018). Social inclusion of the people with mental health issues: Compare international results. *International Journal of Social Psychiatry 2018, 64(4)*, 344–350. DOI: 10.1177/0020764018763941

Douaihy, A., Daley, D., Marlatt, A., & Donovan, D.M. (2016). Relapse prevention: Clinical models and intervention strategies. In R.K. Ries, D.A. Fiellin, S.C. Miller, & R. Saitz (Eds.). *The ASAM principles of addiction medicine* (5th ed.). Wolters Kluwer.

Dowling, G. (2011). *Advances in drug abuse and addiction research from NIDA: Implications for treatment* [Power point presentation]. https://www.bumc.bu.edu/care/files/2011/08/02-Keynote-CRIT-2011.pdf

Dugosh, K., Abraham, A., Seymour, B., McLoyd, K., Chalk, M., & Festinger, D. (2016). A systematic review on the use of psychosocial interventions in conjunction with medications for the treatment of opioid addiction. *Journal of Addiction Medicine, 10(2)*, 93–103. https://doi.org/10.1097/ADM.0000000000000193

Duval, S., & Wicklund, R.A. (1972). *A theory of objective self awareness.* Academic Press.

Easterbrook, J. (1959). The effect of emotion on cue utilisation and the organisation of behavior. *Psychological review, 66*, 183-201. https://doi.org/10.1037/h0047707

Egevari, G., Ciccocioppo, R., Jentsch, J., & Hurd, Y. (2018). Shaping vulnerability to addiction – the contribution of behavior, neural circuits and molecular mechanisms. *Neuroscience & Behavioral Reviews, 85*, 117-125. https://doi.org/10.1016/j.neubiorev.2017.05.019

Ellemers, N., & Haslam, S.A. (2012). Social identity theory. In P.A.M. Van Lange, A.W. Kruglanski, & E.T. Higgins (Eds.), *Handbook of theories of social psychology* (p. 379–398). Sage Publications Ltd. https://doi.org/10.4135/9781446249222.n45

Elliott, K. (2006). Anthetic inner critic work as a method for relapse prevention. *Alcoholism Treatment Quarterly, 24(3)*, 109-119. https://doi.org/10.1300/J020v24n03_07

Ehret, P.J., LaBrie, J.W., Santerre, C., & Sherman, D.K. (2015). Self-affirmation and motivational interviewing: Integrating perspectives to reduce resistance and increase efficacy of alcohol interventions, *Health Psychology Review, 9(1)*, 83-102, DOI: 10.1080/17437199.2013.840953

Enright, R. (2017). Why resentment lasts – And how to defeat it [Web log post]. *Psychology Today.* https://www.psychologytoday.com/ca/blog/the-forgiving-life/201703/why-resentment-lasts-and-how-defeat-it

Epley, N., & Gilovich, T. (2016). The mechanics of motivated reasoning. *Journal of Economic Perspectives, 30(3),* 133-140. http://dx.doi.org/10.1257/jep.30.3.133

Epton, T., Harris, P.R., Kane, R., van Koningsbruggen, G.M., & Sheeran, P. (2015). The impact of self-affirmation on health-behavior change: A meta-analysis. *Health Psychology, 34(3),* 187-96. DOI:10.1037/hea0000116

Evans, J. (2008). Dual-processing accounts of reasoning, judgment, and social cognition. *Annual Review of Psychology, 59,* 255-78. 10.1146/annurev.psych.59.103006.093629

Ewald, D.R., Strack, R.W., & Orsini, M.M. (2019). Rethinking addiction. *Global Pediatric Health.* https://doi.org/10.1177/2333794X18821943

Exline, J.J., & Hill, P.C. (2012). Humility: A consistent and robust predictor of generosity. *The Journal of Positive Psychology, 7(3),* 208–218. https://doi.org/10.1080/17439760.2012.671348

Evans, D.R. (1997). Health promotion, wellness programs, quality of life and the marketing of psychology. *Canadian Psychology, 38(1),* 1–12. https://doi.org/10.1037/0708-5591.38.1.1

Feldman, R., & Dinardo, A. (2009). *Essentials of understanding psychology* (3rd Canadian ed.). McGraw-Hill.

Festinger, L. (1957). *A theory of cognitive dissonance.* Stanford University Press.

Festinger, L. (1957). A theory of social comparison processes. *Human Relations, 7(2),* 117-140. https://doi.org/10.1177/001872675400700202

Festinger, L., & Carlsmith, J.M. (1959). Cognitive consequences of forced compliance. *The Journal of Abnormal and Social Psychology, 58(2),* 203–210. https://doi.org/10.1037/h0041593

Field, M., Mogg, K., & Bradley, B. (2005). Craving and cognitive biases for alcohol cues in social drinkers. *Alcohol & Alcoholism, 40(6),* 504–510. doi:10.1093/alcalc/agh213

Filkowski, M., Cochran, R., & Haas, B. (2016). Altruistic behavior: Mapping responses in the brain. *Neuroscience and Neuroeconomics, 5,* 65-75. https://doi.org/10.2147/NAN.S87718

Finney, J.W., Noyes, C.A., Coutts, A.I., & Moos, R.H. (1998). Evaluating substance abuse treatment process models: I. Changes on proximal outcome variables during 12-step and cognitive-behavioral treatment. *Journal of Studies on Alcohol, 59(4)*, 371–380. https://doi.org/10.15288/jsa.1998.59.371

Fischer, J. (2011). The Four Domains Model: Connecting spirituality, health and well-being. *Religions, 2*, 17-28; doi:10.3390/rel2010017

Fishbein, M. (1979). A theory of reasoned action: Some applications and implications. *Nebraska Symposium on Motivation, 27*, 65–116.

Fishbein, M. & Ajzen, I. (1975) *Belief, attitude, intention, and behavior: An introduction to theory and research.* Addison-Wesley.

Fishbein, M. & Ajzen, I. (2010). *Predicting and changing behavior: The Reasoned Action Approach.* Taylor & Francis.

Fleming, K., & Bartholow, B. (2014). Alcohol cues, approach bias, and inhibitory control: Applying a dual process model of addiction to alcohol sensitivity. *Psychology of Addictive Behaviors: Journal of the Society of Psychologists in Addictive Behaviors, 28(1)*, 85–96. https://doi.org/10.1037/a0031565

Fontenelle, L.F., Oostermeijer, S., Harrison, B.J., Pantelis, C., & Yucel, M. (2011). Obsessive-compulsive disorder, impulse control disorders and drug addiction: Common features and potential treatments. *Drugs, 71(7)*, 827-840. 827-40. DOI:10.2165/11591790-000000000-00000

Fox, K.C., Nijeboer, S., Dixon, M.L., Floman, J.L., Ellamil, M., Rumak, S.P., et al. (2014). Is meditation associated with altered brain structure? A systematic review and meta-analysis of morphometric neuroimaging in meditation practitioners. *Neuroscience & Biobehavioral Reviews, 43*, 48–73. DOI: 10.1016/j.neubiorev.2014.03.016

Franck, E., & De Raedt, R. (2007). Self-esteem reconsidered: Unstable self-esteem outperforms level of self-esteem as vulnerability marker for depression. *Behaviour Research and Therapy, 45(7)*, 1531-1541.

Franken I.H. (2003). Drug craving and addiction: Integrating psychological and neuropsychopharmacological approaches. *Progress in Neuro-Psychopharmacology & Biological Psychiatry, 27(4)*, 563–579. https://doi.org/10.1016/S0278-5846(03)00081-2

Frankl, V. (1959/2006). *Man's search for meaning.* Beacon Press.

French, M.T., McGeary, K.A., Chitwood, D.D., McCoy, C.B., Inciardi, J.A., & McBride, D. (2000). Chronic drug use and crime. *Substance Abuse, 21*, 95–109 (2000). https://doi.org/10.1023/A:1007763129628

Friese, M., & Wänke, M. (2014). Personal prayer buffers self-control depletion. *Journal of Experimental Social Psychology, 51*, 56–59. https://doi.org/10.1016/j.jesp.2013.11.006

Furnham, A. & Cheng, H. (2000) Lay theories of happiness. *Journal of Happiness Studies, 1*, 227–246.

Galanter, M. (2007). Spirituality and recovery in 12-step programs: An empirical model. *Journal of Substance Abuse & Treatment, 33(3)*, 265–272. doi: 10.1016/j.jsat.2007.04.016. S0740-5472(07)00186-9

Galanter, M., Josipovic, Z., Dermatis, H., Weber, J., & Millard, M. (2017). An initial fMRI study on neural correlates of prayer in members of Alcoholics Anonymous. *The American Journal of Drug and Alcohol Abuse, 43(1)*, 44-54. DOI: 10.3109/00952990.2016.1141912

Garavan, H., & Stout, J. (2005). Neurocognitive insights into substance abuse. *Trends in Cognitive Sciences, 9(4)*, 194-201. doi:10.1016/j.tics.2005.02.008

Gardner, M., & Steinberg, L. (2005). Peer influence on risk taking, risk preference, and risky decision making in adolescence and adulthood: An experimental study. *Developmental Psychology, 41(4)*, 625–635. doi: 10.1037/0012-1649.41.4.625.

Garland E. (2011). Trait mindfulness predicts attentional and autonomic regulation of alcohol cue-reactivity. *Journal of Psychophysiology, 25(4)*, 180–189. https://doi.org/10.1027/0269-8803/a000060

Garland, E., Boettiger, C., Gaylord, S., Chanon, V., & Howard, M. (2012). Mindfulness is inversely associated with alcohol attentional bias among recovering alcohol-dependent adults. *Cognitive Therapy and Research, 36(5)*, 441–450. https://doi.org/10.1007/s10608-011-9378-7

Garland, E., Fredrickson, B., Kring, A., Johnson, D., Meyer, P., & Penn, D. (2010). Upward spirals of positive emotions counter downward spirals of negativity: Insights from the broaden-and-build theory and affective neuroscience on the treatment of emotion dysfunctions and deficits in psychopathology. *Clinical Psychology Review, 30*, 849–864. https://doi.org/10.1016/j.cpr.2010.03.002

Garland, E. , Froeliger, B., & Howard, M. (2013). Mindfulness training targets neurocognitive mechanisms of addiction at the attention-appraisal-emotion interface. *Frontiers in Psychiatry, 4*, 173. https://doi.org/10.3389/fpsyt.2013.00173

Garland, E., & Howard, M. (2018). Mindfulness-based treatment of addiction: Current state of the field and envisioning the next wave of research. *Addiction Science & Clinical Practice, 13(1)*, 14. doi:10.1186/s13722-018-0115-3

Gawronski, B. (2012). Back to the future of dissonance theory: Cognitive consistency as a core motive. *Social Cognition, 30(6)*, 652-668.

George, O., & Koob, G. (2010). Individual differences in prefrontal cortex function and the transition from drug use to drug dependence. *Neuroscience & Biobehavioral Review, 35(2)*, 232–47. doi: 10.1016/j.neubiorev.2010.05.002

Gibbons, F.X., Smith, T.W., Ingram, R.E., Pearce, K., Brehm, S.S., & Schroeder, D.J. (1985). Self-awareness and self-confrontation: Effects of self-focused attention on members of a clinical population. *Journal of Personality and Social Psychology, 48(3)*, 662-675. DOI:10.1037//0022-3514.48.3.662

Giovazolias, T., & Themeli, O. (2014). Social learning conceptualization for substance abuse: Implications for therapeutic interventions. *The European Journal of Counselling Psychology, 3(1)*, 69–88. doi:10.5964/ejcop.v3i1.23

Gipson, C.D., Kupchik, Y.M., & Kalivas, P.W. (2014). Rapid, transient synaptic plasticity in addiction. *Neuropharmacology, 76(Pt B - 0 0)*, 276–286. https://doi.org/10.1016/j.neuropharm.2013.04.032

Goldberg, S., Tucker, R., Greene, P., Davidson, R. , Wampold, B., Kearney, D., & Simpson, T. (2018). Mindfulness-based interventions for psychiatric disorders: A systematic review and meta-analysis. *Clinical Psychology Review, 59*, 52–60. https://doi.org/10.1016/j.cpr.2017.10.011

Golden, B. (2019). How self-criticism threatens you in mind and body [Web log post]. *Psychology Today.* https://www.psychologytoday.com/intl/blog/overcoming-destructive-anger/201901/how-self-criticism-threatens-you-in-mind-and-body

Goldstein, R., Craig, A., Bechara, A., Garavan, H., Childress, A., Paulus, M., & Volkow, N. (2009). The neurocircuitry of impaired insight in drug addiction. *Trends in Cognitive Sciences, 13(9)*, 372–380. https://doi.org/10.1016/j.tics.2009.06.004

Goldstein, R., & Volkow, N. (2011). Dysfunction of the prefrontal cortex in addiction: Neuroimaging findings and clinical implications. *Nature Reviews. Neuroscience, 12(11)*, 652–669. https://doi.org/10.1038/nrn3119

Goodman, J., & Packard, M.G. (2016). Memory systems and the addicted brain. *Frontiers in Psychology, 7(24).* https://doi.org/10.3389/fpsyt.2016.00024

Gorski, T.T., & Miller, M. (1982). Counseling for relapse prevention. Herald House/Independence Press.

Grant, S., Colaiaco, B., Motala, A., Shanman, R., Booth, M., Sorbero, M., et al. (2017). Mindfulness-based relapse prevention for substance use disorders: A systematic review and meta-analysis. *Journal of Addiction Medicine, 11(5),* 386–396. https://doi.org/10.1097/ADM.0000000000000338

Grant, B.F., Goldstein, R.B., Saha, T.D., Chou, S.P., Jung, J., Zhang, H., et al. (2015). Epidemiology of DSM-5 Alcohol Use Disorder: Results From the National Epidemiologic Survey on Alcohol and Related Conditions III. *JAMA Psychiatry, 72(8),* 757–766. https://doi.org/10.1001/jamapsychiatry.2015.0584

Greenberg, J., Reiner, K., & Meiran, N. (2012). "Mind the trap:" Mindfulness practice reduces cognitive rigidity. *PloS One, 7(5),* e36206. https://doi.org/10.1371/journal.pone.0036206

Groome, D. (2014). *An introduction to cognitive psychology* (3rd ed.). Routledge.

Grueter, B.A., Rothwell, P.E., & Malenka, R.C. (2012). Integrating synaptic plasticity and striatal circuit function in addiction. *Current Opinion in Neurobiology, 22(3),* 545–551. https://doi.org/10.1016/j.conb.2011.09.009

Guenzel, N., & McChargue, D. (2020). Addiction relapse prevention. *StatPearls.* https://www.ncbi.nlm.nih.gov/books/NBK551500/

Grupe, D., & Nitschke, J. (2013). Uncertainty and anticipation in anxiety: An integrated neurobiological and psychological perspective. *Nature Reviews Neuroscience, 14(7),* 488–501. doi:10.1038/nrn3524

Gu, J., Strauss, C., Bond, R., & Cavanagh, K. (2015). How do mindfulness-based cognitive therapy and mindfulness-based stress reduction improve mental health and wellbeing? A systematic review and meta-analysis of mediation studies. *Clinical Psychology Review, 37,* 1–12. http://dx.doi.org/10.1016/j.cpr.2015.01.006

Guthrie, E.R. (1940). Association and the law of effect. *Psychological Review, 47(2),* 127-148.

Hall, J., & Fincham, F. (2005). Self-forgiveness: The stepchild of forgiveness. *Journal of Social and Clinical Psychology, 24(5),* 621-637. Retrieved from http://citeseerx.ist.psu.edu/viewdoc/download?doi=10.1.1.452.7231&rep=rep1&type=pdf

Hall, J., & Fincham, F. (2008). The temporal course of self-forgiveness. *Journal of Social and Clinical Psychology, 27(2),* 174–202. http://fincham.info/papers/jscp-The%20temporal%20course%20of%20self-forgiveness.pdf

Hammond, C. (2017). The 7 steps of accepting responsibility [Web log post]. *Psych Central.* https://pro.psychcentral.com/exhausted-woman/2016/05/the-7-steps-of-accepting-responsibility-for-wrongdoing/

Hamonniere, T., & Varescon, I. (2018). Metacognitive beliefs in addictive behaviours: A systematic review. *Addictive Behaviors, 85*, 51–63. https://doi.org/10.1016/j.addbeh.2018.05.018

Hardy, B. (2018). Why willpower makes things worse, not better [Web log post]. *Psychology Today.* https://www.psychologytoday.com/us/blog/quantum-leaps/201803/why-willpower-makes-things-worse-not-better

Hardy, J. (2006). Speaking clearly: A critical review of the self-talk literature. *Psychology of Sport and Exercise, 7*, 81-97. doi:10.1016/j.psychsport.2005.04.002

Harter, S. (1999). *The Construction of the Self. A Developmental Perspective.* Guilford Press.

Hartzler, B., & Fromme, K. (2003). Fragmentary and en bloc blackouts: Similarity and distinction among episodes of alcohol-induced memory loss. *Journal of Studies on Alcohol, 64(4)*, 547–550. https://doi.org/10.15288/jsa.2003.64.547

Harvey, M.D., & Enzle, M.E. (1981). A cognitive model of social norms for understanding the transgression-helping effect. *Journal of Personality and Social Psychology, 41(5)*, 866-875.

Harvey, P. & Martinko, M.J. Attribution theory and motivation. In N. Borkowski. (2016). *Organizational behavior, theory, and design in health care* (2nd ed.). Jones & Bartlett Learning.

Hasin, D.S., O'Brien, C.P., Auriacombe, M., Borges, G., Bucholz, K., Budney, A., et al. (2013). DSM-5 criteria for substance use disorders: Recommendations and rationale. *The American Journal of Psychiatry, 170(8)*, 834–851. https://doi.org/10.1176/appi.ajp.2013.12060782

Harvard Medical School. (2020). Understanding the stress response. *Harvard Health Publishing.* https://www.health.harvard.edu/staying-healthy/understanding-the-stress-response

Hatzigiakoumis, D.S., Martinotti, G., Giannantonio, M.D., & Janiri, L. (2011). Anhedonia and substance dependence: Clinical correlates and treatment options. *Frontiers in Psychiatry, 2*, 10. http://doi.org/10.3389/fpsyt.2011.00010

Heavey, C.L., & Hurlburt, R.T. (2008). The phenomena of inner experience. *Consciousness and cognition, 17*, 798–810. doi:10.1016/j.concog.2007.12.006

Heilig, M., Egli, M., Crabbe, J.C., & Becker, H.C. (2010). Acute withdrawal, protracted abstinence and negative affect in alcoholism: Are they linked? *Addiction*

Biology, 15(2), 169–184. https://doi.org/10.1111/j.1369-1600.2009.00194.x

Heinz, A., Löber, S., Georgi, A., Wrase, J., Hermann, D., Rey, E-R., et al. (2003). Reward craving and withdrawal relief craving: Assessment of different motivational pathways to alcohol intake. *Alcohol and Alcoholism, 38(1),* 35-39. https://doi.org/10.1093/alcalc/agg005

Heylighen, F. (1992). Evolution, selfishness and cooperation. *Journal of Ideas, 2(4),* 70-76. https://pdfs.semanticscholar.org/fc6d/93966c24f1ac8b6ded84d53de5d04cdc746f.pdf

Higgins, E.T. (1987). Self-discrepancy: A theory relating self and affect. *Psychological Review, 94(3),* 319–340. https://doi.org/10.1037/0033-295X.94.3.319

Hogarth, L., Balleine, B.W., Corbit, L.H., & Killcross, S. (2013). Associative learning mechanisms underpinning the transition from recreational drug use to addiction. *Annals of the New York Academy of Sciences, 1282,* 12–24. https://doi.org/10.1111/j.1749-6632.2012.06768.x

Holland P.C. (2008). Cognitive versus stimulus-response theories of learning. *Learning & Behavior, 36(3),* 227–241. https://doi.org/10.3758/lb.36.3.227

Hölzel, B.K., Lazar, S.W., Gard, T., Schuman-Olivier, Z., Vago, D.R., & Ott, U. (2011). How does mindfulness meditation work? Proposing mechanisms of action from a conceptual and neural perspective. *Perspectives on Psychological Science, 6(6),* 537–559. https://doi.org/10.1177/1745691611419671

Hooker, S.A., Masters, K.S., & Park, C.L. (2018). A meaningful life is a healthy life: A conceptual model linking meaning and meaning salience to health. *Review of General Psychology, 22(1),* 11–24. https://doi.org/10.1037/gpr0000115

Hsu S., Grow J., & Marlatt A. (2008). Mindfulness and addiction. In: L. Kaskutas & M. Galanter (eds.). *Recent developments in alcoholism.* Springer. https://doi.org/10.1007/978-0-387-77725-2_13

Human Rights Watch. (2016). *US: Disastrous toll of criminalizing drug use.* https://www.hrw.org/news/2016/10/12/us-disastrous-toll-criminalizing-drug-use

Hyman, S.E., Malenka, R.C., & Nestler, E.J. (2006). Neural mechanisms of addiction: The role of reward-related learning and memory. *Annual Review of Neuroscience, 29,* 565-598. doi: 10.1146/ annurev.neuro.29.051605.113009

Hynes, M. (Host). (2019, Sept 20). *Headlines and rejection: Interview with Dr. Steven Stosny* [Radio broadcast interview]. In Meyer, M., & Mahoney, S. (Producers), Tapestry. CBC Radio.

Ingram, R.E. (1990). Self-focused attention in clinical disorders: Review and a conceptual model. *Psychological Bulletin, 107*(2), 156–176. https://doi.org/10.1037/0033-2909.107.2.156

Irani, A. (2018). Positive altruism: Helping that benefits both the recipient and giver [Master's thesis]. *University of Pennsylvania.* https://repository.upenn.edu/mapp_capstone/152

Iversen, L. (2003). Cannabis and the brain. *Brain, 126(6),* 1252–1270. https://doi.org/10.1093/brain/awg143

Jacobsen, L.K., Southwick, S.M., & Kosten, T.R. (2001). Substance use disorders in patients with posttraumatic stress disorder: A review of the literature. *American Journal of Psychiatry, 158(8),* 1184-1190. https://doi.org/10.1176/appi.ajp.158.8.1184

Jankowski, P.J., Sandage, S.J., & Hill, P.C. (2013). Differentiation-based models of forgivingness, mental health and social justice commitment: Mediator effects for differentiation of self and humility. *The Journal of Positive Psychology, 8(5),* 412–424. https://doi.org/10.1080/17439760.2013.820337

Jeppsen, B., Pössel, P., Winkeljohn, S., Bjerg, A. & Wooldridge, D. (2015). Closeness and control: Exploring the relationship between prayer and mental health. *University of Louisville Counseling Psychology Commons.* https://ir.library.louisville.edu/cgi/viewcontent.cgi?article=1174&context=faculty

Jesse, S., Bråthen, G., Ferrara, M., Keindl, M., Ben-Menachem, E., Tanasescu, R., et al. (2017). Alcohol withdrawal syndrome: Mechanisms, manifestations, and management. *Acta Neurologica Scandinavica, 135(1),* 4–16. doi: 10.1111/ane.12671

Johnson, J. (2015). Good, neutral, and bad selfishness [Web log post]. *Psychology Today.* https://www.psychologytoday.com/ca/blog/cui-bono/201501/good-neutral-and-bad-selfishness

Johnson, M.H. (2001). Functional brain development in humans. *Neuroscience, 2,* 475-483. http://www-inst.eecs.berkeley.edu/~cs182/sp06/readings/Johnson%20-%202001.pdf

Kabat-Zinn, J. (1990). *Full catastrophe living: Using the wisdom of your body and mind to face stress, pain and illness.* Delacorte.

Kadam, M., Sinha, A., Nimkar, S., Matcheswalla, Y., & De Sousa, A. (2017). A comparative study of factors associated with relapse in alcohol dependence and opioid dependence. *Indian Journal of Psychological Medicine, 39(5),* 627–633. https://doi.org/10.4103/IJPSYM.IJPSYM_356_17

Kadden, R.M., & Litt, M.D. (2011). The role of self-efficacy in the treatment of substance use disorders. *Addictive Behaviors, 36(12),* 1120–1126. https://doi.org/10.1016/j.addbeh.2011.07.032

Kang, D., Jo, H., Jung, W., Kim, S., Jung, Y., Choi, C., et al. (2013). The effect of meditation on brain structure: Cortical thickness mapping and diffusion tensor imaging. *Social, Cognitive, & Affective Neuroscience, 8,* 27–33. Doi:10.1093/scan/nss056

Karyadi, K., VanderVeen, J., & Cyders, M. (2014). A meta-analysis of the relationship between trait mindfulness and substance use behaviors. *Drug and Alcohol Dependence, 143,* 1–10. https://doi.org/10.1016/j.drugalcdep.2014.07.014

Kauer, J.A., & Malenka, R.C. (2007). Synaptic plasticity and addiction. *Nature Reviews: Neuroscience, 8(11),* 844–58. doi:10.1038/nrn2234

Kelley, A.E. (2004). Memory and addiction: Shared neural circuitry and molecular mechanisms. *Neuron, 44(1),* 161-179. https://doi.org/10.1016/j.neuron.2004.09.016

Kelly, T. M., & Daley, D. C. (2013). Integrated treatment of substance use and psychiatric disorders. *Social Work in Public Health, 28(3-4),* 388–406. https://doi.org/10.1080/19371918.2013.774673

Keng, S., Smoski, M., & Robins, C. (2011). Effects of mindfulness on psychological health: A review of empirical studies. *Clinical Psychology Review, 31(6),* 1041–1056. doi:10.1016/j.cpr.2011.04.006

Kiken, L.G., & Shook, N.J. (2011). Looking up: Mindfulness increases positive judgments and reduces negativity bias. *Social Psychological and Personality Science, 2(4),* 425–431. https://doi.org/10.1177/1948550610396585

Knowlton, B.J. (2014). Basal ganglia: Habit formation. In: D. Jaeger D & R. Jung (eds.). *Encyclopedia of Computational Neuroscience (pp.* 1–17). Springer.

Kobasa, S. C. (1979). Stressful life events, personality, and health: An inquiry into hardiness. *Journal of Personality and Social Psychology, 37(1),* 1-11. http://dx.doi.org/10.1037/0022-3514.37.1.1

Kober, H., Mende-Siedlecki, P., Kross, E. F., Weber, J., Mischel, W., Hart, C. L., & Ochsner, K. N. (2010). Prefrontal-striatal pathway underlies cognitive regulation of craving. *Proceedings of the National Academy of Sciences of the United States of America, 107(33),* 14811–14816. https://doi.org/10.1073/pnas.1007779107

Koenig, H. (2012). Religion, spirituality, and health: The research and clinical implications. *ISRN Psychiatry*, 278730. https://doi.org/10.5402/2012/278730.

Koncz, A., Demetrovics, Z., & Takacs, Z.K. (2020) Meditation interventions efficiently reduce cortisol levels of at-risk samples: A meta-analysis. *Health Psychology Review*. DOI: 10.1080/17437199.2020.1760727

Koob, G.F. (2020). Neurobiology of opioid addiction: Opponent process, hyperkatifeia, and negative reinforcement. *Biological Psychiatry, 87*, 44-53. https://doi.org/10.1016/j.biopsych.2019.05.023

Koob G.F. (2015). The dark side of emotion: The addiction perspective. *European Journal of Pharmacology, 753*, 73–87. https://doi.org/10.1016/j.ejphar.2014.11.044

Koob, G.F., & Le Moal, M. (2008). Review. Neurobiological mechanisms for opponent motivational processes in addiction. *Philosophical Transactions of the Royal Society of London. Series B, Biological Sciences, 363(1507)*, 3113–3123. https://doi.org/10.1098/rstb.2008.0094

Korteling, J., Brouwer, A., & Toet, A. (2018). A neural network framework for cognitive bias. *Frontiers in Psychology.* https://doi.org/10.3389/fpsyg.2018.01561

Kosten, T.R., & O'Connor, P.G. (2003). Drug and alcohol withdrawal. *New England Journal of Medicine, 348(18)*, 1786-95. http://depts.washington.edu/psychres/wordpress/wp-content/uploads/2017/07/100-Papers-in-Clinical-Psychiatry-Substance-Use-and-Addiction-Psychiatry-Management-of-drug-and-alcohol-withdrawal..pdf

Kowalski, J., Wypych, M., Marchewka, A., & Dragan, M. (2019). Neural correlates of Cognitive-Attentional Syndrome: An fMRI study on repetitive negative thinking induction and resting state functional connectivity. *Frontiers in Psychology.* https://doi.org/10.3389/fpsyg.2019.00648

Kraft, B., Jonassen, R., Stiles, T., & Landro, N. (2017). Dysfunctional metacognitive beliefs are associated with decreased executive control. *Frontiers in Psychology.* https://doi.org/10.3389/fpsyg.2017.00593

Krause, N. (2012). Religious involvement, humility, and change in self-rated health over time. *Journal of Psychology and Theology, 40(3)*, 199-210. https://doi.org/10.1177/009164711204000303

Krause, N., & Hayward, R. D. (2012). Humility, lifetime trauma, and change in religious doubt among older adults. *Journal of Religion and Health, 51(4)*, 1002–1016. DOI: 10.1007/s10943-012-9576-y

Krause, N., & Hayward, R. (2013). Prayer beliefs and change in life satisfaction over time. *Journal of Religion and Health, 52(2)*, 674–694. doi:10.1007/s10943-012-9638-1

Kress, L., & Aue, T. (2017). The link between optimism bias and attention bias: A neurocognitive perspective. *Neuroscience and Biobehavioral Reviews, 80*, 688-702. http://dx.doi.org/10.1016

Kus, R. (1995). Prayer and meditation in addiction recovery. *Journal of Chemical Dependency Treatment, 5(2)*, 101-115, DOI: 10.1300/J034v05n02_08

Lacroix, A. (2019). Glucocorticoid effects on the nervous system and behavior. *UpToDate.*

Lafaye, G., Karila, L., Blecha, L., & Benyamina, A. (2017). Cannabis, cannabinoids, and health. *Dialogues in Clinical Neuroscience, 19(3)*, 309–316.

Lambert, N., Fincham, F., LaVallee, D., & Brantley, C. (2012). Praying together and staying together: Couple prayer and trust. *Psychology of Religion and Spirituality, 4(1)*, 1-9. DOI: 10.1037/a0023060

Lambert, N., Fincham, F., Marks, L., & Stillman, T. (2010). Invocations and intoxication: Does prayer decrease alcohol consumption? *Psychology of Addictive Behaviors, 24(2)*, 209-219. DOI: 10.1037/a0018746

Lammers, S. M., Soe-Agnie, S. E., de Haan, H. A., Bakkum, G. A., Pomp, E. R., & Nijman, H. J. (2014). Middelengebruik en criminaliteit: ein overzicht [Substance use and criminality: A review]. *Tijdschrift Voor Psychiatrie, 56(1)*, 32–39.

Lanae, V., & Feinauer, L. (1993). Resilience factors associated with female survivors of childhood sexual abuse. *American Journal of Family Therapy, 2193, 216-24.*

Lander, L., Howsare, J., & Byrne, M. (2013). The impact of substance use disorders on families and children: From theory to practice. *Social Work in Public Health, 28(3-4)*, 194–205. https://doi.org/10.1080/19371918.2013.759005

Larimer, M.E., Palmer, R.S., & Marlatt, A. (1999). An overview of Marlatt's cognitive-behavioral model. *Alcohol Research & Health, 23(2)*, 151-160. https://pubs.niaaa.nih.gov/publications/arh23-2/151-160.pdf

Latt, N. & Dore, G. (2014). Thiamine in Wernicke's encephalopathy. *Internal Medicine Journal, 44,* 911-915. https://doi.org/10.1111/imj.12522

Laudet, A.B., Savage, R., & Mahmood, D. (2002). Pathways to long-term recovery: A preliminary investigation. *Journal of Psychoactive Drugs, 34(3)*, 305–311. https://doi.org/10.1080/02791072.2002.10399968

Law, B.M. (2005). Probing the depression-rumination cycle. *APA Monitor on Psychology, 36(10),* 38.

Lazar, S., Kerr, C., Wasserman, R., Gray, J., Greve, D., Treadway, M., et al. (2005). Meditation experience is associated with increased cortical thickness. *Neuroreport, 16,* 1893–710. Doi:1097/01.wnr.0000186598.66243.19

Le Boutillier, C. & Croucher, A. (2010). Social Inclusion and mental health. *The British Journal of Occupational Therapy. 73(3),* 136-139. 10.4276/030802210X12682330090578.

Lee, H., Roh, S., & Kim, D.J. (2009). Alcohol-induced blackout. *International Journal of Environmental Research and Public Health, 6(11),* 2783–2792. https://doi.org/10.3390/ijerph6112783

Leipold, B., & Greve, W. (2009). Resilience: A conceptual bridge between coping and development. *European Psychologist, 14(1),* 40-50. doi:10.1027/1016-9040.14.1.40

Leventhal, A., Kahler, C., Ray, L., Stone, K., Young, D., Chelminski, I., et al. (2008). Anhedonia and amotivation in psychiatric outpatients with fully remitted stimulant use disorder. *The American Journal on Addictions / American Academy of Psychiatrists in Alcoholism and Addictions,* 17(3), 218–223. http://doi.org/10.1080/10550490802019774

Levy, M.S. (2008). Listening to our clients: The prevention of relapse. *Journal of Psychoactive Drugs, 40(2),* 167-172. DOI: 10.1080/02791072.2008.10400627

Li, W., Howard, M., Garland, E., McGovern, P., & Lazar, M. (2017). Mindfulness treatment for substance misuse: A systematic review and meta-analysis. *Journal of Substance Abuse Treatment, 75,* 62–96. http://dx.doi.org/10.1016/j.jsat.2017.01.008

Lightman, A. (2018). Fact and faith: Why science and spirituality are not incompatible. *Science Focus.* https://www.sciencefocus.com/the-human-body/fact-and-faith-why-science-and-spirituality-are-not-incompatible/

Linehan, M., & Dimidjian, S. (2003). Mindfulness practice. In W. O'Donohue, J.E. Fisher, & S. Hayes (Eds.), *Cognitive behavioral therapy: Applying empirically supported techniques in your practice* (pp. 229-237). John Wiley & Sons.

Lipka, M. (2016). 5 facts about prayer. *Pew Research Center.* http://www.pewresearch.org/fact-tank/2016/05/04/5-facts-about-prayer/

Lloyd, A. (2003). Urge surfing. In W. O'Donohue, J.E. Fisher, & S. Hayes (Eds.), *Cognitive behavioral therapy: Applying empirically supported techniques in your practice* (pp. 451-455). John Wiley & Sons.

Logel, C., & Cohen, G.L. (2012). The role of the self in physical health. *Psychological Science, 23(1),* 53–55. https://doi.org/10.1177/0956797611421936

Loke, A.Y., & Mak, Y.W. (2013). Family process and peer influences on substance use by adolescents. *International Journal of Environmental Research and Public Health, 10(9),* 3868–3885. https://doi.org/10.3390/ijerph10093868

Luciana, M., & Ewing, S.W. (2015). Introduction to the special issue: Substance use and the adolescent brain: Developmental impacts, interventions, and longitudinal outcomes. *Developmental Cognitive Neuroscience, 16,* 1-4. https://doi.org/10.1016/j.dcn.2015.10.005

Luders, E., Toga, A., Lepore, N., & Gaser, C. (2009). The underlying anatomical correlates of long-term meditation: Larger hippocampal and frontal volumes of gray matter. *Neuroimage, 45,* 672–810. Doi:1016/j.neuroimage.2008.12.061

Luks, A. (1988). Helper's high: Volunteering makes people feel good, physically and emotionally. *Psychology Today, 22(10),* 34-42.

Luscher, C., & Malenka, R.C. (2011). Drug-evoked synaptic plasticity in addiction: From molecular changes to circuit remodeling. *Neuron, 69,* 650–663.

Lyubomirsky, S., Kasri, F., & Zehm, K. Dysphoric rumination impairs concentration on academic task. *Cognitive Therapy and Research, 27(3),* 309-330. DOI: 10.1023/A:1023918517378

Lyubomirsky, S., & Nolen-Hoeksema, S. (1995). Effects of self-focused rumination on negative thinking and interpersonal problem solving. *Journal of Personality and Social Psychology, 69(1),* 176–90.

Lyubomirsky, S., & Nolen-Hoeksema, S. (1993). Self-perpetuating properties of dysphoric rumination. *Journal of Personality and Social Psychology, 65(2),* 339-349.

MacInnes D.L. (2006). Self-esteem and self-acceptance: An examination into their relationship and their effect on psychological health. *Journal of Psychiatric and Mental Health Nursing, 13,* 483–489.

Maier, S., & Seligman, M. (2016). Learned helplessness at fifty: Insights from neuroscience. *Psychological review, 123(4),* 349–367. doi:10.1037/rev0000033

Mann, M., Hosman, C.M.H., Schaalma, H.P., & De Vries, N. (2004). Self-esteem in a broad-spectrum approach for mental health promotion. *Health Education Research, 19(4),* 357-72. DOI: 10.1093/her/cyg041

Marcus, M.T., Fine, M., Moeller, F.G., Khan, M.M., Pitts, K., Swank, P.R., et al. (2003). Change in stress levels following mindfulness-based stress reduction in a therapeutic community. *Addictive Disorders & Their Treatment, 2(3),* 63–68. https://doi.org/10.1097/00132576-200302030-00001

Markou, A., Kosten, T., & Koob, G. (1998). Neurobiological similarities in depression and drug dependence: A self-medication hypothesis. *Neuropsycho-pharmacology, 18,* 135–174. Retrieved from https://www.ncbi.nlm.nih.gov/pubmed/9471114

Marlatt, G., & Chawla, N. (2007). Meditation and alcohol use. *Southern Medical Journal, 100(4),* 451.

Marlatt, G.A., & Gordon, J.R. (1985). *Relapse prevention: Maintenance strategies in the treatment of addictive behavior.* Guildford Press.

Martela, F., & Ryan, R.M. (2016). Prosocial behavior increases well-being and vitality even without contact with the beneficiary: Causal and behavioral evidence. *Motivation and Emotion, 40,* 351–357. https://doi.org/10.1007/s11031-016-9552-z

Martela, F., Ryan, R.M. & Steger, M.F. (2018). Meaningfulness as satisfaction of autonomy, competence, relatedness, and beneficence: Comparing the four satisfactions and positive affect as predictors of meaning in life. *Journal of Happiness Studies, 19,* 1261–1282. https://doi.org/10.1007/s10902-017-9869-7

Maslow, A. (1954/1987). *Motivation and personality* (3rd ed.). Pearson Education.

Masters, K.S., & Spielmans, G.I. (2007). Prayer and health: Review, meta-analysis, and research agenda. *Journal of Behavioral Medicine, 30,* 329-338. DOI 10.1007/s10865-007-9106-7

Mathias, C. W., Duffing, T. M., Ashley, A., Charles, N. E., Lake, S. L., Ryan, S. R., Liang, Y., & Dougherty, D. M. (2015). Aggression as a predictor of early substance use initiation among youth with family histories of substance use disorders. *Addictive Disorders & Their Treatment, 14(4),* 230–240. https://doi.org/10.1097/ADT.0000000000000068

Maynes, J. (2015). Critical thinking and cognitive bias. *Informal Logic, 35(2),* 183-203.

Maze, I., & Nestler, E. J. (2011). The epigenetic landscape of addiction. *Annals of the New York Academy of Sciences, 1216,* 99–113. https://doi.org/10.1111/j.1749-6632.2010.05893.x

McCarthy-Jones S., & Fernyhough C. (2011). The varieties of inner speech: Links between quality of inner speech and psychopathological variables in a sample of young adults. *Consciousness and Cognition, 20*, 1586–1593. 10.1016/j.concog.2011.08.005

McCullough, M., Pedersen, E., Tabak, B., & Carter, E. (2014). Conciliatory gestures promote forgiveness and reduce anger in humans. *Proceedings of the National Academy of Sciences, 111(30)*, 11211-11216. doi:10.1073/pnas.1405072111

McCusker, C. (2001). Cognitive biases and addiction: An evolution in theory and method. *Addiction, 96*, 47-56. DOI: 10.1080/09652140020016950

McGee, M. (2008). Meditation and psychiatry. *Psychiatry, 5(1)*, 28–41.

McHugh, R.K., Hearon, B.A., & Otto, M.W. (2010). Cognitive behavioral therapy for substance use disorders. *The Psychiatric Clinics of North America, 33(3)*, 511–525. https://doi.org/10.1016/j.psc.2010.04.012

McKellar, J., Ilgen, M., Moos, B.S., & Moos, R. (2008). Predictors of changes in alcohol-related self-efficacy over 16 years. *Journal of Substance Abuse Treatment, 35(2)*, 148–155. doi:10.1016/j.jsat.2007.09.003

McQuaid, R.J., Jesseman, R., & Rush, B. (2018). Examining barriers as risk factors for relapse: A focus on the Canadian treatment and recovery system of care. *The Canadian Journal of Addiction, 9(3)*, 5-12. doi: 10.1097/CXA.0000000000000022

Means, J.R., Wilson, G.L., Sturm, C., Biron, J.E., & Bach, P.J. (1990). Humility as a psychotherapeutic formulation. *Counselling Psychology Quarterly, 3(2)*, 211–215. https://doi.org/10.1080/09515079008254249

Melemis S.M. (2015). Relapse prevention and the five rules of recovery. *The Yale Journal of Biology and Medicine, 88(3)*, 325–332. https://www.ncbi.nlm.nih.gov/pmc/articles/PMC4553654/

Midlarsky, E. (1991). Helping as coping. In M.S. Clark (Ed.), *Review of personality and social psychology, Vol. 1). Prosocial behavior* (pp. 238–264). Sage Publications, Inc.

Millar, M.G., Millar, K.U., & Tesser, A. (1988). The effects of helping and focus of attention on mood states. *Personality and Social Psychology Bulletin, 14*(3), 536–543. https://doi.org/10.1177/0146167288143012

Moeller, S.J., Hajcak, G., Parvaz, M.A., Dunning, J.P., Volkow, N.D., & Goldstein, R.Z. (2012). Psychophysiological prediction of choice: Relevance to insight and drug addiction. *Brain, 135(11)*, 3481–3494. https://doi.org/10.1093/brain/aws252

Mongrain, M., Chin, J.M., & Shapira, L.B. (2011). Practicing compassion increases happiness and self-esteem. *Journal of Happiness Studies, 12(6)*, 963-981. https://doi.org/10.1007/s10902-010-9239-1

Moos, R., & Timko, C. (2008). Outcome research on twelve-step and other self-help programs. In M. Galanter, & H. Kleber (Eds.), *Textbook of substance abuse treatment* (4th ed.) (pp. 511-521). American Psychiatric Press. https://www.mentalhealth.va.gov/providers/sud/selfhelp/docs/4_moos_ti mko_chapter.pdf

Morin, A. (2018). 7 ways to overcome toxic self-criticism [Web log post]. *Psychology Today*. https://www.psychologytoday.com/intl/blog/what-mentally-strong-people-dont-do/201801/7-ways-overcome-toxic-self-criticism

Morin, A. (2011a). Self-awareness part 1: Definition, measures, effects, functions, and antecedents. *Social and Personality Psychology Compass 5(10)*, 807-823. DOI: 10.1111/j.1751-9004.2011.00387.x

Morin, A. (2011b). Self-awareness part 2: Neuroanatomy and the importance of inner speech. *Social and Personality Psychology Compass, 5(12)*, 1004-1017. 10.1111/j.1751-9004.2011.00410.x

Morisano, D., Babor, T. F., & Robaina, K. A. (2014). Co-occurrence of substance use disorders with other psychiatric disorders: Implications for treatment services. *Nordic Studies on Alcohol and Drugs, 31(1)*, 5–25. https://doi.org/10.2478/nsad-2014-0002

Morse, E. (2017). Addiction is a chronic medical illness. *North Carolina Medical Journal, 79(3)*, 163-165. doi: 10.18043/ncm.79.3.163

Moynihan, R., Heath, I., & Henry, D. (2002). Selling sickness: The pharmaceutical industry and disease mongering. *British Medical Journal, 324(7342)*, 886–891. https://doi.org/10.1136/bmj.324.7342.886

Mruck, C. (2006). *Self-esteem research, theory, and practice: Toward a positive psychology of self-esteem* (3rd ed.). Springer.

Mughal, A.S. (2018). Reasons of relapse in hindrance or treatment in substance related addictive disorder: A qualitative study. *Journal of Alcoholism & Drug Dependence, 6(2)*. DOI: 10.4172/2329-6488.1000310

Muhuri, P.K., Gfoerer, J.C., & Davies, M.C. (2013). Associations of nonmedical pain reliever use and initiation of heroin use in the united states. *SAMHSA CBHSQ Data Review*. https://www.samhsa.gov/data/sites/default/files/DR006/DR006/nonme dical-pain-reliever-use-2013.htm

Murayama, K. (2018). The science of motivation. *American Psychological Association.* https://www.apa.org/science/about/psa/2018/06/motivation

Nasiry, Rodsari, A.B., & Nasiry, S. (2014). The prediction of tendency to substance abuse on the basis of self-esteem and components of emotional intelligence. *Research on Addiction Quarterly Journal of Drug Abuse, 8(31),* 103 – 111.

National Drug Early Warning System (NDEWS). (2020). *NDEWS.* http://ndews.org/

National Institute on Drug Abuse (NIDA). (2020). *Addiction and health.* https://www.drugabuse.gov/publications/drugs-brains-behavior-science-addiction/addiction-health

National Institute on Drug Abuse (NIDA). (2017). *"All scientific hands on deck" to end the opioid crisis.* https://www.drugabuse.gov/about-nida/noras-blog/2017/05/all-scientific-hands-deck-to-end-opioid-crisis

National Institute on Drug Abuse (NIDA). (2016). *Cocaine.* https://www.drugabuse.gov/publications/drugfacts/cocaine

National Institute on Drug Abuse (NIDA). (2020). *Drugs and the brain.* https://www.drugabuse.gov/publications/drugs-brains-behavior-science-addiction/drugs-brain

National Institute on Drug Abuse (NIDA). (2020). *Common comorbidities with substances use disorders research report.* https://www.drugabuse.gov/publications/research-reports/common-comorbidities-substance-use-disorders/introduction

National Institute on Drug Abuse (NIDA). (2020). *Commonly used drug charts.* https://www.drugabuse.gov/drug-topics/commonly-used-drugs-charts

National Institute on Drug Abuse (NIDA). (2010). Comorbidity: Addiction and other mental illnesses. *Research Report Series.* https://www.drugabuse.gov/sites/default/files/rrcomorbidity.pdf

National Institute on Drug Abuse (NIDA). (2020). *Drug misuse and addiction.* https://www.drugabuse.gov/publications/drugs-brains-behavior-science-addiction/drug-misuse-addiction

National Institute on Drug Abuse (NIDA). (n.d.). *Drug Topics.* https://www.drugabuse.gov/drug-topics

National Institute on Drug Abuse (NIDA). (2003). *Epidemiology.* https://archives.drugabuse.gov/publications/diagnosis-treatment-drug-abuse-in-family-practice-american-family-physician-monograph/epidemiology

National Institute on Drug Abuse (NIDA). (2019). Hallucinogens. *DrugFacts.*
https://www.drugabuse.gov/publications/drugfacts/hallucinogens

National Institute on Drug Abuse (NIDA). (2014). Hallucinogens and dissociative
drugs. *Research Report Series.*
https://www.drugabuse.gov/sites/default/files/hallucinogensrrs.pdf

National Institute on Drug Abuse (NIDA). (2020). *How effective is drug addiction
treatment?* https://www.drugabuse.gov/publications/principles-drug-
addiction-treatment-research-based-guide-third-edition/frequently-asked-
questions/how-effective-drug-addiction-treatment

National Institute on Drug Abuse (NIDA). (2020). *How is methamphetamine different
from other stimulants, such as cocaine?*
https://www.drugabuse.gov/publications/research-
reports/methamphetamine/how-methamphetamine-different-other-
stimulants-such-cocaine

National Institute on Drug Abuse (NIDA). (2020). *How is methamphetamine
manufactured?* https://www.drugabuse.gov/publications/research-
reports/methamphetamine/how-methamphetamine-manufactured

National Institute on Drug Abuse (NIDA). (2011). *Inhalants research report.*
https://www.drugabuse.gov/publications/research-
reports/inhalants/letter-director

National Institute on Drug Use (NIDA). (n.d.). *Infographics.*
https://www.drugabuse.gov/drug-topics/trends-statistics/infographics

National Institute on Drug Use (NIDA). (2020). *Is there a link between marijuana use
and psychiatric disorders?*
https://www.drugabuse.gov/publications/research-
reports/marijuana/there-link-between-marijuana-use-psychiatric-
disorders

National Institute on Drug Abuse (NIDA). (2019). Marijuana. *DrugFacts.*
https://www.drugabuse.gov/publications/drugfacts/marijuana

National Institute on Drug Use (NIDA). (2020). MDMA (ecstasy/molly). *DrugFacts.*
https://www.drugabuse.gov/publications/drugfacts/mdma-ecstasymolly

National Institute on Drug Use (NIDA). (2020). *Monitoring the Future.*
https://www.drugabuse.gov/drug-topics/trends-statistics/monitoring-
future

National Institute on Drug Use (NIDA). (2018). *National Survey on Drug Use and
Health (NSDUH).* https://www.drugabuse.gov/drug-topics/trends-
statistics/national-survey-drug-use-health-nsduh

National Institutes on Drug Abuse (NIDA). (2020). *Opioid overdose crisis.* https://www.drugabuse.gov/drug-topics/opioids/opioid-overdose-crisis

National Institutes on Drug Abuse (NIDA). (2017). *Opioid prescribers can play a key role in stopping the opioid overdose epidemic.* https://www.drugabuse.gov/publications/improving-opioid-prescribing

National Institute on Drug Abuse (NIDA). (2020). *Part 1: The Connection Between Substance Use Disorders and Mental Illness.* https://www.drugabuse.gov/publications/research-reports/common-comorbidities-substance-use-disorders/part-1-connection-between-substance-use-disorders-mental-illness on 2020, June 19

National Institute on Drug Abuse (NIDA). (2018). *Prescription CNS depressant drug facts.* https://www.drugabuse.gov/publications/drugfacts/prescription-cns-depressants

National Institute on Drug Abuse (NIDA). (2018). *Principles of drug addiction treatment: A research-based guide* (3rd ed.). https://www.drugabuse.gov/publications/principles-drug-addiction-treatment-research-based-guide-third-edition

National Institute on Drug Abuse (NIDA). (2003). *Relationships matter: Impact of parental, peer factors on teen, young adult substance abuse.* https://archives.drugabuse.gov/news-events/nida-notes/2003/08/relationships-matter-impact-parental-peer-factors-teen-young-adult-substance-abuse

National Institute on Drug Abuse (NIDA). (2016). *Synthetic cathinones ("Bath Salts").* https://www.drugabuse.gov/publications/drugfacts/synthetic-cathinones-bath-salts

National Institute on Drug Abuse (NIDA). (2019). Treatment Approaches for Drug Addiction *DrugFacts.* https://www.drugabuse.gov/publications/drugfacts/treatment-approaches-drug-addiction

National Institute on Drug Use (NIDA). (n.d.). *Trends & statistics.* https://www.drugabuse.gov/drug-topics/trends-statistics

National Institute on Drug Abuse (NIDA). (2018). *What is drug addiction?* https://www.drugabuse.gov/publications/drugs-brains-behavior-science-addiction/drug-misuse-addiction

National Institute on Drug Abuse (NIDA). (2020). *Why is there comorbidity between substance use disorders and mental illnesses?* https://www.drugabuse.gov/publications/research-reports/common-comorbidities-substance-use-disorders/why-there-comorbidity-between-substance-use-disorders-mental-illnesses

National Institutes of Health (NIH). (2015). *10 percent of US adults have drug use disorder at some point in their lives*. https://www.nih.gov/news-events/news-releases/10-percent-us-adults-have-drug-use-disorder-some-point-their-lives#:~:text=The%20study%2C%20funded%20by%20the,some%20time%20in%20their%20lives.

National Library of Medicine. (2020). Substance use disorder. *Medline Plus*. https://medlineplus.gov/ency/article/001522.htm

National Survey on Drug Use and Health (NSDUH). (2020). *What is NSDUH?* https://nsduhweb.rti.org/respweb/homepage.cfm

Nennig, S.E., & Schank, J.R. (2017). The Role of NFkB in drug addiction: Beyond inflammation. *Alcohol and Alcoholism, 52(2)*, 172–179. https://doi.org/10.1093/alcalc/agw098

Nordstrom, B.R., & Dackis, C.A. (2011). Drugs and crime. *The Journal of Psychiatry & Law, 39(4)*, 663–687. https://doi.org/10.1177/009318531103900407

Nestler E.J. (2013). Cellular basis of memory for addiction. *Dialogues in Clinical Neuroscience, 15(4)*, 431–443. https://www.ncbi.nlm.nih.gov/pmc/articles/PMC3898681/

Nielsen, D.A., Utrankar, A., Reyes, J.A., Simons, D.D., & Kosten, T.R. (2012). Epigenetics of drug abuse: Predisposition or response. *Pharmacogenomics, 13(10)*, 1149–1160. https://doi.org/10.2217/pgs.12.94

Nielsen, R. & Marrone, J. (2018). Humility: Our current understanding of the construct and its role in organizations. *International Journal of Management Reviews, 20*, 805-824. doi:10.1111/ijmr.12160

Noël, X., Bechara, A., Brevers, D., Verbanck, P., & Campanella, S. (2010). Alcoholism and the loss of willpower: A neurocognitive perspective. *Journal of Psychophysiology, 24(4)*, 240–248. doi:10.1027/0269-8803/a000037

Nolen-Hoeksema, S., Stice, E., Wade, E., & Bohon, C. (2007). Reciprocal relations between rumination and bulimic, substance abuse. *Journal of Abnormal Psychology, 116(1)*, 198–207. DOI:10.1037/0021-843X.116.1.198

Nordfjærn, T. (2011) Relapse patterns among patients with substance use disorders. *Journal of Substance Use, 16(4)*, 313-329. DOI: 10.3109/14659890903580482

O'Donnell, J., Gladden, R.M., Mattson, C.L., Hunter, C.T., & Davis, N.L. (2020). Vital signs: Characteristics of drug overdose deaths involving opioids and stimulants — 24 states and the District of Columbia, January–June 2019.

CDC Morbidity and Mortality Weekly Report, 69, 1189–1197. DOI: http://dx.doi.org/10.15585/mmwr.mm6935a1

Okun, M.A., Yeung, E.W., & Brown, S. (2013). Volunteering by older adults and risk of mortality: A meta-analysis. *Psychology and Aging, 28(2),* 564–577. https://doi.org/10.1037/a0031519

Oscar-Berman, M., & Marinković, K. (2007). Alcohol: Effects on neurobehavioral functions and the brain. *Neuropsychology Review, 17(3),* 239–257. https://doi.org/10.1007/s11065-007-9038-6

Otake, K., Shimai, S., Tanaka-Matsumi, J., Otsui, K. & Fredrickson, B.L. (2006). Happy people become happier through kindness: A counting kindness intervention. *Journal of Happiness Studies, 7,* 361–375. DOI 10.1007/s10902-005-3650-z

Pagano, M.E., Friend, K.B., Tonigan, J.S., & Stout, R.L. (2004). Helping other alcoholics in alcoholics anonymous and drinking outcomes: Findings from project MATCH. *Journal of Studies on Alcohol, 65(6),* 766–773. https://doi.org/10.15288/jsa.2004.65.766

Paine, D.R., Sandage, S.J., Rupert, D., Devor, N.G., & Bronstein, M. (2015). Humility as a psychotherapeutic virtue: Spiritual, philosophical, and psychological foundations. *Journal of Spirituality in Mental Health, 17,* 3–25. DOI: 10.1080/19349637.2015.957611

Palmgren, S.E. (2007). The efficacy of self-affirmation in debiasing defenses against continuation of substance abuse treatment. *Dissertation Abstracts International: Section B: The Sciences and Engineering, 67(11-B),* 6744.

Pardini, D., Plante, T., Sherman, A., & Stump, J. (2000). Religious faith and spirituality in substance abuse recovery: Determining the mental health benefits. *Journal of Substance Abuse Treatment, 19,* 347-354. DOI: 10.1016/s0740-5472(00)00125-2

Pathan, H., & Williams, J. (2012). Basic opioid pharmacology: An update. *British Journal of Pain, 6(1),* 11–16. https://doi.org/10.1177/2049463712438493

Penneback, J. (2016). Does confessing our secrets improve our mental health? *Scientific American Mind, 27(2),* 71. doi:10.1038/scientificamericanmind0316-71a

Perkins, R. & Repper, J. (2018). Thinking about recovery and well-being in a social context. *Mental Health and Social Inclusion, 22(4),* 161-166. https://doi.org/10.1108/MHSI-08-2018-058

Perlovsky, L. (2013). A challenge to human evolution-cognitive dissonance. *Frontiers in Psychology, 4,* 179. https://doi.org/10.3389/fpsyg.2013.00179

Pesut, B., Fowler, M., Taylor, E.J., Reimer-Kirkham, S. & Sawatzky, R. (2008). Conceptualising spirituality and religion for healthcare. *Journal of Clinical Nursing, 17,* 2803–2810. doi: 10.1111/j.1365-2702.2008.02344.x

Pew Research Center. (2014). Frequency of prayer. *Religious Landscape Study.* https://www.pewforum.org/religious-landscape-study/frequency-of-prayer/

Pew Research Center. (2015). *Religious practices and experiences.* https://www.pewforum.org/2015/11/03/chapter-2-religious-practices-and-experiences/#private-devotions

Post, S. (2005). Altruism, happiness, and health: It's good to be good. *International Journal of Behavioral Medicine, 12(2),* 66-77.

Post, S., Johnson, B., Lee, M., & Pagano, M. (2015). Positive psychology in Alcoholics Anonymous and the 12 Steps: Adolescent recovery in relation to humility. *The American Psychological Association Addictions Newsletter,* 18-20. http://www.helpingotherslivesober.org/documents/publications/Positive_Psychology_in_Alcoholics_Anonymous_and_the_12_steps_Adolescent_Recovery_in_Relation_to_Humility.pdf

Post, S., Pagano, M., Lee, M., & Johnson, B. (2016). Humility and 12-Step recovery: A prolegomenon for the empirical investigation of a cardinal virtue in alcoholics anonymous. *Alcoholism Treatment Quarterly, 34(3),* 262–273. doi:10.1080/07347324.2016.1182817

Priddy, S., Howard, M., Hanley, A., Riquino, M., Friberg-Felsted, K., & Garland, E. (2018). Mindfulness meditation in the treatment of substance use disorders and preventing future relapse: Neurocognitive mechanisms and clinical implications. *Substance Abuse and Rehabilitation, 9,* 103–114. doi:10.2147/SAR.S145201

Priester, P., Scherer, J., Steinfeldt, J., Jana-Masri, A., Jashinsky, T., Jones, J., et al. (2009). The frequency of prayer, meditation and holistic interventions in addictions treatment: A national survey. *Pastoral Psychology, 58,* 315. https://doi.org/10.1007/s11089-009-0196-8

Proulx, A. (2020). *A trip through the 12 steps with a doctor and therapist.* Recovery Folio.

Pruett, J., Nishimura, N. & Priest, R. (2007). The role of meditation in addiction recovery. *Counseling and Values, 52,* 71-84. doi:10.1002/j.2161-007X.2007.tb00088.x

Psychology Today. (2020). *Learned helplessness.* https://www.psychologytoday.com/ca/basics/learned-helplessness

Puchalski, C. M. (2001). The role of spirituality in health care. *Proceedings (Baylor University. Medical Center), 14(4),* 352–357. https://www.ncbi.nlm.nih.gov/pmc/articles/PMC1305900/

Ramirez, R., Hinman, A., Sterling, S., Weisner, C., & Campbell, C. (2012). Peer influences on adolescent alcohol and other drug use outcomes. *Journal of Nursing Scholarship, 44(1),* 36–44. https://doi.org/10.1111/j.1547-5069.2011.01437.x

Ramo, D. E., & Brown, S. A. (2008). Classes of substance abuse relapse situations: A comparison of adolescents and adults. *Psychology of Addictive Behaviors, 22(3),* 372–379. https://doi.org/10.1037/0893-164X.22.3.372

Rasmussen N. (2008). America's first amphetamine epidemic 1929-1971: A quantitative and qualitative retrospective with implications for the present. *American Journal of Public Health, 98(6),* 974–985. https://doi.org/10.2105/AJPH.2007.110593

Renthal, W., & Nestler, E. J. (2008). Epigenetic mechanisms in drug addiction. *Trends in Molecular Medicine, 14(8),* 341–350. https://doi.org/10.1016/j.molmed.2008.06.004

Reese, S. (2014). Drug abuse among doctors: Easy, tempting, and not uncommon. *Medscape Business of Medicine.* https://www.medscape.com/viewarticle/819223

Rice, K.G., Ashby, J.S., & Slaney, R.B. (1998). Self-esteem as a mediator between perfectionism and depression: A structural equations analysis. *Journal of Counseling Psychology, 45(3),* 304–314. https://doi.org/10.1037/0022-0167.45.3.304

Richardson, C.G., Kwon, J.Y., & Ratner, P.A. (2013). Self-esteem and the initiation of substance use among adolescents. *Canadian Journal of Public Health,104(1),* e60-e63.

Rinn, W., Desai, N., Rosenblatt, H., & Gastfriend, D. (2002). Addiction denial and cognitive dysfunction: A preliminary investigation. *Journal of Neuropsychiatry and Clinical Neuroscience, 14(1),* 52-57. https://neuro.psychiatryonline.org/doi/pdf/10.1176/jnp.14.1.52

Riso, L.P., du Toit, P.L., Blandino, J.A., Penna, S., Dacey, S., Duin J.S. et al. (2003). Cognitive aspects of chronic depression. *Journal of Abnormal Psychology, 112(1),* 72–80.

Robinson, T., & Berridge, K. (2008). The incentive sensitization theory of addiction: Some current issues. *Philosophical Transactions of the Royal Society of London. Series B, Biological Sciences, 363(1507),* 3137–3146. https://doi.org/10.1098/rstb.2008.0093

Robinson, T.E., & Berridge, K.C. (1993). The neural basis of drug craving: An incentive-sensitization theory of addiction. *Brain Research Review, 18*, 247–91. doi:10.1016/0165-0173(93)90013-P

Robison, A.J., & Nestler, E.J. (2011). Transcriptional and epigenetic mechanisms of addiction. *Nature Reviews: Neuroscience, 12(11)*, 623–637. https://doi.org/10.1038/nrn3111

Rogawski M.A. (2005). Update on the neurobiology of alcohol withdrawal seizures. *Epilepsy Currents, 5(6)*, 225–230. https://doi.org/10.1111/j.1535-7511.2005.00071.x

Rooke, S., Hine, D., & Thorsteinsson, E. (2008). Implicit cognition and substance use: A meta-analysis. *Addictive Behavior, 33*, 1314–1328.

Rosen, L.G., Sun, N., & Rushlow, W. (2015). Molecular and neuronal plasticity mechanisms in the amygdala-prefrontal cortical circuit: Implications for opiate addiction memory formation. *Frontiers in Neuroscience, 9(399).* doi: 10.3389/fnins.2015.00399

Rosenkranz, M., Davidson, R., MacCoon, D., Sheridan, J., Kalin, N., & Lutz, A. (2013). A comparison of mindfulness-based stress reduction and an active control in modulation of neurogenic inflammation. *Brain, Behavior, and Immunity, 27*, 174–184. https://doi.org/10.1016/j.bbi.2012.10.013

Ross, H., & Dolan, S. (2017). Forgiveness and its importance in substance use disorders. *Journal of Psychology and Christianity, 36(3)*, 250-266. https://www.researchgate.net/publication/322339237_Forgiveness_and_I ts_Importance_In_Substance_Use_Disorders

Ruiz, F., & Tanaka, K. (2001). The relationship between cognitive dissonance and helping behaviors. *Japanese Psychological Research, 43(2)*, 55-62.

Russo, S. J., Dietz, D. M., Dumitriu, D., Morrison, J. H., Malenka, R. C., & Nestler, E. J. (2010). The addicted synapse: Mechanisms of synaptic and structural plasticity in nucleus accumbens. *Trends in Neurosciences, 33(6)*, 267–276. https://doi.org/10.1016/j.tins.2010.02.002

Saavedra, J., Perez, E., Crawford, P., & Arias, S. (2018). Recovery and creative practices in people with severe mental illness: Evaluating well-being and social inclusion. *Disability And Rehabilitation, 40(8)*, 905-911. http://dx.doi.org/10.1080/09638288.2017.1278797

Sachdeva, A., Choudhary, M., & Chandra, M. (2015). Alcohol withdrawal syndrome: Benzodiazepines and beyond. *Journal of Clinical and Diagnostic Research, 9(9)*, VE01–VE07. https://doi.org/10.7860/JCDR/2015/13407.6538

Sack, D. (2012). Does willpower play a role in addiction recovery? [Web log post]. *Psychology Today.* https://www.psychologytoday.com/ca/blog/where-science-meets-the-steps/201211/does-willpower-play-role-in-addiction-recovery

Samek, D.R., & Hicks, B.M. (2014). Externalizing disorders and environmental risk: Mechanisms of gene-environment interplay and strategies for intervention. *Clinical Practice, 11(5),* 537–547. https://doi.org/10.2217/CPR.14.47

Sancho, M., De Gracia, M., Rodríguez, R., Mallorqui, N., Sanchez, J., Trujols, J., et al. (2018). Mindfulness-based interventions for the treatment of substance and behavioral addictions: A systematic review. *Frontiers in Psychiatry, 9,* 95. https://doi.org/10.3389/fpsyt.2018.00095

Sarvet, A.L., & Hasin, D. (2016). The natural history of substance use disorders. *Current Opinion in Psychiatry, 29(4),* 250–257. https://doi.org/10.1097/YCO.0000000000000257

Schacter, D. (1999). The seven sins of memory: Insights from psychology and cognitive neuroscience. *American Psychologist, 54(3),* 182-203. https://www.researchgate.net/profile/Daniel_Schacter/publication/13099 436_The_seven_sins_of_memory_-_Insights_from_psychology_and_cognitive_neuroscience/links/0c96052f3f8 1c5ece0000000.pdf

Schofield, T.J., Conger, R.D., & Robins, R.D. (2015). Early adolescent substance use in Mexican origin families: Peer selection, peer influence, and parental monitoring. *Drug and Alcohol Dependence, 157,* 129. DOI: 10.1016/j.drugalcdep.2015.10.020

Schuckit, M.A. (2014). Recognition and management of withdrawal delirium (delirium tremens). *The New England Journal of Medicine, 371(22),* 2109-2113. DOI: 10.1056/NEJMra1407298

Schumann, K., & Dweck, C. (2014). Who accepts responsibility for their transgressions? *Personality an Social Psychology Bulletin, 40(12),* 1598-1610. https://doi.org/10.1177/0146167214552789

Schunk, D.H. (2012). *Learning theories* (6th ed.). Pearson.

Schwabe, L., Dickinson, A., & Wolf, O.T. (2011). Stress, habits, and drug addiction: A psychoneuroendocrinological perspective. *Experimental and Clinical Psychopharmacology, 19(1),* 53–63. doi:10.1037/a0022212

Schwabe, L., & Wolf, O.T. (2009). Stress prompts habit behavior in humans. *Journal of Neuroscience, 29(22),* 7191–8. doi:10.1523/JNEUROSCI.0979-09.2009

Schwartz, C. (2007). Altruism and subjective well-being: Conceptual model and empirical support (Ch. 4). In S.G. Post: *Altruism and health: Perspectives from empirical research* (pp. 33-42). Oxford University Press.

Schwartz, C.E., Meisenhelder, J.B., Ma, Y. & Reed, G. 2003. (2003). Altruistic social interest behaviors are associated with better mental health. *Psychosomatic Medicine, 65*, 778–785. DOI: 10.1097/01.PSY.0000079378.39062.D4

Scully J. L. (2004). What is a disease? *EMBO Reports, 5(7)*, 650–653. https://doi.org/10.1038/sj.embor.7400195

Secades-Villa, R., Garcia-Rodríguez, O., Jin, C. J., Wang, S., & Blanco, C. (2015). Probability and predictors of the cannabis gateway effect: A national study. *The International Journal on Drug Policy, 26(2)*, 135–142. https://doi.org/10.1016/j.drugpo.2014.07.011

Seppälä, E. (2013). 20 Scientific reasons to start meditating today [Web log post]. *Psychology Today* https://www.psychologytoday.com/blog/feeling-it/201309/20-scientific-reasons-start-meditating-today

Setorg, S., Kazemi, H., & Raisi, Z. (2014). Effectiveness of meta-cognitive therapy on craving beliefs and substance-related beliefs in substance abuse disorder patients. *Journal of Research on Addiction, 7(28)*, 147-162. http://etiadpajohi.ir/article-1-285-en.html

Shah, M., & Huecker, M.R. (2020). Opioid withdrawal. *StatPearls.* https://www.ncbi.nlm.nih.gov/books/NBK526012/

Shahar, G. (2017). The hazards of self-criticism [Web log post]. *Psychology Today*. https://www.psychologytoday.com/ca/blog/stress-self-and-health/201708/the-hazards-self-criticism

Shahar, B., Britton, W., Sbarra, D., Figueredo, A., & Bootzin, R. (2010). Mechanisms of change in Mindfulness-Based Cognitive Therapy for depression: Preliminary evidence from a randomized controlled trial. *International Journal of Cognitive Therapy, 3(4)*, 402-418. https://doi.org/10.1521/ijct.2010.3.4.402

Shapero, B.G., Greenberg, J., Pedrelli, P., de Jong, M., & Desbordes, G. (2018). Mindfulness-based interventions in psychiatry. *Focus (American Psychiatric Publishing), 16(1)*, 32–39. https://doi.org/10.1176/appi.focus.20170039

Shapiro, S., Oman, D., Thoresen, C., Plante, T., & Flinders, T. (2008). Cultivating mindfulness: Effects on well-being. *Journal of Clinical Psychology, 64(7)*, 840-862. doi:10.1002/jclp.20491

Sharot, T. (2011). The optimism bias. *Current Biology, 21(23)*, R941-R945. https://doi.org/10.1016/j.cub.2011.10.030

Sharot, T., Guitart-Masip, M., Korn, C. W., Chowdhury, R., & Dolan, R. J. (2012). How dopamine enhances an optimism bias in humans. *Current Biology, 22(16)*, 1477–1481. https://doi.org/10.1016/j.cub.2012.05.053

Sharot, T., Korn, C. W., & Dolan, R. J. (2011). How unrealistic optimism is maintained in the face of reality. *Nature Neuroscience, 14*, 1475–1479. https://doi.org/10.1038/nn.2949

Sharot, T., Riccardi, A., Raio, C., & Phelps, E. (2007). Neural mechanisms mediating optimism bias. *Nature 450*, 102–105. https://doi.org/10.1038/nature06280

Sherman, D.K., & Cohen, G.L. (2006). The psychology of self-defense: Self-affirmation theory. In M.P. Zanna (Ed.) *Advances in Experimental Social Psychology* (Vol. 38) (pp. 183-242). Academic Press.

Shi, L., Zhang, D., Wang, L., Zhuang, J., Cook, R., & Chen, L. (2017). Meditation and blood pressure: A meta-analysis of randomized clinical trials. *Journal of Hypertension, 35(4)*, 696-706. doi: 10.1097/HJH.0000000000001217

Shonin, E. & Van Gordon, W. (2016). The mechanisms of mindfulness in the treatment of mental illness and addiction. *International Journal of Mental Health & Addiction, 14*, 844. https://doi.org/10.1007/s11469-016-9653-7

Shpancer, N. (2015). How to stop worrying and get on with your life [Web log post]. *Psychology Today.* https://www.psychologytoday.com/ca/blog/insight-therapy/201501/how-stop-worrying-and-get-your-life?collection=168048

Shuler, P., Gelberg, L., & Brown, M. (1994). The effects of spiritual/religious practices on psychological well-being among inner city homeless women. *Nurse Practitioner Forum, 5(2)*, 106-113.

Simão, T., Caldeira, S., & de Carvalho, E. (2016). The effect of prayer on patients' health: Systematic literature review. *Religions, 7(11)*. doi:10.3390/rel7010011

Sin, N. L., & Lyubomirsky, S. (2009). Enhancing well-being and alleviating depressive symptoms with positive psychology interventions: A practice-friendly meta-analysis. *Journal of Clinical Psychology, 65(5)*, 467–487. https://doi.org/10.1002/jclp.20593

Skinner, W. (2016). *A bio-psycho-social plus approach to addiction and recovery.* [Author's copy].

Skinner, M.D., Lahmek, P., Pham, H., & Aubin, H.J. (2014). Disulfiram efficacy in the treatment of alcohol dependence: A meta-analysis. *PloS One, 9(2)*, e87366. https://doi.org/10.1371/journal.pone.0087366

Slade, M., Rennick-Egglestone, S., Blackie, L., Lewellyn-Beardsley, J., Franklin, D., Thornicroft, G., et al. (2019). Post-traumatic growth in mental health recovery: Qualitative study of narratives. *British Medical Journal Open, 9,* e029342. doi:10.1136/bmjopen-2019-029342

Smith, R.H. (2000). *Handbook of social comparison.* Springer.

Smith, S. (2004). Exploring the interaction of trauma and spirituality. *Traumatology, 10(4),* 231-243. https://doi.org/10.1177/153476560401000403

Smith, J.M., & Alloy, L.B. (2009). A roadmap to rumination: A review of the definition, assessment, and conceptualization of this multifaceted construct. *Clinical Psychology Review, 29(2),* 116–128. https://doi.org/10.1016/j.cpr.2008.10.003

Snoek, A., Levy, N., & Kennett, J. (2016). Strong-willed but not successful: The importance of strategies in recovery from addiction. *Addictive Behaviors Review, 4,* 102-17. https://doi.org/10.1016/j.abrep.2016.09.002

Soleimani, M., Sharif, S., Zadeh, A., & Ong, F. (2016). Relationship between hardiness and addiction potential in medical students. *International Journal of Psychology & Behavioral Science, e6225.* DOI: 10.17795/ijpbs-6225

Solomon, R.L. & Corbit, J.D. (1974). An opponent-process theory of motivation: I. Temporal dynamics of affect. *Psychology Review, 81,* 119-145.

Spada, M., Caselli, G., Nikčević, A., & Wells, A. (2015). Metacognition in addictive behaviors. *Addictive Behaviors, 44,* 9–15. http://dx.doi.org/10.1016/j.addbeh.2014.08.002

Spada, M., Caselli, G., & Wells, A. (2013). A triphasic metacognitive formulation of problem drinking. *Clinical Psychology & Psychotherapy, 20(6),* 494–500. https://doi.org/10.1002/cpp.1791

Spada, M., Caselli, G., & Wells, A. (2009). Metacognitions as a predictor of drinking status and level of alcohol use following CBT in problem drinkers: A prospective study. *Behaviour Research and Therapy, 47(10),* 882–886. DOI:10.1016/j.brat.2009.06.010

Stacy, A, & Wiers, R.W., 2010. Implicit cognition and addiction: A tool for explaining paradoxical behavior. *Annual Review of Clinical Psychology, 6,* 551–575. https://doi.org/10.1146/annurev.clinpsy.121208.131444

Staub, E. (2011). Altruism born of suffering: The value of kindness [Web log post]. *Psychology Today.* https://www.psychologytoday.com/blog/in-the-garden-good-and-evil/201112/altruism-born-suffering

Staub, E., & Vollhardt, J. (2008). Altruism born of suffering: The roots of caring and helping after victimization and other trauma. *American Journal of Orthopsychiatry, 78(3)*, 267-80. doi: 10.1037/a0014223.

Stauffer, B. (2016). *Every 25 seconds: The human toll of criminalizing drug use in the United States.* https://www.hrw.org/report/2016/10/12/every-25-seconds/human-toll-criminalizing-drug-use-united-states

Steakley, L. (2013). How the brain processes trauma and why support, altruism can ease fear. *Stanford Medicine Scope.* https://scopeblog.stanford.edu/2013/04/16/how-the-brain-processes-trauma-and-why-support-altruism-can-ease-fear/

Steele, C. M. (1988). The psychology of self-affirmation: Sustaining the integrity of the self. In L. Berkowitz (Ed.), *Advances in experimental social psychology* (Vol. 21) (pp. 261-302). Academic Press.

Steele, C.M., & Liu, T.J. (1983). Dissonance processes as self-affirmation. *Journal of Personality and Social Psychology, 45(1)*, 5-19.

Stinckens, N., Lietaer, G., & Leijssen, M. (2013). Working with the inner critic: Process features and pathways to change. *Person-Centered & Experiential Psychotherapies, 12(1)*, 59-78, DOI: 10.1080/14779757.2013.767747

Stoeber, J. (2003). Self-pity: Exploring the links to personality, control beliefs, and anger. *Journal of Personality, 71(2)*, 183-220. https://doi.org/10.1111/1467-6494.7102004

Stoicea, N., Costa, A., Periel, L., Uribe, A., Weaver, T., & Bergese, S.D. (2019). Current perspectives on the opioid crisis in the US healthcare system. *Medicine, 98(20)*, e15425. doi: 10.1097/MD.0000000000015425

Substance Abuse and Mental Health Services Administration (SAMHSA). (1999). *Brief interventions and brief therapies for substance abuse.* Center for Substance Abuse Treatment. https://www.ncbi.nlm.nih.gov/books/NBK64947/

Substance Abuse and Mental Health Services Administration (SAMHSA). (2004). Chapter 2: Impact of substance abuse on families. *Treatment Improvement Protocol (TIP) Series, No. 39.* https://www.ncbi.nlm.nih.gov/books/NBK64258/

Substance Abuse and Mental Health Services Administration (SAMHSA). (2019). *Key substance use and mental health indicators in the United States: Results from the 2018 National Survey on Drug Use and Health.* https://www.samhsa.gov/data/sites/default/files/cbhsq-reports/NSDUHNationalFindingsReport2018/NSDUHNationalFindingsReport2018.pdf

Substance Abuse and Mental Health Services Administration (SAMHSA). (2009). Incorporating alcohol pharmacotherapies into medical practice Chapter 2 – acamprosate. *Treatment Improvement Protocol (TIP) Series, 49.* https://www.ncbi.nlm.nih.gov/books/NBK64035/

Substance Abuse and Mental Health Services Administration (SAMHSA) and National Institute on Alcohol Abuse (NIAA). (2015). *Medication for the treatment of alcohol use disorder: A brief guide.* HHS Publication No. (SMA) 15-4907. Rockville, MD: Substance Abuse and Mental Health Services Administration. https://store.samhsa.gov/sites/default/files/d7/priv/sma15-4907.pdf

Tang, S-H., & Hall, V.C. (1995). The overjustification effect: A meta-analysis. *Applied Cognitive Psychology, 9,* 365-404.

Tang, Y., Hölzel, B., & Posner, M. (2015). The neuroscience of mindfulness meditation. *Nature Reviews of Neuroscience, 16(4),* 213–25. https://doi.org/10.1038/nrn3916

Tang, Y., & Leve, L. (2016). A translational neuroscience perspective on mindfulness meditation as a prevention strategy. *Translational Behavioral Medicine, 6(1),* 63–72. https://doi.org/10.1007/s13142-015-0360-x

Tang, Y., Posner, M., Rothbart, M., & Volkow, N. (2015). Circuitry of self-control and its role in reducing addiction. *Trends in Cognitive Sciences, 19(8),* 439-444. https://doi.org/10.1016/j.tics.2015.06.007

Tang, Y., Tang, R., & Posner, M. (2013). Brief meditation induces smoking reduction. *Proceedings of the National Academy of Sciences, 110(34),* 13971-13975. DOI: 10.1073/pnas.1311887110

Tang, Y., Tang, R., & Posner, M. (2016). Mindfulness meditation improves emotion regulation and reduces drug abuse. *Drug and Alcohol Dependence, 163(Supp 1),* S13-S18. https://doi.org/10.1016/j.drugalcdep.2015.11.041

Tang, S-H., & Hall, V.C. (1995). The overjustification effect: A meta-analysis. *Applied Cognitive Psychology, 9,* 365-404.

Tanyi, R.A. (2002). Towards clarification of the meaning of spirituality. *Journal of Advanced Nursing, 39(5),* 500-509. https://doi.org/10.1046/j.1365-2648.2002.02315.x

Tartakovsky, M. (2018). Why ruminating is unhealthy and how to stop it [Web log post]. *PsychCentral.* https://psychcentral.com/blog/why-ruminating-is-unhealthy-and-how-to-stop/

Telles, S., Gerbarg, P., & Kozasa, E. (2015). Physiological effects of mind and body practices. *Biomedical Research International.* http://dx.doi.org/10.1155/2015/983086

Tesser, A. (2000). On the confluence of self-esteem maintenance mechanisms. *Personality and Social Psychology Review, 4(4),* 290-299.

The Self-Help Alliance (2010). *Building better boundaries.* https://www.ualberta.ca/anesthesiology-pain-medicine/media-library/documents/workbookbuilding-better-boundariesfeb2011.pdf

Thoits, P.A., & Hewitt, L.N. (2001). Volunteer work and well-being. *Journal of Health and Social Behavior, 42(2),* 115–131. https://doi.org/10.2307/3090173

Thomsen, D.K. (2006). The association between rumination and negative affect: A review. *Cognition and Emotion, 20(8),* 1216-1235. DOI: 10.1080/02699930500473533

Tiffany, S.T., & Conklin, C.A. (2000). A cognitive processing model of alcohol craving and compulsive alcohol use. *Addiction, 95(8 Suppl 2),* 145-153. DOI:10.1080/09652140050111717

Toneatto, T. (1999). Metacognition and substance use. *Addictive Behaviors, 24(2),* 167–174.

Torregrossa, M.M., Corlett, P.R., & Taylor, J.R. (2011). Aberrant learning and memory in addiction. *Neurobiology of Learning and Memory, 96(4),* 609–623. https://doi.org/10.1016/j.nlm.2011.02.014

Trevisan, L.A., Boutros, N., Petrakis, I.L., & Krystal, J.H. (1998). Complications of alcohol withdrawal. *Pathophysiological Insights, 22(1),* 61-66.

Tsaousides, T. (2015). 7 things you need to know about fear [Web log post]. *Psychology Today.* https://www.psychologytoday.com/ca/blog/smashing-the-brainblocks/201511/7-things-you-need-know-about-fear

Tudor, K. (1996/2013). *Mental health promotion: Paradigms and practice.* Routledge.

Tuesta, L.M., & Zhang, Y. (2014). Epigenetic memory and addiction. *The Embo Journal, 33(10),* 1091-1103. DOI 10.1002/embj.201488106

Turrigiano, G.G. (1999). Homeostatic plasticity in neuronal networks: The more things change, the more they stay the same. *Trends in Neuroscience, 22,* 221–227.

Umberson, D., & Montez, J. K. (2010). Social relationships and health: A flashpoint for health policy. *Journal of Health and Social Behavior, 51(Suppl),* S54–S66. doi:10.1177/0022146510383501

United Nations International Narcotic Control Board (INCB). (2011). *Narcotic drugs: Estimated world requirements for 2012 and statistics for 2010.*

https://www.incb.org/documents/Narcotic-Drugs/Technical-Publications/2011/Part_FOUR_Comments_NAR-Report-2011_English.pdf

U.S. Centers for Medicare & Medicaid Services (HealthCare.gov). (n.d.). *Mental health & substance abuse coverage.* https://www.healthcare.gov/coverage/mental-health-substance-abuse-coverage/

U.S. Department of Health & Human Services. (2019). Mental health and substance use disorders. *MentalHealth.gov.* https://www.mentalhealth.gov/what-to-look-for/mental-health-substance-use-disorders

Vanderplasschen, W., Yates, R., & Miovský, M. (2017). Bridging the gap between research and practice in therapeutic communities (TCs) for addictions. *Journal of Groups in Addiction & Recovery, 12(2-3),* 63-67. DOI: 10.1080/1556035X.2017.1331598

van der Schier, R., Roozekrans, M., van Velzen, M., Dahan, A., & Niesters, M. (2014). Opioid-induced respiratory depression: Reversal by non-opioid drugs. *F1000 Prime Reports, 6,* 79. https://doi.org/10.12703/P6-79

van Niekerk, B. (2018). Religion and spirituality: What are the fundamental differences? *HTS Theological Studies, 74(3),* 1-11. https://dx.doi.org/10.4102/hts.v74i3.4933

van Osch, Y., Zeelenberg, M., & Breugelmans, S.M. (2018). The self and others in the experience of pride. *Cognition and Emotion, 32(2),* 404-413. DOI: 10.1080/02699931.2017.1290586

Verdejo-García, A., Bechara, A., Recknor, E., & Pérez-García, M. (2006). Executive dysfunction in substance dependent individuals during drug use and abstinence: An examination of the behavioral, cognitive and emotional correlates of addiction. *Journal of the International Neuropsychological Society, 12,* 405–415. DOI: 10.10170S1355617706060486

Verdejo-García, A., & Perez-Garcia, M. (2008). Substance abusers' self-awareness of the neurobehavioral consequences of addiction. *Psychiatry Research, 158(2),* 172-180. https://doi.org/10.1016/j.psychres.2006.08.001

Volkow, N.D., Baler, R.D., Compton, W.M., & Weiss, S.R. (2014). Adverse health effects of marijuana use. *The New England Journal of Medicine, 370(23),* 2219–2227. https://doi.org/10.1056/NEJMra1402309

Volkow, N.D., & Koob, G. (2015). Brain disease model of addiction: Why is it so controversial? *The Lancet: Psychiatry, 2(8),* 677–679. https://doi.org/10.1016/S2215-0366(15)00236-9

Vollhardt, J.R. (2009). Altruism born of suffering and prosocial behavior following adverse life events: A review and conceptualization. *Social Justice Research, 22(1),* 53-97. doi:10.1007/s11211-009-0088-1

Vollhardt, J. R., & Staub, E. (2011). Inclusive altruism born of suffering: The relationship between adversity and prosocial attitudes and behavior toward disadvantaged outgroups. *American Journal of Orthopsychiatry, 81*(3), 307–315. https://doi.org/10.1111/j.1939-0025.2011.01099.x

von der Goltz, C., & Kiefer, F. (2009). Learning and memory in the aetiopathogenesis of addiction: Future implications for therapy? *European Archives of Psychiatry and Clinical Neuroscience, 259,* 183. https://doi.org/10.1007/s00406-009-0057-6

Voss, P., Thomas, M., Cisneros-Franco, J., & de Villers-Sidani, É. (2017). Dynamic brains and the changing rules of neuroplasticity: Implications for learning and recovery. *Frontiers in Psychology, 8,* 1657. https://doi.org/10.3389/fpsyg.2017.01657

Wakeman, S.E., Larochelle, M.R., Ameli, O., Chaisson, C.E., McPheeters, J.T., Crown, W.H., Azocar, F., et al. (2020). Comparative effectiveness of different treatment pathways for opioid use disorder. *Journal of the American Medical Association, 3(2),* e1920622. doi:10.1001/jamanetworkopen.2019.20622

Walach, H., & Reich, K.H. (2005). Reconnecting science and spirituality: Toward overcoming a taboo. *Zygon, 40(2),* 423-441.

Warren, R. (2012). *The purpose driven life.* Zondervan.

Watson, P., de Wit, S., Hommel, B., & Wiers, R. (2012). Motivational mechanisms and outcome expectancies underlying the approach bias toward addictive substances. *Frontiers in Psychology.* https://doi.org/10.3389/fpsyg.2012.00440

Wegela, K. (2010). How to practice mindfulness meditation. *Psychology Today.* https://www.psychologytoday.com/ca/blog/the-courage-be-present/201001/how-practice-mindfulness-meditation

Weidman, A., Cheng, J., & Tracy, J. (2018). The psychological structure of humility. *Journal of Personality and Social Psychology, 114(1),* 153-178. http://dx.doi.org/10.1037/pspp0000112

Weiner, B. (1992). *Human Motivation: Metaphors, Theories and Research.* Sage Publications.

Weiner, B. (2000). Intrapersonal and interpersonal theories of motivation from an attributional perspective. *Educational Psychology Review, 12(1),* 1-14.

Weinstein, A., & Cox, W. (2006). Cognitive processing of drug-related stimuli: The role of memory and attention. *Journal of Psychopharmacology, 20(6)*, 850–859. doi: 10.1177/0269881106061116

Weir, K. (2017). Forgiveness can improve mental and physical health. *American Psychological Association Continuing Education, 48(1)*, 30. https://www.apa.org/monitor/2017/01/ce-corner

Weiss, H.M., & Knight, P.A. (1980). The utility of humility: Self-esteem, information search, and problem-solving efficiency. *Organizational Behavior & Human Performance, 25(2)*, 216–223. https://doi.org/10.1016/0030-5073(80)90064-1

Wenk-Sormaz, H. (2005). Meditation can reduce habitual responding. *Alternative Therapies in Health and Medicine, 11*, 42–58. https://pdfs.semanticscholar.org/99f2/9a5f6f4277d98a582cc50e9b4490f7e2442b.pdf

Wheeler, S.B. (2010). Effects of self-esteem and academic performance on adolescent decision-making: An examination of early sexual intercourse and illegal substance use. *Journal of Adolescent Health, 47*, 582–590. doi:10.1016/j.jadohealth.2010.04.009

Whelan, P.J., & Remski, K. (2012). Buprenorphine vs. methadone treatment: A review of evidence in both developed and developing worlds. *Journal of Neurosciences in Rural Practice, 3(1)*, 45–50. https://doi.org/10.4103/0976-3147.91934

White, N.M. (1996). Addictive drugs as reinforcers: Multiple partial actions on memory systems. *Addiction, 91(7)*, 921–950. doi: 10.1111/j.1360-0443.1996.tb03586.x

White, A.M., Signer, M.L., Kraus, C.L., & Swartzwelder, H.S. (2004). Experiential aspects of alcohol-induced blackouts among college students. *The American Journal of Drug and Alcohol Abuse, 30(1)*, 205–224. https://doi.org/10.1081/ADA-120029874

Whittington, B., & Scher, S. (2010). Prayer and subjective well-being: An examination of six different types of prayer. *The International Journal for the Psychology of Religion, 20*, 59-68. https://doi.org/10.1080/10508610903146316

Wiers, C., Gladwin, T., Ludwig, V., Gropper, S., Stuke, H., Gawron, C., et al. (2017). Comparing three cognitive biases for alcohol cues in alcohol dependence. *Alcohol and Alcoholism, 52(2)*, 242–248. doi: 10.1093/alcalc/agw063

Wild, L.G., Flisher, A.J., Bhana, A., & Lombard, C. (2004). Associations among adolescent risk behaviours and self-esteem in six domains. *Journal of Child*

Psychology and Psychiatry 45(8), 1454–1467. doi: 10.1111/j.1469-7610.2004.00330.x

Williams, K.M.B. (1985). Self-awareness theory and decision theory: A theoretical and empirical integration [Doctoral dissertation]. *Retrospective Theses and Dissertations*, 7895. https://lib.dr.iastate.edu/rtd/7895

Williams, L.A., & DeSteno, D. (2009). Pride: Adaptive social emotion or seventh sin? *Psychological Science, 20(3)*, 284–288. doi: 10.1111/j.1467-9280.2009.02292.x

Williams, L.A., & DeSteno, D. (2008). Pride and perseverance: The motivational function of pride. *Journal of Personality and Social Psychology. 94(6)*, 1007–1017. doi: 10.1037/0022-3514.94.6.1007.

Wilson, N., Kariisa, M., Seth, P., Smith, H., & Davis, N.L. (2020). Drug and opioid-involved overdose deaths — United States, 2017–2018. *MMWR Morbidity and Mortality Weekly Report, 69*, 290–297. DOI: http://dx.doi.org/10.15585/mmwr.mm6911a4external icon

Winch, G. (2014). The key difference between pride and arrogance [Web log post]. *Psychology Today.* https://www.psychologytoday.com/ca/blog/the-squeaky-wheel/201407/the-key-difference-between-pride-and-arrogance

Winters, K.C., & Arria, A. (2011). Adolescent brain development and drugs. *The Prevention Researcher, 18(2)*, 21–24.

Winters, K.C., & Lee, C.Y. (2008). Likelihood of developing an alcohol and cannabis use disorder during youth: Association with recent use and age. *Drug and Alcohol Dependence, 92(1-3)*, 239–247. https://doi.org/10.1016/j.drugalcdep.2007.08.005

Wong, Y.I., Stanton, M.C., & Sands, R.D. (2014). Rethinking social inclusion: Experiences of persons in recovery from mental illness. *American Journal of Orthopsychiatry, 84(6)*, 685–695. http://dx.doi.org/10.1037/ort0000034

Woodward, C., & Joseph, S. (2003). Positive change processes and post-traumatic growth in people who have experienced childhood abuse: Understanding vehicles of change. *Psychology and Psychotherapy, 76*(Pt 3), 267–283. https://doi.org/10.1348/147608303322362497

World Health Organization (WHO). (1994). Assessment of fracture risk and its application to screening for postmenopausal osteoporosis: Report of a WHO study group. *WHO Technical Report Series, 843*, 1-129. https://pubmed.ncbi.nlm.nih.gov/7941614/

Wright, J.C., Nadelhoffer, T., Perini, T., Langville, T., Echols, M., & Venezia, K. (2017). The psychological significance of humility. *The Journal of Positive Psychology, 12(1)*, 3-12. doi: 10.1080/17439760.2016.1167940

Wubben, M.J., De Cremer, D., & van Dijk, E. (2012). Is pride a prosocial emotion? Interpersonal effects of authentic and hubristic pride. *Cognition & Emotions, 26(6),* 1084-1097. doi:10.1080/02699931.2011.646956

Yang, C., Zhou, Y., Cao, Q., Xia, M., & An, J. (2019). The relationship between self-control and self-efficacy among patients with substance use disorders: Resilience and self-esteem as mediators. *Frontiers in Psychiatry, 10,* 388. doi: 10.3389/fpsyt.2019.00388

Young, M., DeLorenzi, L. & Cunningham, L. (2011). Using meditation in addiction counseling. *Journal of Addictions & Offender Counseling, 32,* 58-71. doi:10.1002/j.2161-1874.2011.tb00207.x

Zeidan, F., Martucci, K., Kraft, R., Gordon, N., McHaffie, J., & Coghill, R. (2011). Brain mechanisms supporting modulation of pain by mindfulness meditation. *The Journal of Neuroscience, 31(14),* 5540–5548. http://doi.org/10.1523/JNEUROSCI.5791-10.2011

Zemore, S. (2007). A role for spiritual change in the benefits of 12-step involvement. *Alcoholism: Clinical & Experimental Research, 31(S3),* 76S–79S. DOI: 10.1111/j.1530-0277.2007.00499.x

Zemore, S.E., & Pagano, M.E. (2008). Kickbacks from helping others: Health and recovery. *Recent Developments in Alcoholism, 18,* 141–166. https://doi.org/10.1007/978-0-387-77725-2_9

Zgierska, A., Rabago, D., Zuelsdorff, M., Coe, C., Miller, M., & Fleming, M. (2008). Mindfulness meditation for alcohol relapse prevention: A feasibility pilot study. *Journal of Addiction Medicine, 2(3),* 165–173. doi: 10.1097/ADM.0b013e31816f8546.

Zhang, M., Ying, J., Wing, T., Song, G., Fung, D., & Smith, H. (2018b). Cognitive biases in cannabis, opioid, and stimulant disorders: A systematic review. *Frontiers in Psychology.* https://doi.org/10.3389/fpsyt.2018.00376

Zoellner, T., & Maercker, A. (2006). Posttraumatic growth in clinical psychology - a critical review and introduction of a two component model. *Clinical Psychology Review, 26(5),* 626–653. https://doi.org/10.1016/j.cpr.2006.01.008

Zubaran, C., Fernandes, J.G., & Rodnight, R. (1997). Wernicke-Korsakoff syndrome. *British Medical Journal Postgraduate Medical Journal, 73,* 27-31. https://doi.org/10.1136/pgmj.73.855.27

Zucker, D.M., Dion, K., & McKeever, R.P. (2014). Concept clarification of grief in mothers of children with an addiction. *Journal of Advanced Nursing, 71(4),* 751–767. doi: 10.1111/jan.12591

Made in the USA
Middletown, DE
29 September 2024

61650528R10119